W9-DAG-020

VANISHING LIVES
Style and Self in Tennyson,
D. G. Rossetti, Swinburne, and Yeats

VANISHING LIVES,

Style and Self in Tennyson, D. G. Rossetti, Swinburne, and Yeats

———— ❧ ————

by

James Richardson

UNIVERSITY PRESS OF VIRGINIA

Charlottesville

This is a title in the series

VIRGINIA
VICTORIAN
STUDIES

THE UNIVERSITY PRESS OF VIRGINIA
Copyright © 1988 by the Rector and Visitors
of the University of Virginia

First published 1988

Printed in the United States of America

Library of Congress Cataloging-in-Publication Data

Richardson, James, 1950–
    Vanishing lives : style and self in Tennyson, D.G.
Rossetti, Swinburne, and Yeats / by James
Richardson.
        p. cm.—(Virginia victorian)
    Includes index.
    ISBN 0-8139-1165-6
    1. English poetry—19th century—History and
criticism.   2. Self in literature.   3. Death in
literature.   4. Tennyson, Alfred Tennyson, Baron,
1809–1892—Criticism and interpretation. 5.
Rossetti, Dante Gabriel, 1828–1882—Criticism and
interpretation. 6. Swinburne, Algernon Charles,
1837–1909—Criticism and interpretation.   7.
Yeats, W. B. (William Butler), 1865–1939—
Criticism and interpretation.   I. Title.   II. Series
PR595.S44R53 1988
821'.8'09353—dc19   87-25269
                                          CIP

*This book is for
James Everette Richardson
and
Betty Behrer Richardson,
who began it,
and for Catherine,
who ended it.*

Contents

Acknowledgments

This book was begun with a fellowship from the
National Endowment for the Humanities and a
sabbatical from Harvard University and nearly
completed on a leave from Princeton University. It has
acquired many debts along the way. Jerome Buckley,
Jerome McGann, and David Perkins read the first draft
and furnished the generous but exact criticism that
ensured it would not be the last. Jack Kolb and Daniel
Albright read a much later version and provided
extremely helpful suggestions I have tried to do justice
to. I am grateful to the late Walker Cowen, Director of
the University Press of Virginia, for many kindnesses
and courtesies, not the least of which was securing
readings with a speed not likely to be bettered until
manuscripts are transmitted telepathically, and to
Gerald Trett for the intelligent rigor of his editing.
Because Cecil Lang (to whom I owe, among many
other things, my enthusiasm for Victorian and Pre-
Raphaelite poetry) has read more versions of this essay
than he cares to, or can, remember, he could easily be
forgiven for not getting far enough in this one to see
his prodigious labors acknowledged. I would very
much like to thank Professor Constance W. Hassett of
Fordham University for secretarial and editorial
assistance. Unfortunately, she did not type a word of
this book, and declined the privilege of assisting in the
proofreading. As the senior Victorianist of our
household, however, she thought every thought of it
with me. I would be hard put to say where her help
begins and ends, but even debts too great for words are
not exempt from them. And since her own *The Elusive
Self in the Poetry of Robert Browning* obviated the
hundred or so pages on the other Victorian poet that
this essay once contained, the reader may well, in the
very near future, want to add thanks to mine. Finally,

anyone who has spent much time in a classroom recently will realize how much of what follows came out of one. This book is too late for the students who, with both insight and intelligent bafflement, unwittingly contributed to it, and is perhaps too condensed for their successors, but I hope it will be of some use to all those who share with me the task of explaining how poetry works and why it matters.

An early version of the chapter on Rossetti first appeared in the *Journal of Pre-Raphaelite Studies*. Thanks to editor Francis Golffing for permission to reprint. Selections from William Carlos Williams are from *Collected Poems Volume I:1909–1939* ed. A. Walton Litz and Christopher MacGowan (Copyright 1938 by New Directions Publishing Corporation) and are reprinted with the permission of New Directions and Carcanet New Press Ltd. All extracts from the poetry and prose of W. B. Yeats appear with the permission of A. P. Watt Ltd. on behalf of Michael Yeats and Macmillan London Ltd. *W. B. Yeats: Interviews and Recollections,* ed. E. H. Mikhail is quoted with the permission of Macmillan London Ltd. Selections from Yeats's poetry are reprinted with permission of Macmillan Publishing Company from *The Collected Poems of W. B. Yeats* (Copyright 1912, 1916, 1918, 1924, 1928, 1933 by Macmillan Publishing Company. Copyrights renewed 1940, 1944, 1946, 1952, 1956, 1961 by Bertha Georgie Yeats). Selections from *Essays and Introductions* (Copyright Mrs. W. B. Yeats 1961) are reprinted with permission of Macmillan Publishing Company. Excerpts from *Autobiography* (Copyright 1916, 1936 by Macmillan Publishing Company, renewed 1944, 1964 by Bertha Georgie Yeats), *Mythologies* (Copyright Mrs. W. B. Yeats, 1959), *A Vision* (Copyright 1937 by W. B. Yeats, renewed 1965 by Bertha Georgie Yeats and Anne Butler Yeats), *Explorations* (Copyright Mrs. W. B. Yeats 1962), and *The Variorum Edition of the Poems of W. B. Yeats* edited by Peter Allt and Russell K. Alspach (Copyright 1957 by Macmillan Publishing Company) are used by permission of Macmillan Publishing Company.

VANISHING LIVES

Style and Self in Tennyson,
D. G. Rossetti, Swinburne, and Yeats

Introduction

the dark dissolving human heart
                    The Princess—Tennyson

WHAT IS real in our lives is "that continual vanishing away, that strange, perpetual weaving and unweaving of ourselves."[1] Pater said it; Tennyson could have, for the remark distills the poignance of his poetry. Whether contemplating geological upheaval or the fading of the personal past or recording the smallest shifting and blurring of the moment, Tennyson gives to transience, the oldest theme, a new intimacy and subtlety. In the instabilities of the self he found what amounted to new sources of both sadness and exhilaration.

Even Gerard Manley Hopkins, the Victorian poet furthest from Tennyson in sensibility, felt this, and he spoke for thousands of his contemporaries when he called Tennyson "always new, *touching,* beyond other poets."[2] Or so he "used to think," for already in 1864 Tennysonian imitators, Tennyson's imitations of himself, and the first sharp winds of modernism were combining to obscure, for several generations, that first freshness. And yet, Hopkins continues, he still finds "divine, terribly beautiful" the section of *In Memoriam* beginning

> Sad Hesper o'er the buried sun
>   And ready, thou, to die with him,
>   Thou watchest all things ever dim
> And dimmer, and a glory done:

(Ricks 971)

> The team is loosened from the wain,
>   The boat is drawn upon the shore;
>   Thou listenest to the closing door,
> And life is darkened in the brain.

These are perhaps not the lines everyone would choose to represent Tennyson at his best, but their twilit losses could hardly be more typical. "Dim / And dimmer," things blur with the motion of their passing, which seems inseparable from the mind's fading—"And life is darkened in the brain"—as it lets them go. Dimness is one of the most characteristic features of Victorian poetry, and this kind of elegiac "dissolve" is one of its most characteristic actions.

For finally, as Hopkins says with whimsical regret, Tennyson is, "one must see it, what we used to call Tennysonian," and "Tennysonian" inevitably means "elegiac." *In Memoriam,* his lament for his strangely intense friendship with Arthur Henry Hallam, made him poet laureate, and yet this long elegy, which duty sometimes stiffens and generalizes, is neither the finest nor the purest example of the Tennysonian. Tennyson's love poems, his narratives, even his exhortations against his own elegiac tendencies—"Ulysses," for example—are all in their various ways elegies. Tennyson is primarily an elegist of the *self,* and what he renders more fully than any other poet is the sense of life as transparent, ghostlike, dissolving, ungraspable, nearly unrememberable. "I have never *lived* a day, but daily die" (Ricks 269).

The dimness and fluidity of Victorian poetry are not merely a matter of twilight, of mists, shadows, deep horizons and flowing waters, though these are, over and over, the features of its central landscape. More important are the blurrings of attention, of memory, of the Tennysonian version of desire—the "weaving and unweaving of ourselves"—to which they correspond. "Dimness" is by no means limited to the pictorial, or restricted to individual words and images. It can inhere in syntax, repetition, or the hypnotic, defocusing rhythms favored by Tennyson, Swinburne, and the early Yeats. Pater's "weaving and unweaving" of the self is not only the theme of much of the greatest poetry between Wordsworth and Yeats but a part of its very texture and movement. Take, for example, this well-known section of *In Memoriam:*

(Ricks 973)

There rolls the deep where grew the tree.
    O earth, what changes hast thou seen!
    There where the long street roars, hath been
The stillness of the central sea.

The hills are shadows, and they flow
 From form to form, and nothing stands;
 They melt like mist, the solid lands,
Like clouds they shape themselves and go.

But in my spirit will I dwell,
 And dream my dream, and hold it true;
 For though my lips may breathe adieu,
I cannot think the thing farewell.

Such vertigo could be seen as the response to the chasms of space and time that science had newly opened under the nineteenth century. Tennyson often stared into them, and he once called astronomy and geology the "terrible Muses" (Ricks 1411), but surely there is as much fascination as terror in his intuition of a silent, flowing ghost behind the din of London. This is a moment of recognition and comprehension. Lyell's geology has given Tennyson an image for his own vanishing life, for a "prehistory" deeper, shiftier, more lost than that of the planet. And this dimness and fluidity are already deeply incorporated in his language and his patterns of feeling. Alan Sinfield comments:

> If we were to reduce [lines 7–8] to a more straightforward form, say "The solid lands melt like mist and shape themselves and go like clouds," we would not alter the grammatical function of any of the words or phrases, but the order in which we encounter them. The subject, verbs and complements act in the same way, but Tennyson has put them into a more expressive arrangement. "The solid lands," instead of coming first, are sandwiched between the mist and the clouds so that they seem completely engulfed by images of insubstantiality; and "go" is made starkly to end the sentence and the stanza so that the solid lands seem to slide suddenly away into an indefinite void.[3]

"They melt like mist, the solid lands"—the bedrock dissolves even before its appearance in the sentence, as the poem stutters with speed. But it moves swiftly nowhere. The first stanza is a circle beginning and ending with the sea, which seems final whether it images past or present. Even "There where the long street roars," the only island of solidity, recalls in sound and conception the rolling and breaking of waves. The hills also move without progress, "From *form* to *form*" (and *from,* as any bad typist knows, is hardly different from *form*). There is a shortage of transitivity in the images and syntax. The most prominent direct object is in fact reflexive—"they shape themselves"—action in a ring. The poet dreams his dream, and the circling of the syntax becomes a kind of encirclement in elegiac flux. What remains is the transparency, the elusiveness of experience. The landscape vanishes at a touch, and thought never quite rises to specificity. "I cannot think the *thing* farewell," Tennyson says, only half-concluding. "Thing" is the most abstract way of being specific, and it is a feature not only of Tennyson's but of Wordsworth's diaphanous grasp. Does the line mean he cannot let the past go, or that he cannot make it be over? Tennyson's intelligent melancholy would have been aware of the alternatives, and of their possible simultaneity.

Prosodic considerations are also important in defining the Tennysonian flow. Later in this essay, metrical and formal matters will be discussed in some detail, and fairly technically. But for now, a few impressions. First, Saintsbury on Tennyson's *a b b a* tetrameter: "the *In Memoriam* quatrain is much more continuous, and has a more bird-like motion than the ordinary 'long measure' [*a b a b* tetrameter] of which it is a displacement, and yet . . . it invites to continuation though its own internal movement is so perfect."[4] It is a bit difficult to know what audience is imagined for this little dance on the high wire—prosodists are easily reduced to talking to themselves. But Saintsbury, as often, is making important points. The apparently unhelpful "bird-like" is probably a reference to Tennyson's own deft characterization of his stanza. Here "she" is sorrow (or the Muse—in Tennyson they are seldom different):

(Ricks 905)

> Nor dare she trust a larger lay,
>> But rather loosens from the lip
>> Short swallow-flights of song, that dip
> Their wings in tears, and skim away.

Tennyson is obliquely referring to his stanza's tendency to engage emotion lightly ("dip") in its close *b b* rhyme and let it go in the more distant final rhyme ("and skim away"). Christopher Ricks also feels that the quatrain "rises to a momentary chime and then fades." G. K. Chesterton found "the last line like an echo of something distant, a sound heard years before"[5] This is the dying fall Tennyson manages to discover in every form.

Saintsbury's sense that the stanza "invites to continuation" is related. He is seconding an 1850 review by Charles Kingsley, who found that "the mournful minor rhyme of each first and fourth line always leads the ear to expect something beyond, and enables the poet's thoughts to wander sadly on, from stanza to stanza and poem to poem."[6] *In Memoriam,* that is, is full of a feeling characteristic of Tennyson in general—not conclusiveness, but endless ending. Each stanza trails off, so markedly that more than one section of *In Memoriam* could end with a fine elegiac fade after *any* of its stanzas.

Saintsbury incautiously seems to attribute these qualities to the form itself. He probably knew better; Tennyson certainly did. When Coventry Patmore published an essay assigning to several poetic forms inherent emotions, Tennyson, with slightly more enthusiasm than was necessary, sent him a doleful extemporaneous poem in a meter Patmore had defined as "rapid and high-spirited" and a positively skippy performance in what should have been "the most solemn of all our English measures" (*AT Mem.* 1:469–70). Language and feeling are too full of possibilities to be completely determined by a choice of rhythms or an arrangement of rhymes. It is a poet's characteristic *use* of a form or meter—not any "innate" quality—that is always in question.

Tennyson, for his part, thought he had invented the *In Memoriam* stanza, but readers eagerly and somewhat to his annoyance supplied him with seventeenth-century predecessors. Here is Lord Herbert of Cherbury's Celinda, speaking on love after death:

> I speak not this with a false heart,
>   (Wherewith his hand she gently strain'd)
>   Or that would change a love maintain'd
> With so much faith on either part.
>
> Nay, I protest, though Death with his
>   Worst Counsel should divide us here,
>   His terrors could not make me fear,
> To come where your lov'd presence is.

Only if loves fire with the breath
  Of life be kindled, I doubt,
  With our last air 'twill be breath'd out,
And quenched with the cold of death.

Both the stanza and the subject are Tennysonian, but there is no danger of mistaking this for an excerpt from *In Memoriam*. The rhythmic "flow" is utterly different. Tennyson's lines, whether perceived as slow or fast (readers differ here), will be described as smooth or effortless. In contrast, Herbert's lines are deliberately tight rhythmically—to place his stresses correctly, to avoid false steps (reading metrically is like dancing) requires timing and attention. Tennyson would have found this whole passage—perhaps especially lines 1 and 9—frustrating. He would probably have said that its emotions were blocked.

Herbert's *sound* is different, too. He speaks through comparatively pursed lips. The tense monosyllabism (there are five purely monosyllabic lines) of "I speak not this with a false heart" is a far cry from the liquid consonants and moaning vowels of "The hills are shadows and they flow." Tennyson can also write a line of monosyllables, but the hypnotic repetitions, easier rhythm, and smoother sound-transitions of "And dream my dream, and hold it true" make it an entirely different experience.

Tennyson also tends to have more straight-ahead syntactical momentum, even when it takes him in circles. His most important conjunction is the undiscriminating "and," which gathers images one by one, and, one by one, lets them go. Herbert, more deliberate, can drop into parentheses ("Wherewith . . .") or into the parenthetical ("I doubt"). This is related to occasional differences in the right margin. In Herbert's more reluctant momentum, we are more likely to hear a run-on as steep, carved: "Nay, I protest, though Death with his / Worst Counsel should divide us here." Tennyson's lines and stanzas can also draw us on, but his drop from line to line seldom seems precipitous in quite the same way. It is likely to be less sharp. The new line is encountered, like an ascending escalator, already in motion: "The hills are shadows, and they flow / From form to form, and nothing stands."

A reader with another case to make might find in Herbert's terseness and tightness a kind of emotional precision. Herbert's version of the stanza, indeed, intensifies attention, while Tennyson's blurs and dissolves it. Herbert conceives the stanza as something to work constantly *against*—as a result, we can hardly hear it whole. Reading *In Memoriam,* however, we "hear back" over an entire stanza, perhaps over two. Tennyson turns the quatrain into an undulation, into the fade and flow characteristic of his deepest emotions.

From the phantasmal glide of Tennyson to the strenuous attention of Hopkins, nineteenth-century poetic styles are implicated in the fluidity of the self. Variations among the poets in rhythm, impedance, imagery, lineation, syntax, and quality of sound express their senses of the speed, continuity, and feel of our passing. Their poetry is almost a sensuous equivalent of a flux it both imitates and strives against, balancing life's intensity and particularity with its vagueness and swiftness.

What follows will attempt to define mainstream Victorian poetic style in order to link the motions of poetry to the poets' sense of the self and its movement through time. There is not much critical machinery for dealing with notions so fluid and dim as "dimness" and "flow," and this essay may try the reader's patience by reaching after words for habits, visions, and stances that are perhaps essentially preverbal. The psychological biases under consideration are less ideas than feelings, less feelings, even, than ways or forms or styles of feeling. They are so universal in the nineteenth century that they may not seem to call for comment, but for all their vagueness, and perhaps because of it, they are deep, powerful, resistant to change—and an essential stratum of the experience of Victorian poetry.

Dimness in all its variations was perceived by early twentieth-century poets as absolutely central to the Victorianism they were struggling to move beyond. They said so directly: Pound guessed that the nineteenth century would be remembered as a "rather blurry . . . sort of a period" and wrote "Against the Crepuscular Spirit" of his lesser contemporaries. And they said so indirectly: the

Yeats concordance lists eighty-one uses of the word *dim* in his poetry, but only three of them are from after 1906. Yeats began as a Tennysonian, though he saw Tennyson in soft focus through Rossetti. "The Yeats of the Celtic twilight," Eliot once quipped, "seems to me to have been more the Yeats of the pre-Raphaelite twilight."[7] When both life and poetry seemed about to fail him, he had to move out of a dimness that was for him not just a pictorial quality but an aesthetic, a style, a morality, not only a way of art to be revised, but a way of living to be outgrown—a Tennysonian way. He reached toward those edges, restraints, geometries, and cleanlinesses that have by now become as much the standard fare of the late twentieth century as shadows and dimnesses and pale ladies were of the late nineteenth. But even after Yeats is well on his way toward achieving "clean outline, instead of those outlines of lyric poetry that are blurred with desire and vague regret" (*V. Ed.* 849), his best and most central poems are those that respond directly to the problems of focus and flow, of self and time, posed by his Victorian predecessors. Moving from "pale brows, still hands and dim hair" (*CP* 59) to "beauty like a tightened bow" (*CP* 89) is for Yeats both an erotic and a technical project. The recasting of poetic flow and texture is hardly separable from the revision of desire and of the very architecture of the self.

TENNYSON

I

Vanishing Lives,
Vanishing Landscapes

the city . . . built
To music, therefore never built at all,
And therefore built for ever.

— *Gareth and Lynette*

THOUGH RELATIONS between the two most prominent Victorian poets were probably more complex than the surviving evidence implies, they were at least cordial enough that Tennyson, never long on tact, could "rally Browning playfully on his harshness of rhythm, the obscurity and length of his poems," and the latter could reply, "I cannot alter myself: the people must take me as they find me," as if a reviewer, not the poet in the same room, had addressed him, and as if only his popularity were under discussion (*AT Mem.* 2:230). Browning perhaps did not think it worthwhile to confront Tennyson, whose sensitivity to criticism was legendary, with his own shortcomings, though the natural frustrations of his nearly lifelong eclipse by the laureate may occasionally have made petty revenge tempting. Their fascination with each other seems, to us, inevitable. Their mutual affection was apparently quite strong, their mutual admiration real but not unmixed with those reservations two temperaments so radically different and so variously successful must harbor for each other. This undoubtedly would have made the friendship, had it not been conducted mostly at great distances, something of a strain. Indeed, when Browning, traveling with his son Pen not long after the death of Elizabeth Barrett Browning, sighted the Tennyson family unexpectedly in the Amiens station, he pulled his hat over his face to avoid recognition and perhaps the consequent explanations and condolences.

His action is perfectly understandable, but it sets a clear limit on a friendship that, for Browning at least, must have begun to take on uncomfortably mythic proportions—ten years earlier he had also been surprised to encounter Tennyson abroad, this time in Paris. "Odd, is it not, to leave Florence twice, and twice meet, for the first English face—Tennyson's!"[1] More than odd, he must have thought.

As a dramatic poet, Browning was free of that false humility which excuses itself from the labors of politeness on the pretense that its insincerities would immediately be detected, and his letters to Tennyson loudly praise some of his least interesting work.[2] Tennyson, with his finely developed instincts for self-preservation, acquired the habit of thanking his friends for their books before he had read them.

In true Tennysonian fashion, Tennyson admired Browning from a distance even in the same room, but was perhaps unsuccessful at penetrating either the man or his poetry. "He has a mighty intellect," said the poet whose best ideas were barely distinct from emotions and who could not have been sure he thought intellect in poetry very important, but "he seldom attempts the marriage of sense with sound, although he shows a spontaneous felicity in the adaptation of words and ideas to feelings" (*AT Mem.* 2:285). "If the pronunciation of the English language were forgotten," he extemporized to the unfailingly sympathetic Allingham—twice in the same month—"Browning would be held the greatest of modern poets, having treated the greatest variety of subjects in a powerful manner."[3] This is, again, real admiration, but it comes from a poet who had but one subject, and who felt the flow of his language—which had already acquired the description "Tennysonian"—to be inseparable from that subject. He despaired (with everyone but Rossetti and his circle) over *Sordello* and lamented (with everyone including Rossetti, who thought the poem satirized him) *Fifine at the Fair,* but he praised many poems in *Men and Women* and *Dramatis Personae,* for their sentiment, their picturesqueness, and above all their cleverness, and found the first section of *The Ring and the Book,* after a reading by the poet, "full of strange vigour and remarkable in many ways" (*AT Mem.* 2:59). In his more confident moods he defended Browning against his many detractors, apparently reserving the privilege of criticism to himself as an equal. He admired such disputatious pieces as "Bishop Blougram" for their intellectual agility, but "Evelyn Hope" is the poem he liked to recommend to doubters as a *poem.* It is an elegy for a sixteen-year-old girl spoken by a much older admirer, and one of the very few Browning poems one could imagine Tennyson writing.

What is perhaps most interesting about Tennyson's contradictory feelings for Browning's poetry is that he cannot quite see its oddness, toughness, and knottiness as a style in itself. He thinks of his rival not in terms of his success at being Browning but in terms of his failure to be a second Tennyson. Browning is not a strange and independent being to be regarded with wonder but rather, like Ida of the *The Princess,* a "false self." He becomes an impeded version of the laureate, who said of him—one can imagine with what plaintive emphasis—"He has plenty of music in him, but he cannot get it out" (*AT Mem.* 2:285). This places Browning on one end of a scale of which Tennyson occupies the happy middle. The opposite extreme is Swinburne, who according to Tennyson is "a reed through which all things blow into music," "all things" implying a failure of moral selectivity (*AT Mem.* 2:285). For Tennyson, the poet of the dimly erotic dissolutions, Browning's insistence on the resistance of the other, the effort of feeling, seemed a nervous tic. All the contradictions, collisions, and tensions Browning reveled in seemed to Tennyson not the very basis of consciousness but flaws, bars to the smoother, purer, and more anonymous Tennysonian pleasures: "One is constantly aware of the greatness of the man," he said to Allingham, "yet somehow baulked of satisfaction."[4]

In an early letter to Elizabeth Barrett, Browning, for his part, saw Tennyson as infused with the elegiac dimness and dewiness of one of his own landscapes, as "a LONG, hazy kind of a man" with "something 'naif' about him" whose "genius" was clearly visible, and who seemed to need the help of his solicitous publisher to navigate the evening. Insofar as he believed in his own art, Browning had to have reservations about that of his contemporary, and in a letter of 1870 to Isa Blagden, they pour out, apparently compounded by years of exasperation. *The Holy Grail and Other Poems* is "all out of my head already." He deplores its cultivated smoothness of effect with "the monotony, however, you must expect if the new is to be of a piece with the old." It is not clear here whether Browning is objecting to weaknesses he perceived in a particular volume or to the inalienably Tennysonian, for smoothness, even unmemorableness, is part of Tennyson's perception of a life that seems to slide by without touching us. Going on to "Pelleas and Ettarre," Browning accuses Tennyson of being a decorative landscapist: "We look at the object of art in poetry so differently! Here is an Idyll about a knight being untrue to his friend and yielding to the temptation of that friend's mistress after having engaged to assist him in his suit. I should judge the conflict in the knight's soul the proper subject to describe: Tennyson thinks he should describe the castle, and effect of the moon on its towers, and anything *but* the soul."[5]

On the other hand, Browning, like Tennyson, sometimes took it upon himself to rescue his fellow from the depredations of lesser critics. In response to Julia Wedgwood's confession of "want of fervour" for Tennyson's poetry, Browning writes that "nobody has more fully found out at the beginning what he was born to do,—nor done it more perfectly."[6] But the praise may also be a reservation. "Perfect" is, in the context of this friendship, a loaded word. Tennyson apparently on more than one occasion urged Browning to "make his work as perfect as possible" (*AT Mem.* 2:230). For Browning, perhaps partly as a result, the word weighs in the other scale: "What's come to perfection perishes" says "Old Pictures in Florence." In the same letter he criticizes "Enoch Arden," a poem he had praised in a letter to Tennyson six weeks earlier as "the perfect thing" (*AT Mem.* 2:16). Browning, it must be remembered, is the poet who wrote of the failed but nevertheless "faultless painter" Andrea del Sarto in what is, perhaps not coincidentally, one of his most Tennysonian monologues—and a monologue that his letter to Julia Wedgwood, fifteen years later, seems to echo:

> Eh? the whole seems to fall into a shape
> As if I saw alike my work and self
> And all that I was *born to be and do,*
> A twilight-piece.
>
> . . . . .
>
> Ah, but a man's reach should exceed his grasp,
> Or what's a heaven for? All is silver-gray
> Placid and *perfect* with my art: the worse!

(ll. 46–49, 97–99; my emphasis)

For Browning, artist of the imperfect, the soulless perfection of Andrea del Sarto's art could easily resemble the sentimental smoothness of "Enoch Arden." Andrea, Enoch Arden, and perhaps Tennyson himself might seem to share the elegiac sadness of a life lived as though it were already over.

Browning may or may not have had Tennyson's "twilight-pieces" particularly in mind when he anatomized the elegiac tendencies of the Victorian age in "Andrea del Sarto," and he was certainly hyperbolic in his characterization of Tennyson as a descriptive poet, but his points are worth considering, especially if one keeps in mind that both Browning and Tennyson are poets of the Paterian flow of the self. Faced with death or failure or love, Browning's speakers find themselves in a state of flickering and uncertain identity—"Do I live, am I dead?" Over and over, with a kind of insomniac fervor, they explain themselves to themselves, trying to change the past, seemingly dissolving and reforming as they tell and untell their stories.

Tennyson is undeniably more of a landscapist than Browning, but though his pictorialism can be excessive, it has always been clear that his landscapes are mental landscapes. They are, as much as Browning's monologues, places inside the mind. If Tennyson's poems seem less individualized than Browning's, it is because they work further from the will and closer to sleep, death, and desire, where we are more alike, and where fewer and more general words serve to murmur of our disappearance. Dimmed in trance, swept up in flow or mist, lost in the opening horizon, blurred by ghosts, the Tennysonian poem is also a borderline state of consciousness.

Tennyson's landscape is a vanishing landscape, and his poems, like Browning's though with broader and less personal gestures, limn the dissolutions and crystallizations of the self.

Tennyson was quite conscious that his interest in landscape was really an interest in its transparency to the mind. "It is the distance that charms me in the landscape," he once remarked, "the picture and the past and not the immediate today in which I move."[7] The stress or thisness of the present that so fascinated Browning, Hopkins, and Lawrence is at best a matter of ambivalence for Tennyson, who looks instead for "distance," "the past"—the confusion, even the equation, of space and time is quintessentially Tennysonian. He recalls that even as a child "the words 'far, far away' had always a strange charm" for him (*AT Mem.* 1:11), as well they might have, given his nightmarish family life, and the six stanzas he made out of this spell in 1888 are six disappearances:

> What sight so lured him through the fields he knew
> As where earth's green stole into heaven's own hue,
>   Far-far-away?

> What sound was dearest in his native dells?
> The mellow lin-lan-lone of evening bells
>   Far-far-away.

> What vague world-whisper, mystic pain or joy,
> Through those three words would haunt him when a
>   boy,
>   Far-far-away?

> A whisper from his dawn of life? a breath
> From some fair dawn beyond the doors of death
>   Far-far-away?

> Far, far, how far? from o'er the gates of Birth,
> The faint horizons, all the bounds of earth,
>   Far-far-away?

> What charm in words, a charm no words could give?
> O dying words, can Music make you live
>   Far-far-away?

(Ricks 1405–6)

Typically, the boy's interest is in the horizon, the dim fusion of field and sky that "lures" the dimming soul into it, and in the "lin-lan-lone" of bells softened and lowered by distance and evening. Tennyson cited that phrase as one of his best, and it provides an instructive contrast to the metallic over-the-shoulder suddenness of the "*Hy, Zy, Hine*" of vespers in Browning's "Soliloquy of the Spanish Cloister." But the poem's perspective is somewhat more complex. It is also bounded by a horizon of time. "Far-Far-Away" cherishes a memory more than seventy years old. Looking to the far verge of the past, Tennyson sees a boy staring, listening for the size of space, a double distance. And what does the boy hear? Perhaps another memory, a "whisper from his dawn of life." Or perhaps an intuition of what the aged poet, with only a few years to live, himself hears from "beyond the doors of death." Vistas within vistas, the poem finally encircles us with the ambiguous Tennysonian mood—"pain or joy"—and loses itself in itself. For Tennyson, the "charm in words, a charm no words could give," is their power to make such worlds. In this regard, the poem's incantation of the word *word* and the third stanza's near-identifications of *word* and *world* are revealing. The process of a Tennysonian poem is often such a letting-go into a "spaciousness" which we can only describe in terms of space or time, but which, being a mental phenomenon, is both and neither. The cities built to music in "Tithonus," "Tiresias," and the *Idylls* are only special cases of the dimmer, interior spaces Tennyson is always opening, raising with words.

Neither in this poem nor in his remarks about the distance in landscape does Tennyson imagine anything specific at the end of geography. Nor does he, outside of a few set pieces such as "Anacaona" (Ricks 283) of the "cocoa-shadowed coves" and a failed attempt to inflame Wordsworth's imagination by relating a tale of a tropical island covered entirely with red foliage (*AT Mem.* 1:209), show an important interest in the exotic or even in the merely foreign. He yearns for distance itself—the space he finds in dimmed and echoing language, in the climbing, dissolving repetition of "far, far" and the long vista "away" uncoils into. This is the poet who responded to his brother's jitters before a dinner party with "Fred, think of Herschel's great star-patches, and you will soon get over all that" (*AT Mem.* 1:20). His own form of spacious resignation, according to his son, was the simple prayer "O Thou Infinite, Amen" (*AT Mem.* 1:325).

Tennyson's vistas of time are similarly vague in their horizons. Though his famous "passion of the past" first appears as a phrase in a late poem, "The Ancient Sage," he told Knowles it was what he had "always felt even from a boy,"[8] and it is a lifelong theme. "Past," however, has a limited meaning. Tennyson was not a cultivator of historical exotics. His sense of otherness is neither so strong nor so patient as Browning's, and he exhibits nothing really comparable to the latter's reconstructions of Italy's artistic past. What figures of history and myth he touches turn immediately transparent—through them we see Tennyson, though in that mood of sad distance where he is nearly no one, "A white-haired shadow roaming like a dream / The ever-silent spaces of the East" (Ricks 1114).

The past in Tennyson's poetry is almost completely private, but it is also, paradoxically, impersonal. We know very little from the poems themselves of either the terrors or the pleasures of Tennyson's early years, though the labors of his biographers have more than adequately established that he had no Eden to mourn for. In a real sense, Tennyson's past never happened to him. His losses are things he never had, continually surprising, painful, and fascinating vacancies. Only with the death of Arthur Hallam was he granted an utterable tragedy, and even then *In Memoriam* is weakest when it tries to imagine his friend as a character rather than as a loss. Tennyson's past, particularly in the early poems, is The Past. It is almost completely without detail. In the juvenile "Written by an Exile of Bassorah," for example, Noureddin gazes into a dim horizon of the self, that, typically, is full of twilight and distance, streaming and waving and haze. It promotes a very Tennysonian confusion—as in "Far-Far-Away" it is difficult at first to tell whether the poet is primarily interested in a receding landscape or a vanishing past:

(Ricks 96)   The far-distant hills, and the groves of my childhood,
                        Now stream in the light of the sun's setting ray;

And the tall-waving palms of my own native wild-wood
In the blue haze of distance are melting away.

Distance is more important than the distant; loss overshadows the lost.

The sadness of "Tears, idle tears" is similar:

Tears, idle tears, I know not what they mean,
Tears from the depth of some divine despair
Rise in the heart, and gather to the eyes,
In looking on the happy Autumn-fields,
And thinking of the days that are no more.

Fresh as the first beam glittering on a sail,
That brings our friends up from the underworld,
Sad as the last which reddens over one
That sinks with all we love below the verge;
So sad, so fresh, the days that are no more.

(Ricks 784–86)

Ah, sad and strange as in dark summer dawns
The earliest pipe of half-awakened birds
To dying ears, when unto dying eyes
The casement slowly grows a glimmering square;
So sad, so strange, the days that are no more.

Dear as remembered kisses after death,
And sweet as those by hopeless fancy feigned
On lips that are for others; deep as love,
Deep as first love, and wild with all regret;
O Death in Life, the days that are no more.

Tennyson reports that "this song came to me on the yellowing autumn-tide at Tintern Abbey, full for me of its bygone memories" (Ricks 784n) and he is probably remembering both Arthur Hallam, who was buried nearby, and Wordsworth, whose own "Tintern Abbey" is a wellspring of the retrospection and regret, the sense of vanishing past and dissolving identity, that stream through Tennyson's poetry. Neither is remembered particularly, but memory in general deepens the scene. At the end of every stanza "the days that are no more" become a kind of mental horizon into which Tennyson's emotions flow, a mental horizon for which his poems are constantly finding physical equivalents. Here, for example, the sail that "sinks with all we love below the verge" recalls similar elegiac fade-outs in "Ulysses":

> To follow knowledge like a sinking star,
> Beyond the utmost bound of human thought.
>
> Yet all experience is an arch wherethrough
> Gleams that untravelled world, whose margin fades
> For ever and for ever when I move.

(Ricks 564, 563)

There may be another horizon in the poem, equally important but less visible. Graham Hough notes of "Tears, idle tears" that "each line is self-contained—yet does not end with a snap, but trails away, suggesting a passage into some infinite beyond." Hough remarks that "very few people notice" that the poem is unrhymed. Saintsbury makes a similar observation about the blank verse of "Tithonus"—"I have never, from first reading at first appearance to the present day, been able to persuade myself that the first ten lines, and especially the first four, are not a regular stanza."[9]

Several features of Tennysonian verse are responsible for this sense of "trailing away." First, "Tears, idle tears" is full of the kind of edgeless near-rhyme with which Tennyson frequently half-shapes his blank verse. *Despair–more–world–verge–more–birds–square–more–more* form a shifting sequence. Second, many of the lines, including the repeated "*So* sad, so strange, the days that are no *more*," open and close with related sounds, or open with the sound that concludes the previous line, or both:

> *Tears,* idle tears, I know not what they *mean,*
> *Tears* from the depth of some divine *despair*
> *Rise* in the heart, and gather to the *eyes,*

The result is an ambiguous momentum. The end pauses, vaguely remembering the beginning; the beginning shoves wearily off what had seemed an end.

A large part of the effect can be attributed to Tennyson's typically long—even moaning—terminal vowels ("divine despair," "are no more") combined with a characteristically weak enjambment that allows lines to float free, and with the peculiar momentum of his blank verse, a momentum probably best described as bodiless. The phantom rhyme heard by readers is a recurrent, long fade into the right margin. Between the lines we are swung into some larger and vaguely apprehended realm. Distance and disconnection somehow yawn beneath the high polish of the verse. Whether the lines are heard as slow or fast (this is a very difficult subjective determination), they seem to gather a momentum that is dissipated in the echoing white space. The total effect, as often in Tennyson's poetry, is of experience passing without touching—one finishes each line having missed something, having not quite focused, hearing a rhyme almost reached, a space opened.

Tennyson once said of the sadness of "Tears, idle tears" that "it was not real woe" but "rather the yearning that young people occasionally experience for that which seems to have passed away from them forever" (*AT Mem.* 2:73). But the woe is quite genuine: "not real" should probably be translated as "objectless." He mourns not lost things but the loss—whether through repression or erosion—of the past itself. His characteristic poetic mood is the sadness that radiates from such tremors in the foundation of his identity. The past, the distance—these are the vast realm of absence into which Tennyson's feelings are always flowing, but which he is seldom allowed to touch.

Speaking of a poem's "spaciousness" in this peculiar sense may seem excessively literal—we do not quite walk around in a poem as we do in a room. But the alternative, regarding poems as flocks of black characters resident on a page, is even more literal. Like a room or a landscape, a poem occurs in the brain, where it in part ceases to be distinct words and becomes associations, instructions, images. There, it can seem to occupy more or less of us, seem more or less definite, more or less strange. And whatever else it is, a poem is something that *works*. It is a program the brain loads and runs, with the difference that the brain gradually adapts to run it more successfully: the poem in effect runs part of the brain.

It is certainly true that for many nineteenth-century poets,

Tennyson prominent among them, poetry may feel like a place, whether or not it describes one. Once the movement of poetry is yoked to the Paterian fluidity of the self, the poet is "inside" the poem as he is inside his mind. This sense of interiority or placeness is commonly—though of course not inevitably—imaged as landscape. The feeling of being in a poem is translated into being in a scene. But for poets of less confident sublimity than Wordsworth, "inside" too easily implies "outside"—spaciousness modulates into enclosure. Placeness then finds its metaphors in rooms, bowers, islands, towers and is infused with feelings of alienation and unreality. The existence of outside compromises the reality of inside (and vice versa) so that Tennyson must admonish himself to leave "The Palace of Art," Keats must constantly ask "Do I wake or sleep?" and Yeats, echoing Keats's description of *Endymion* as "a little Region to wander in,"[10] deplores the tendency of his early poetry to be an encompassing "region" rather than an objective "action" (*LKT* 82–83)

Whatever spaces there are behind the eyes cannot be the same as those we think we see before us. More likely, the spaciousness of a poem is best described not in terms of length, width, and height but as a quality of attention, and perhaps this is equivalent to the manner in which the poem *mixes* with the mind. The "dreaminess" or "regionality" felt by Yeats and Keats is a dimmed or blurred consciousness that can be at least partially analyzed in terms of the features of style—rhythm, syntax, diction, repetition, etc.—that control attention. The issue seems to be *flow*. The very vagueness of the word is useful, for in Tennyson, flow is not only an image (a feature of landscapes) but also a theme and a stylistic aspiration.

This is certainly true of "The Kraken," one of Tennyson's earliest and most fantastic worlds apart. The poem fades, both pictorially and stylistically, into deep fluidity and nervous fascination:

(Ricks 246–47)

> Below the thunders of the upper deep;
> Far, far beneath in the abysmal sea,
> His ancient, dreamless, uninvaded sleep
> The Kraken sleepeth: faintest sunlights flee

About his shadowy sides: above him swell
Huge sponges of millennial growth and height;
And far away into the sickly light,
From many a wondrous grot and secret cell
Unnumbered and enormous polypi
Winnow with giant arms the slumbering green.
There hath he lain for ages and will lie
Battening upon huge seaworms in his sleep,
Until the latter fire shall heat the deep;
Then once by man and angels to be seen,
In roaring he shall rise and on the surface die.

Tennyson's poems often repay literal-minded examination of their spaces, if only with the discovery that they quickly repel the literal. Postponing its subject until the fourth line, the opening sentence, with its series of prepositional phrases, draws us along and, seemingly, in and down. "Upper deep" should be the first shock, but like most Tennysonian shocks it passes almost without conscious effect. Had Tennyson written "Below the thunders of the deep," we could stand on shore. But "upper deep" implies depth above and below. Its near-paradox is one of those suddenly blurred borders or horizons with which Tennyson's poems surround us. "The Kraken" is, after all, less about a sea monster than about the unfocusing, the half-reality of the self.

The increasingly uncertain topography is mirrored in the syntax. Hardly anything happens, but everything is connected—following the directionlessness directions of prepositional phrases, attention generalizes. The very continuation of the sentence becomes associated with increasing dimness and distance, an effect reinforced by what W. David Shaw, characterizing the line "His ancient, dreamless, uninvaded sleep," calls "the weakening of poetic shape, produced by the drift of adjectives."[11] The sentence reduces to "The Kraken sleepeth . . . his sleep." Another Tennysonian world rises from a lengthened tautology.

Tennyson often, as here, devotes elaborate stanzas to the discovery of shapelessness rather than shape—or to musical coherence rather than sculptural contour. The rhyme scheme of "The Kraken" is *a b a b c d d c e f e a a f e,* hardly a scheme at all. In theory, then, six rhyme sounds control its fifteen lines. But *a, b,* and *f* (*deep, sea, green*) are assonantally very close, as are *d* and *e* (*height, lie*), so that there are in fact only three distinct rhymes. Thirteen of the lines end with two of these—and "deep" and "sleep" are repeated exactly, as by a hypnotist. So frequent are their returns that the rhyme sounds lose all closural effect and most of their reality as words. They blur and swarm, becoming one of the poem's dimmed borders, part of its musical, involving spaciousness.

Alliteration is also enlisted. The effect of a density of repeated sounds is, of course, largely dependent on context. In these lines from Daniel, "Care-charmer Sleep, son of the sable Night, / Brother to Death, in silent darkness born," the relatively clear-sounding and predominantly initial alliteration seems both to balance the lines internally and to propel them. But in

> From many a wondrous grot and secret cell
> Unnumbered and enormous polypi
> Winnow with giant arms the slumbering green

the effect is quite different. These lines are, first of all, strongly reminiscent of "The moan of doves in immemorial elms / And murmuring of innumerable bees" from "Come down, O maid," another poem that invites us down from a "height" into a deeper, murmuring, more personal realm. (When Tennyson steals from himself or others, he is as likely to lift a sound pattern as an idea or image. Compare Wordsworth's "she is in her grave, and, Oh / the difference to me!" to Tennyson's "In more of life true life no more / And love the indifference to be" or Herrick's "Then, methinks, how sweetly flows / The liquefaction of her clothes" to Tennyson's "And on the liquid mirror glows / The clear perfection of her face"). The repeated sounds of "The Kraken," softer, more complex, spreading to noninitial syllables, might be described not as balanced but as inwoven. Far from pushing off each other, they blend and blur. The present of the poem dims, slows, deepens.

Tennyson, in addition, employs two noticeably different rhythms for creating (descending into) and dispersing (ascending from) this poetic space. In the first ten lines, we find two of the poem's three spondees, "Fár, fár" and "Húge spónges." Spondees late in the line can be absorbed by, can indeed contribute to, the line's momentum. These, lying heavily on the opening syllables, are hollow and slow. The caesuras are mostly feminine (occurring after an unstressed syllable). In contrast to the more distinct masculine caesura, these typically give the line a softer, more trailing or sagging pause: "His ancient, / / dreamless, / / uninvaded sleep / The Kraken sleepeth. / / Faintest sunlights flee."

Finally, the characteristic rhythmic variation of the first ten lines is the second- or third-foot pyrrhic (I retain the questionable entity "foot" as a familiar way to locate and name rhythmic phenomena). These will often (the former especially, and especially in this slowed and polysyllabic environment) contribute to a kind of drop or sag in the line: "Far, far beneath in the abysmal sea," "Huge sponges of millennial growth and height," "Unnumbered and enormous polypi."

All these features contribute to a sense of slowed, viscous time and moaning interiority. In lines 11–15, however, the syntax straightens out, alliteration thins and clears, caesuras are overridden and the recurring rhythmic variation is the more gliding *fourth*-foot pyrrhic. The poem accelerates and skims towards its climax, which is a kind of overflow: "The Kraken" is one line longer than a sonnet, and its last line is one foot longer than a pentameter. It does not conclude. It expires:

> There hath he lain for ages and will lie
> Battening upon huge seaworms in his sleep,
> Until the latter fire shall heat the deep;
> Then once by man and angels to be seen,
> In roaring he shall rise and on the surface die.

As with many of Tennyson's poems, it is less useful to ask "What does it mean?" than "Why was Tennyson attracted to the subject?" One might say that the poem's fascinated evasion of its own center is a young poet's typical strategy. Tennyson is tapping a poetic potential he cannot name—and will not name, for a young poet, indeed a young *person,* finds in such definition the threat of limitation and exhaustion. "The Kraken," like "The Hesperides," is in part about a life at once feared and hoarded—in either case unlived—and Ricks is surely correct in finding Tennyson here, as in "Mariana," "The Lady of Shalott," and more poems than one can conveniently name, entranced by "a life which is no life."[12] This is his familiar world of fluidity and dimness, its monstrous center (like those deeply encircled ladies), hardly visible. The Kraken's sleep is impenetrable, "uninvaded." Even its nourishment is absorbed frictionlessly and unconsciously, "Battening upon huge seaworms in its sleep." Life happens without participation or awareness. All time passes without touching.

Or almost. Tennyson's timeless worlds apart are always underlain by the faint, anxious pulse of the future. The end will always seem to be coming—this poet is more interested in dreading the end than in the end itself. When it comes here, the monster breaks the surface with a passion gigantic, objectless, and ineffectual—he almost seems to die from being "seen." Culler calls the Kraken an "analogue of the 'Lady of Shalott,' "[13] and indeed for the beauty as well as the beast, exposure, individuation, and death occur in the same moment, a moment that is a blend of swan song, prophetic rage, and something very like embarrassment.

The best-known and most determined of Tennyson's places apart is the island of "The Lotos-Eaters." The world of that poem tempts readers toward words like *timeless,* but as in "The Kraken," its Tennysonian languor is inseparable from a terrible swiftness. Somewhere under its narcotized cadences "time driveth onward fast," and the mariners have already become the past, disinherited by the future:

(Ricks 434)

> all hath suffered change:
> For surely now our household hearths are cold:
> Our sons inherit us: our looks are strange:
> And we should come like ghosts to trouble joy.

Not only its blend of languor and swiftness, stupor and dread, but its techniques of spaciousness are reminiscent of "The Kraken:

(Ricks 430)

> "Courage!" he said, and pointed toward the *land,*
> "This mounting wave will roll us shoreward soon."

In the *afternoon* they came unto a *land*
In which it seem̀ed always *afternoon*.
All round the coast the languid air did swoon,
Breathing like one that hath a weary dream.
Full-faced above the valley stood the moon;
And like a downward smoke, the slender stream
Along the cliff to fall and pause and fall did seem.

A land of streams! some, like a downward smoke,
Slow-dropping veils of thinnest lawn, did go;
And some through wavering lights and shadows broke,
Rolling a slumbrous sheet of foam below.
They saw the gleaming river seaward flow
From the inner land: far off, three mountain-tops,
Three silent pinnacles of aged snow,
Stood sunset-flushed: and, dewed with showery drops,
Up-clomb the shadowy pine above the woven copse.

The first two lines are given a kind of wooden, heroic momentum, which Tennyson deflates suddenly with the inspired flatness of
the *land–land* rhyme. " 'The strand' was, I think, my first reading,"
he said, "but the no rhyme of 'land' and 'land' was lazier" (Ricks
430n). "Lazier," certainly, or even "deeper," since the circling of
land around to land seems not only to stop time but to enclose us, a
phenomenon Tennyson describes, with characteristic indirection,
in the "swoon" of the "languid air" "all round the coast." When
"afternoon" lies wearily down on "afternoon," the poem, sighing
itself asleep, seems incapable even of finding its next words.
    The Spenserian stanza uses only three rhymes to organize nine
lines and, as in "The Kraken," Tennyson effectively reduces the
number to two by half-rhyming his *a*'s and *b*'s (*land–soon–land–
noon–swoon–moon* in the first stanza and *smoke–go–broke–below–
flow–snow* in the second). Because the rhyme sounds recur so
frequently and prominently, the line-ends are flattened, and because
Tennyson's terminal vowel is often very long, they are blurred and
slowed. As in "Tears, idle tears" there is an audible moan at the end
of lines, a moan in which their momentum is largely dissipated. In a
line with Miltonic thrust an initial trochee or spondee can act as a

kind of swimmer's turn, pushing forcefully off the left margin. But with a slowed line and a flat line-ending preceding it, with little rhythmic or syntactical momentum, an initial substitution can be positively weary, especially when, as in "breathing" and "weary dream," the initial and terminal sounds of the line are identical: "All round the coast the languid air did swoon, / Breathing like one that hath a weary dream."

Enjambment, which can in other poems be a major source of propulsion, is in this peculiar rhythmic context another source of weariness. When a line overflows, it can seem to fall exhausted, here partly because of the shift from falling rhythm to an initial anapest:

> They saw the gleaming river seaward flow
> From the inner land.

The same sense of exhausted continuation is provided by the final alexandrine, which, as in Pope's gibe, "like a wounded snake, drags its slow length along," especially when Tennyson loads it with spacious vowels and an image that unsays its motion:

> And like a downward smoke, the slender stream
> Along the cliff to fall and pause and fall did seem.

"Some like a downward smoke," the next stanza goes on—by picking up a phrase and refusing to go on. Manifold repetitions surround us, blurring into the same kind of fluidity and dimness the stanzas take it upon themselves to describe: a scene of streaming, rolling, gleaming, slumbrous, flowing waters and wavering, shadowy objects.

Tennyson's pictorialism is usually, and at its best, somewhat antipictorial in that it involves the creation of emotional dimness. This is a necessary Tennysonian equation. The more thoroughly he images one of his landscapes, the less real it becomes. An odd consequence is visible in these stanzas:

> All round the coast the languid air did swoon
> Breathing like one that hath a weary dream.
> Full-faced above the valley stood the moon;

And the like a downward smoke, the slender stream
Along the cliff to fall and pause and fall did seem.

Aspects of the landscape are compared to a dreamer, a face, and
a smoke, all of which could literally occur in this land of mist and
dark-faced dreamers, and all of which, in one form or another, later
do occur. Tenor and vehicle merge, a confusion Tennyson encourages by shifting their order in the sentences. A related phenomenon
appears later in the poem:

There is sweet music here that softer falls
Than petals from blown roses on the grass,
Or night-dews on still waters between walls
Of shadowy granite, in a gleaming pass.

(ll. 46–49)

With its series of four locational phrases ("on . . . between . . . of . . . in"), the last two lines create an illusion of
movement, and with each qualification the original subject—"music"—fades further, until the deep pool between the twilit granite
cliffs detaches itself almost completely and is remembered not as a
metaphor but as an actual feature of lotos-land. The self-reflexive
quality of Tennyson's mind counteracts the subordinations and
hierarchies of logic so that progression and digression are equivalent. On large scales, as well as small: the choric song of the lotos-
eaters, at first apparently a digression like a song in a play, takes over
the poem completely. In Tennyson, real and half-real merge. Poems
drift through strange depths and simultaneities.

But to call Tennyson a poet of escape raises more questions
than it answers. He is often, indeed, a poet of distance and unreality,
but these are states he reflected, whether or not he sought them. For
though he was too dutiful a Victorian to say that distance and
unreality are our natural conditions, he often came close: "Annihi-
late within yourself these two dreams of Space and Time. To me
often the far-off world seems nearer than the present, for in the
present is always something unreal and indistinct" (*AT Mem.* l:171–
72). What Tennyson's poems say over and over is, not that we
should flee the present, but that we cannot reach it, not that we
escape life, but that we lose it.

II

The Language of Absence

I see their unborn faces shine
Beside the never-lighted fire.

In Memoriam

TENNYSON'S SIMPLEST and most profound delight in language is with its ability to say yes and no at the same time. In a very early poem, never published in his lifetime, he is already rehearsing the ambiguities of dimness, training his mind's eye on the invisible: "As rays of many a rolling central Star / Aye flashing earthward have not reached us yet" (Ricks 167).

The paradox that seems to have fascinated the nineteen-year-old poet is that of absent presence. The future, fully formed, rushes toward him, still unknown. The rays of the distant stars "have not reached us," yet "flashing"—which is early and late Tennyson's favorite word for the quick touch of experience—half-puts them before us. One of his best-known lines, from "Mariana," works similarly: "Unlifted was the clinking latch." This is the kind of image that can be cited, somewhat carelessly, as an instance of Tennyson's particularity. But every reader who has delighted in it knows that its power depends on the unsaying of the very detail it seems to present. "Unlifted" contains the "lift" we imagine despite the completed meaning of the sentence, and the latch "clinks" as if it had been lifted. The alternatives are also confused by the similarity of "lifted" and "clinking" in sound. There is a palimpsest, a dimness, in the line. "No," it says, "but yes." In the Silent Isle episode of "The Voyage of Maeldune," Tennyson achieves a similar effect through an explicit exclusion of one of the senses. The repetition of "silent" cushions the fall of the sea: "Where a silent ocean always broke on a silent shore" (Ricks 1277).

To discuss the participation of the senses in the abstraction of language is to risk literal-mindedness and to invite disagreement, for readers visualize to widely differing degrees, and there is no word analogous to *visualize* for even the sense of hearing. But surely it is impossible to imagine intentionally a silent ocean. Though many of the images of the sea that slip uncalled-for into memory may be without sound, "Do not think of *X*" immediately produces an image of *X,* especially here where Tennyson has taken particular care to make his "silent" line mimic the dull crash of distant surf. Nor is this an isolated instance. He repeats the trick in the next line: "and the long waterfalls / Poured in a thunderless plunge." In "The Lotos-Eaters," the near oxymoron "dark faces pale" also takes away what it gives, as does a line from "Youth:" "I sit among the scentless flowers" (Ricks 579). There are, of course, odorless flowers, but they are not on the poet's mind. Smells release memory powerfully, but compared to sights and sounds, they are difficult to recall at will—or in a poem—and rarely enter memory unsummoned. Our sensory indexer seems to work much more efficiently from smell to memory than in the other direction, with the practical consequence that the past is usually odorless. And these flowers, it turns out, *are* in the past. The speaker, Tennyson tells us, lives entirely in the memory of "natal bowers." Tennysonian images of absent presence, that is, may be related to our inevitable distance or pastness. At any given moment we are nearly all memory. The poems, at any rate, often associate the unreality or pastness of the present with the presence of the past. In this context, the "weird seizures" the hero of *The Princess* is subject to are not weird at all. They merely embody a discovery that Tennyson over and over delights in remaking—that the present, as we see it, blends with the mind's pastness and becomes part ghost:

> Then I remembered that burnt sorcerer's curse
> That one should fight with shadows and should fall;
> And like a flash the weird affection came:

(Ricks 815)
> King, camp and college turned to hollow shows;
> I seemed to move in old memorial tilts,
> And doing battle with forgotten ghosts,
> To dream myself the shadow of a dream.

"All things were and were not" the Prince elsewhere says of his trances, making him the ideal mate for the southern Mariana, "Dreaming, she knew it was a dream: / She felt he was and was not there" (Ricks, p. 365).

The sudden transparency of detail that expresses absent presence—and provides a good part of Tennyson's poetic excitement—is not always explicit or even noticeable. Take these oddly effective lines from "The Lotos-Eaters": "All things have rest, and ripen toward the grave / In silence; ripen, fall and cease" (Ricks 433). The primary antecedent of "All things" is "fruits." The secondary reference is "men." But fruit does not "cease," nor does a man. Fruit decays, men die; a *sound* or an *action* may "cease." "Cease" suggests sudden and total absence, suggests fruit that vanishes as it touches the ground—Keats's "To cease upon the midnight with no pain" is shaded the same way. Reading the poem, one does not, of course, think this through. There is only, encountering the verb, a slight shock of unreality as the image dematerializes.

Absent presence is for Tennyson an irresistible oxymoron. The dead Hallam becomes "a life removed" and "dark freight / A vanished life." His future absence is elaborated almost into a parallel universe as the poet imagines the nephews his sister Emily and Arthur would have given him: "I see their unborn faces shine / Beside the never-lighted fire" (Ricks 931).

The chance lost and the life never lived may be Tennyson's—and the Victorian age's—most haunting absence, but the transparency of the Tennysonian present is most consistently manifest in the characteristics of what might be called his central landscape. "All the world is ghost" to him (Ricks 1368). Morning and evening he surveys "sad and undistinguishable things" and "imperfect half-seen objects" that typically "flash," "flicker," "shimmer," "shiver," "gleam," "fail," "shake" (Ricks 116, 111). It is almost as if he sees the world reflected in water, as he literally does in "The Lady of Shalott," "A Dream of Fair Women," and "The Miller's Daughter." Phrases such as "waning woods," "white kine glimmered," and "Now fades the last long streak of snow" turn solid objects into dimming lights (Ricks 935, 946, 967). Even images of sudden violence seem to flash by only half apprehended. Compare, for example, "And wildly dashed on tower and tree / The sunbeam strikes *along* the world" (Ricks 877) to Wordsworth's "Felt in the blood, and felt *along* the heart" from "Tintern Abbey." Both images achieve their effect through a surprising attribution of length. But where Wordsworth's "along" expands the heart and suggests a warmth felt throughout the body in a prolonged moment, Tennyson's underscores the headlong velocity and distance of experience.

Though he uses the *word* less frequently than his followers, "dimness" is the most striking *feature* of the Tennysonian landscape, and the one he passed on to the Pre-Raphaelites and the early Yeats. When he writes of a "dim land" (Ricks 1607), "dim" describes not only a physical condition of objects but his own state of being. Accordingly he can say "I dimly pace" or speak of a "dim brain" or his "own dim life" (Ricks 77, 240, 892), and he associates the dimness, mists, streamings of his poetry with the pastness of the moment. He sees each moment through the "haze of grief" (Ricks 886) that is its own vanishing. Watching stars dimmed by fog, in fact, he imagines they are past: "As your memories / More than yourselves ye look" (Ricks 164). Conversely, thinking of Enoch Arden fading in the memories of his children, he imagines him shrouded in morning mist:

> Uncertain as a vision or a dream,
> (Ricks 1138)   Faint as a figure seen in early dawn
> Down at the far end of an avenue.

Dim, to take the simplest case, is a strange word. For Tennyson, as for the Pre-Raphaelites and early Yeats, it means partial absence. Though it normally occurs in pictorial passages, it is in its very meaning an admission that language fails at its tasks of depiction. Poetry can be more intense than life—it must be—but its sensuousness compared to that of the senses is very likely to seem dim, merely remembered. The nineteenth century's increasing devotion to literary particularity is therefore almost inevitably both an expression of and a response to the *loss* of particularity—"fallings from us, vanishings." A picture in a poem expresses the loss of the real picture. As Yeats said of the kind of poetry he was trying to outgrow, "Pictures make us sorrowful. We share the poet's separation from what he describes" (*Expl.* 163):

(*In
Memoriam
73*)

We pass; the path that each man trod
    Is dim, or will be dim, with weeds:
        What fame is left for human deeds
In endless age? It rests with God.

Shakespeare of the sonnets is a constant presence in *In Memoriam,* but this is not quite his "devouring time." Tennyson's path does not suffer the down-razing, delving, or defacing with which Shakespeare aligns the energy of language and the depredations of time. Tennyson's path "dims." Rather than being destroyed like an object, it fades like a memory. The only dimness in Shakespeare's sonnets—"And often is his gold complexion dimmed," comparing the sun's mutability to the perfections of a young man—is quite different. Shakespeare's *dim* represents an eclipse of value—it is clearer, both morally and imagistically. Section 72, an observance of the anniversary of Hallam's death, clarifies the contrast:

(My
emphasis)

Risest thou thus, *dim dawn,* again,
    And howlest, issuing out of night,
    With blasts that blow the poplar white,
And lash with storm the streaming pane?

Day, when my crowned estate begun
    To pine in that reverse of doom,
    Which sickened every living bloom,
And *blurred* the splendour of the sun.

For "blurred," Shakespeare might have written "stained" or "blackened," evoking beauty destroyed or virtue spotted. Tennyson's loss attacks not so much the order of the moral world as the integrity of the self. He dims along with his image of the lost past. Loss becomes a problem of disturbed focus, of unreality.

Perhaps because dimness is the mixing of the mind's pastness with the present, it is often in Tennyson's poetry associated with verbal, formal, and thematic repetitions, which might be seen as the

soft meeting of two moments. The connection between Tennysonian repetition and the swoon into the dim spaciousness of half-
existence is explicit in the poet's comments on his habits of meditation: "A kind of waking trance I have frequently had, quite up from
boyhood, when I have been all alone. This has generally come upon
me thro' repeating my own name two or three times to myself
silently, till all at once, as it were out of the intensity of consciousness of individuality, the individuality itself seemed to dissolve and
fade away into boundless being" (*AT Mem.* 1:320). Many of Tennyson's most characteristic effects have something in them of this
trance induced

> When we dwell upon a word we know
> (Ricks 1649)   Repeating, till the word we know so well
> Becomes a wonder and we know not why

—these very lines, with their inwoven repetitions of "word,"
"know," "we" and the sounds of *w, l, o,* are a good example. In the
long returns of Tennyson's mind, sounds, words, objects, images,
emotions grow "dim / And dimmer."

The dimmings of repetition inform some of Tennyson's best
images, for example the almost weightless reptile of "Oenone":
"The lizard, with his shadow on the stone, / Rests like a shadow"
(Ricks 386). The breathtaking stasis of the image typically comes
from a tautology not quite stated—a shadow is like a shadow. And
from another ambiguous motion. The verb given so much impulse
by syntactical suspension and steep enjambment turns out to be the
intransitive and motionless "rest." Irresistible force meets nonexis-
tent object, and there is a ghostly dispersion. Perhaps even more
impressive is this passage from the "The Lotos-Eaters," discussed
above in another context:

> There is sweet music here that softer falls
> Than petals from blown roses on the grass,
> Or night-dews on still waters between walls
> (Ricks 431)   Of shadowy granite, in a gleaming pass;
> Music that gentlier on the spirit lies,
> Than tired eyelids upon tired eyes.

The landscape becomes both tired and musical with Tennysonian repetition of sounds and whole words—it is not even necessary, though neither is it accidental, that the most conspicuous repetitions *include* "tired" and "music." And the near-unreality of touch is also evoked by *conceptual* repetitions, by the silent collisions of like and like: dews and water, petals and grass, eyelids and eyes.

Tennyson's dimness has large implications for his emotional life. Through a kind of negation, he comprehends people, landscapes, and himself in the sadness of half-absence and imminent vanishing. His love is loss; his loss is love. Not surprisingly, then, the Tennysonian woman is often seen through the haze of distance or the blur of recession, as if she, too, were a vanishing landscape. Indeed, much of the Tennysonian woman *is* landscape—flowers, light—and much of the Tennysonian landscape floats on sad desire. Both, of course, are brimming with the past. The line "gaze until their eyes are dim / With gazing on the light and depth of thine" (Ricks 317–18) would seem out of context to be about men gazing at a woman, a Rossettian woman perhaps. It actually depicts the days of the speaker's life gazing at the one day that contained his happy hour of love. The past is transformed into a beautiful woman. As in "Ode to Memory," where Tennyson implores memory to "Visit my low desire!," the erotic and the memorial are closely associated. Conversely, but even more typically, Tennyson discovers his attraction to "Adeline" in her pastness:

> Whence that aery bloom of thine,
>   Like a lily which the sun
> Looks through in his sad decline,
>   And a rose-bush leans upon,
> (Ricks 216)   Thou that faintly smilest still,
>   As a Naiad in a well,
>   Looking at the set of day,
>   Or a phantom two hours old
>   Of a maiden past away.

In being desired, even in being perceived, Adeline is distanced and dimmed. She is "faint," she is twice seen in (or as) the fading light of evening, given a vague translucent depth. And as she is assimilated into the twilight of desire, she becomes "a maiden past away," a love-loss. One wonders incidentally, whether William Allingham, his imagination and life so completely dominated by Tennyson, was vaguely remembering this poem when he recorded, a bit self-consciously, the passage Grigson singles out as the most haunting in the *Diary:* "In the evening walked sadly along the shore of the Solent eastwards by Pylewell—returning, brought home a glow-worm and put it in a white lily, through which it shone."[1] If the sunset, the lily's translucence, and the sadness are indeed from "Adeline," Allingham would not be the only Victorian for whom Tennyson was a ruling presence even in solitude.

The women Tennyson looks *at* (in contrast to the poet-surrogates, such as Mariana, that he looks out *from*) are likely first to be landscape and second to be composed less of matter than of their effect on the viewer:

>   she stood,
> A single stream of all her soft brown hair
> Poured on one side: the shadow of the flowers
> Stole all the golden gloss, and, wavering
> Lovingly lower, trembled on her waist—
> Ah, happy shade—and still went wavering down.
>
>   · · · · ·
>   Half light, half shade,
> She stood, a sight to make an old man young.

(Ricks 514–15)

This is pretty awful for a number of reasons, but it is also instructive. The gardener's daughter, frozen in time but "wavering," is turned into a stream—later her breast becomes a "bounteous wave." She is less a separate being than an image of the self dissolving in desire. Half-lit, half in shade, she is Tennyson's erotic equivalent of a mermaid.

In Tennyson desire often becomes as much a matter of fluid spaces as of erotic objects, and the landscape, as in "Now sleeps the crimson petal," can entirely replace the beloved:

> Now sleeps the crimson petal, now the white;
> Nor waves the cypress in the palace walk;

(Ricks 834–35)

Nor winks the gold fin in the porphyry font:
The fire-fly wakens: waken thou with me.

Now droops the milkwhite peacock like a ghost,
And like a ghost she glimmers on to me.

Now lies the Earth all Danaë to the stars,
And all thy heart lies open unto me.

Now slides the silent meteor on, and leaves
A shining furrow, as thy thoughts in me.

Now folds the lily all her sweetness up,
And slips into the bosom of the lake:

So fold thyself, my dearest, thou, and slip
Into my bosom and be lost in me.

Ricks notes that " 'Nor' . . . stands in such complete parallel-ism to 'Now' as to seem at first a misprint for it," and indeed the gradual equation of yes and no, "now" and "nor" (another instance, by the way, of Tennyson's line-initial half-rhyme) opens the typical Tennysonian space of dim half-existence.[2] "Now sleeps the crim-son petal, now the white" is difficult to imagine—or perhaps it would be better to say difficult to *literalize*. Petals do not "sleep," and we think of whole flowers, not single petals, folding up. Petals could be standing in for flowers, but this discussion begins to sound hopelessly fussy. Like many of Tennyson's images, this one works intensely in two nearly opposite ways. In bothering to discriminate among petals (and among sounds—"Now sleeps the crimson pe-tal" is almost painfully precise in its front-mouth articulation) Tennyson verges on hypersensitivity, even preciosity. But this am-plified particularity is all involved with vanishing. With "sleeps," these particulars, the scene, and the reader all dim. If anything, we might expect the *petals* to "droop," but that word is reserved for the parallel dematerialization of the peacock, which we might expect to "sleep" as the petals do. Perhaps our unconscious referral of the adjectives to their more likely companions contributes to a sense of nonlinearity. There and not there, details float ghostlike in an unfocused depth of desire. The technique is repeated. The cypress waves (not). Nor does the gold fin "wink," that strategic verb

referring both to the half-seen fish and to our half-seeing it. "Fin,"
typically, "winks" in assonance if not in fact. In Tennyson's world,
which often seems submarine even when it is not, fish are something more like photons than animals. In "The Kraken" they are
glimpsed in "faintest sunlights flee / About his shadowy sides," and
in "The Miller's Daughter" "minnows everywhere / In crystal
eddies glance and poise."

With their particularity dimmed and dissolved, selves merge
shocklessly in desire. One lover is a mere "glimmer" on another.
The lily "slips into the bosom of the lake," and of its otherness only
the faint ripple of plosives remains—one recalls the slee*p* of *p*etals.
The meteor glides like a thought, and the earth is miraculously "all
Danaë to the stars." The noun "Danaë" where an adjective is
expected (and one almost hears in Danaë a -*y* adjective) creates a
chasm in the grammar that is partly responsible for the image's
evocation of an unimaginable freedom and openness.

Suspended between here and not here, the poem can hardly be
said to progress, nor does it have to. The final exhortation to "be
lost in me" restates the blurring of borders on which the poem has
depended from its very first line. "Now sleeps the crimson petal"
offers, as Ricks says, "a drowning, a loss of identity, that creates the
mutuality of love"—and is the essence of the Tennysonian fluidity.
What the poem does not have, and does not, for itself, need, is any
real sense of the particularity of love or the otherness of lovers, for
the anonymity of desire is a fairly constant feature of Tennyson's
work, and a deep need. Ricks notes with regard to *Maud*'s "un-
precedented evocation of the fear of love" that "among the things
which he cannot bear about Maud is precisely the dread of her as a
unique person":[3]

> Cold and clear-cut face, why come you so cruelly meek,
>
> . . . . .
>
> Growing and fading and growing upon me without a
>   sound,
> Luminous, gemlike, ghostlike, deathlike, half the night
>   long
> Growing and fading and growing, till I could bear it no
>   more.

(Ricks
1047–48)

Growing and fading and growing, Maud becomes an ominous circumference, a landscape which, like the long lines, surges and withdraws, dims and presses. The passage embodies the threat of sharpness, of particularity and individuality, that Tennyson's poems of self and circumference, the subject of the next chapter, strive so urgently to dim and dissolve.

III

The Limit of the Self

Till her eyes were darkened wholly,
And her smooth face sharpened slowly.

The Lady of Shalott (1832)

BEGINNING WITH Hallam's praise of his "vivid, picturesque delineation of objects," Tennyson has repeatedly been cited for his scientifically scrupulous attention to detail. But Hallam's sentence, which begins with objects, ends with "the peculiar skill with which he holds all of them *fused,* to borrow a metaphor from science, in a medium of powerful emotion."[1] In Tennyson, dimness and sharp particularity are states of consciousness held in tension. He is less a poet of subject or object than of circumference, and the looming and fading of details is the looming and fading of the border of the self.

Early in his career especially, consciousness is a charmed circle defined by the vague fears that are resisted, if not quite named, in "The Poet's Mind" ("Dark-browed sophist, come not anear," [Ricks 224]) and "The Hesperides," where their swelling and subsidence is both represented and mastered by the half-nervous, half-hypnotized rhythm.

> The golden apple, the golden apple, the hallowed fruit,
> Guard it well, guard it warily,
> Singing airily, . . .
>
>   . . . . .
>
> If ye sing not, if ye make false measure,
> We shall lose eternal pleasure,
> Worth eternal want of rest.

(Ricks 424–25)

If the music stops, the circle will undergo gravitational collapse. A watcher will peer in or the center will exhaust itself. We cannot know exactly—what defines this kind of fear is that its object has not been imagined. Commentary often insists on reducing such poems to parables about the world of life intruding on the secret world of art. The poet and his friends, it is true, sometimes saw the problem in those terms—"The Palace of Art" was inspired, according to the poet, by R. C. Trench's remark "Tennyson we cannot live in art" (*AT Mem.* 1:118).[2] But the problems of "art vs. reality" are a special and rather narrow case of the repetitions of vision, language, and behavior which do not adequately express us, and which are our flight from death. In dealing with Tennyson's poetry of encirclement, it is probably useful to insist that art is a metaphor for life, and not vice versa.

Tennyson's most effective image of besieged consciousness is an isolated or bereft woman, and she is less an image than a stance, for in "Mariana" and "The Lady of Shalott" she is largely transparent. In "Mariana," for example, Tennyson is concerned less with the nature of another self than with the borders of his own. The poem expands and contracts through a series of unstable circumferences or distances—room, house, wall, sluice ("about a stonecast from the wall") and, at the outer edge of the world, or in the back of the mind, the trembling poplar. As the poem opens, we see what Mariana might see. "She" does not appear until the refrain:

> With blackest moss the flower-plots
> Were thickly crusted, one and all:
> The rusted nails fell from the knots
> That held the pear to the gable-wall.
> The broken sheds looked sad and strange:
> Unlifted was the clinking latch;
> Weeded and worn the ancient thatch
> Upon the lonely moated grange.
> She only said, "My life is dreary,
> He cometh not," she said;
> She said, "I am aweary, aweary,
> I would that I were dead."

(Ricks 187–88)

One hardly needs to point out the accumulation of images of decay, but the usual equation of decay and desolation is imprecise.

"Mariana" is sad, obsessed, even exhilarated, not depressed. And part of the poem's strange blend of relentlessness and helplessness is the result of an ambiguity in its details.

First, the moss. In a thicker line from an earlier poem, it is "The wet moss crusts the parting wall" (Ricks 159). The direction of the action is clear. But reading "With blackest moss the flower-plots / Were thickly crusted," one thinks of Keats's "To bend with apples the *moss'd* cottage-trees"—in both lines, moss is not just an object but something that *happens*. Similarly, the nails are "rusted," not "rusty," and the thatch is in ambiguous disarray because "weeded," a word that usually means "cleared of weeds," is forced to mean "weedy" as well. Things have *happened* to helpless objects, and there is a sense of causeless effect. Not "no one lifted the latch," but "Unlifted was the clinking latch," which refuses even to imagine a being capable of working a latch. Its silent clinking therefore becomes a ghostly attack. Similarly, nails work loose often enough, but having them fall emphasizes the unpredictability of a Tennysonian world in which the stabilizing forces of friction and process often fail. Even the tense of the verb is tuned this way. "Had fallen" would have located the nails' failure completely in the past. Even "fall" might indicate that they were even now in the process of working loose—past tenses, somewhat surprisingly, are often superior for rendering effects of suddenness and disconnection. "Fell" best carries the subliminal suggestion that the nails are in mid-plunge.

Another such discontinuity is concealed in the not especially conspicuous phrase "The broken sheds." *Break* is a verb for small or abstract destructions. A glass can be broken or a vow, a pencil point or a toy; but not a planet or a shed, except by a cataclysm (unless we are talking about the "broken" *spirit* of a shed, a related story). It is precisely a cataclysm that the phrase's distortion of scale both implies and understates, and that we feel obliquely in the word *strange*. Indeed, cut loose from cause and context, almost all the details of "Mariana" seem to be the wrong size, out of place, estranged. Thus Carol Christ: "The striking characteristic of Tennyson's use of detail here is his distortion of natural focus. It is as if he collapses the distance between each object he contemplates and the beholder. He creates no sense of surrounding context or natural perspective but represents each object in the same intensity and detail. Objects therefore appear isolated, much like a series of disjunct, close-up, still photographs."[3]

"Isolation," "distortion," "collapse of distance" are surely relevant. "Still photographs" probably are not, since the details of "Mariana" are not stunned for memorial contemplation. They are degrees of nearness, and the very *instability* of their distance is a threat. They seem to crystallize like guilty thoughts:

> All day within the dreamy house,
>   The doors upon their hinges creaked;
> The blue fly sung in the pane; the mouse
> (ll. 61–68)   Behind the mouldering wainscot shrieked,
> Or from the crevice peered about.
>   Old faces glimmered through the doors,
>   Old footsteps trod the upper floors,
> Old voices called her from without.

The "dreamy house" is the Tennysonian state of emotional dimness, but it is sharply violated. Ghosts are tracked from room to room by the creak of hinges. The sudden random sounds, especially the footsteps on the upper floors, predict Rossetti's technique of concentration through distraction in "My Sister's Sleep" ("in the room over us / There was a pushing back of chairs"). The mouse and the fly (the nasality of "sung" finely reproducing the vibrations of the window glass) are suddenly huge, suddenly piercing, much as in "Godiva," where the intimate threat of uncontrollable detail to the naked rider is explicit:

> The little wide-mouthed heads upon the spout
> Had cunning eyes to see: the barking cur
> (Ricks 734)   Made her cheek flame: the palfrey's footfall shot
> Light horrors through her pulses: the blind walls
> Were full of chinks and holes; and overhead
> Fantastic gables, crowding, stared.

Detail reaches around a line break to touch her—a dog's bark lights her cheek, a footfall unsteadies her pulse. Both women are being watched, but whether by voyeurs or their own interiors cannot be clear. In the stanza from "Mariana," the sharpness of the present is blurred by the passing of ghosts—"old faces," "old voices," "old footsteps"—and this association of marauding memory with the disproportions of the present at least suggests a causal connection. The repressed past, circumventing the conscious, seizes random detail as its symbol. Objects assault her with fear, shame, and strange relation. *In Memoriam* 6 depends on an odd version of this effect:

> O father, whereso'er thou be,
>   Who pledgest now thy gallant son;
>   A shot, ere half thy draught be done,
> Hath stilled the life that beat from thee.
>
> O mother, praying God will save
>   Thy sailor,—while thy head is bowed,
>   His heavy-shotted hammock-shroud
> Drops in his vast and wandering grave.
>
>   . . . . .
>
>   And, having left the glass, she turns
> Once more to set a ringlet right;
>
> And, even when she turned, the curse
>   Had fallen, and her future Lord
>   Was drowned in passing through the ford,
> Or killed in falling from his horse.

(Ricks 869–70)

Here the simultaneity of detail and fatality seems so magical that innocent actions—the bow or turn of a head, the tilting of a glass—seem almost to *cause* the deaths.

Rhythmically, imagistically, and syntactically dissolved, objects are ranged around Mariana at an unstable distance and in uncertain relation. Lifted from causality, they alternately press and withdraw, loom and fade. The very stanzas become circumferences that a strategic enjambment can violate: "the oxen's low / Came to her" (lines 28–29), an effect rehearsed in the juvenilia—"the owlet's desolate wail / Comes to mine ear"—and repeated in "Margaret"— "Lulled echoes of laborious day / Come to you" (Ricks 97, 454)—

(before Tennyson had discovered the superiority of the past tense for effects of disconnection) and three times in the section of *In Memoriam* quoted above.

The recurring poplar is a microcosm of the detail in "Mariana." It should probably not be said that the mysterious tree "is" the missing Angelo, or Mariana, though at times it is like both. The poplar seems to poise exactly on the border where, buffeted by the mind, reality trembles but does not quite dissolve. "Hard by a poplar shook alway." The tree's separateness does recall the un-reachable Angelo, but only because it first recalls Mariana's isola-tion—in a way strongly reminiscent of Wordsworth's "Intima-tions" ode:

<blockquote>
—But there's a Tree, of many, one,
A single Field which I have looked upon,
Both of them speak of something that is gone.
</blockquote>
(ll. 51–53)

The mind is identified, limited, symbolized by whatever solidifies against its flow, and objects say, besides themselves, their own vanishing.

When the "wild wind" of Mariana's incantation subsides, the poplar, approaching from outside or rising from her depths, falls "Upon her bed, across her brow," touching her like a ghost, or a painful thought. Its last appearance introduces another ambiguity:

<blockquote>
The sparrow's chirrup on the roof,
   The slow clock ticking, and the sound
Which to the wooing wind aloof
   The poplar made, did all confound
Her sense.
</blockquote>
(ll. 73–77)

Aloof was originally a nautical term meaning "into the wind"—a landing ship would "keep aloof" in order to avoid being blown onto shore. But the more usual sense is also relevant. "Aloof" from the wooing wind of Mariana's desire (though "woo" is surely also the sound wind makes), the poplar is as inaccessible as Angelo. Or is it that, as the syntax allows, the "wooing wind" is itself "aloof," that Mariana simultaneously denies and desires the pain symbolized by the poplar's distance. Her obsession deeply resists change, though change is, on the surface, what she yearns for.

The time sense of "Mariana" is profoundly desynchronized. On one hand, time is slow—we are told that nothing happens, that nothing changes, and the refrain comes around again and again to prove it. But half-concealed in the images are cataclysms. And the poem has all the self-generated swiftness of the most intense and repetitive obsession. It can hardly wait to insist "He will not come, he will not come." Time goes nowhere, but rapidly. "Mariana" is the swiftest possible description of eternity, a characterization that might also apply to such poems as "The Lady of Shalott" and "Tithonus."

Rhythm contributes to this ambiguous time sense. "Mariana" is essentially iambic tetrameter, alternating, in the refrain, with trimeter, and it is also dipodic. Like so many of Tennyson's poems— "The Lady of Shalott," "The Hesperides," "Locksley Hall"—it systematically recognizes two degrees of stress and is based not simply on the slack-stress of the iambic foot, but on slack–heavy stress—slack–lighter stress. The symbol is used for the heavier degree of stress: "With bláckest móss // the flower-plots/Were thickly crusted // one and all."

Dipodic rhythm is often found in nursery rhymes—"Four and twenty black birds"—and is usually chantlike, but it is seldom so supercharged with alliteration, patterned pausing, and rhyme as it is here. The interval between the heaviest stresses of this dipodic rhythm is chasmic (three syllables and a caesura), and yet its length is so rigidly enforced that other features of language may be distorted to equalize it. Some of the effects of the rhythm may be bound up with the lengths of vowels, pauses, and junctures. In phrases such as "blackest moss" and "flower-plots," the swift, light endings of the disyllables are almost overwhelmed by the preceding strong stresses, but their near-disappearance brings two heavy syllables too close together and the line slows without roughness, forming islands of the pattern stress–slack–stress (as often in "The Lotos-Eaters" with single words such as "afternoon" and "galingale"). Languor and swiftness coexist without strain. We pronounce the achingly unsatisfying "I am aweary, aweary" almost as a single polysyllable whose continuous articulation thwarts the tension and release even regular iambic rhythm normally supplies. Reading it is rather like rounding a curve. We feel continuous centrifugal force, acceleration (in the scientific sense—change of direction *or* speed). Here and in general the Tennysonian line seems to be governed almost as much by blending velocities as by competing stress patterns, by self-restraining undulation more than by normal kinds of metrical "tension."

All this bears on Tennyson's fondness (Sinfield notes its frequency in *In Memoriam*)[4] for "falling rhythm," which is the use of trochaic rhythm *or* the overlaying of the iambic pattern with words whose *individual* stress patterns seem trochaic, as in this line from "The Lotos-Eaters": "They saw the gleaming river seaward flow."

This is perfectly regular iambic, but all the disyllables are in themselves trochaic, and some of the monosyllables may group themselves as faint, virtual trochees. Two rhythmic currents are meeting, but there is no "tension" in the received sense. There is almost a cancellation of momentum, a sense of being slightly out of step. A stopwatch might find this long-voweled line to be slow, and Wimsatt and Beardsley would probably agree:

> *Maybe some of the languor and soft drag of Tennyson's verse, for instance, comes sometimes from the interplay between the rising iambic motion of the line and the falling trochaic character of a series of important words.*

> *"It little profits that an idle king"*

> *"To follow knowledge like a sinking star"*[5]

One suspects, however, that the "absolute" speed of *these* lines (from "Ulysses") is higher than those quoted from "The Lotos-Eaters," and the reason seems to be the shorter, less spacious vowels. The lines may, in fact, be *faster* than equivalent lines without initially stressed disyllables. Charles O. Hartman, noting the same phenomenon, appears to attribute to it this opposite effect: "A simple example is the trick known to any careful writer of iambic verse: a two-syllable word crossing a foot boundary will tend to speed the line up, while one that coincides with the foot will slow it down."[6]

I introduce the apparently conflicting assessments of Hartman and Wimsatt-Beardsley not for the sake of contentiousness but because both, especially in the Tennysonian context, seem correct in some ways. First of all, lines are normally blends of rising and falling rhythm. Pure examples of either are rare—and odd:

> Willows whiten, aspens quiver   (falling)
> Pierre resides behind Lamont   (rising)

Both of these lines will be heard as strangely rigid—there is some kind of heavy marking between the words. Which is faster? On principle, Hartman might say the former, Wimsatt and Beardsley the latter. But rhythm is complex, and so is speed. Stress, for example, seems to have at least three components—pitch, duration, and loudness—and they do not always work in concert.

Those insisting on the speed of lines of falling rhythm might say that the first line—and certainly a less stiffly patterned line, such as "To follow knowledge like a sinking star," exhibits a kind of muting or flattening of the rhythm that allows for speed. There are two reasons for this. First, the stressed vowel in an initially stressed disyllable will generally be shorter than the equivalent vowel in a terminally stressed disyllable. *Lady* and *delay* contain the same two sounds in reverse order—but the *a* of *lady* is much shorter than that of *delay*. Since in a poetic line stressed syllables are normally longer, the addition of initially stressed disyllables will mute one difference between stresses and slacks. Their alternation in value may therefore in some cases be less conspicuous. Second, I suspect that in "Willows whiten" the difference in *pitch* between stressed and unstressed syllables is less than in rising rhythm. This may be why we hear dominantly falling rhythm (as *Hiawatha*) as literally monotonous.

On the other hand, it may be that the falling–rhythm line has greater differences in the *loudness* of syllables (perhaps to compensate for the muting of the other differences). Certainly it falls more easily than the line of rising rhythm into dipodic chant. But even here the effect on perceived speed is ambiguous. The exaggerated up-and-down of dipody may seem slow, but the fierce insistence of this very basic English pattern may seem to seize the line and run off with it.

Probably the most constant feature of falling rhythm, accounting for the general sense that it trails or fades (or falls!), and thus for Tennyson's attraction to it, is that it leaves us vaguely unsatisfied, waiting for stress, for more distinct iambics, for rising rhythm. In this it is analogous to feminine (essentially "falling") rhyme, which, as Swinburne knew, also invites continuation:

Before our lives divide for *ever*,

While time is with us and hands are free,

(Time, swift to fasten and swift to *sever*

Hand from hand as we stand by the sea)

(*PS* 1:39,
1–4)

Falling rhythm, that is, "wants" to move faster, however fast or slow it is actually moving. It seems to demand continuation, to be reaching after more closure than it can itself provide. And its muting of certain expected features of the language can produce a flatness that may contribute to speed. When it does not, as in "They saw the gleaming river seaward flow," we feel the potential, the need for speed working against some virtually invisible impedance (Wimsatt and Beardsley's "soft drag"?). Tennyson's use of falling rhythm thus becomes another example of restraint without tension. Whether the lines are slow or quick, they are moving, we feel, as fast as they *can*. One pattern tries to catch up with another. A reader emphasizing the attempt will find that the lines rush—a reader hearing the failure will sense "soft drag." Like Tennysonian time, the Tennysonian line can move slowly and quickly in the same moment.

The real miracle of "Mariana" is that a poem so long and so utterly dependent on detail does not at once clog and degenerate into a descriptive sketch, a danger not completely avoided by its companion poem. "Mariana in the South" seems to contain all the right Tennysonian elements, but is conspicuously weaker, perhaps partly because of its relative ornateness. Though Millais painted a version of "Mariana," the exciting disconnection of that first poem is antipictorial. The southern Mariana is more readily imaginable in the darkly furnished and tapestried chambers of Pre-Raphaelite yearning:

> She, as her carol sadder grew,
>   From brow and bosom slowly down
> Through rosy taper fingers drew
>   Her streaming curls of deepest brown
> To left and right, and made appear
>   Still-lighted in a secret shrine,
>   Her melancholy eyes divine,
> The home of woe without a tear.
>   And "Ave Mary," was her moan,
>   "Madonna, sad is night and morn,"
>   And "Ah," she sang, "To be all alone,
>   To live forgotten, and love forlorn."

(Ricks 363)

"Rosy taper fingers" and "melancholy eyes divine" have the lingering adjectival fullness of Rossetti's *House of Life*. Also Rossettian is the fascination with hair and the detachment of religious particulars from their meaningful contexts to suggest the darkness and complexity of passion, which here, as so often in Rossetti, has some of the closeness of self-worship. The stanza does not have the breathtaking disconnections of the first "Mariana." Its sentences hover, qualify, attempt to penetrate—they are draped over the line-endings, prolonged and thickened as they might be in Rossetti or Keats. Instead of detail converging on the mind, we have mind fixing on detail.

The detail of "Mariana," far from being heavy and over-whelming, is tantalizing, thrillingly unsatisfying—we return eagerly to the refrain, to an obsession repeated until its terrible fact is smoothed down. The poem circles full speed nowhere. One cannot ask whether, as in *Measure for Measure,* Angelo will return. In the curved space of Mariana's closed universe, further out is further in, and there is, almost by definition, no "outside."

This is less true of "The Lady of Shalott," in many ways the real companion poem to "Mariana." Nearer to the edge of revolution, the Lady of Shalott is "half sick of shadows." She can only view the world in a mirror, but this device, introduced well into the poem, is only a confirmation of what we sense immediately when the opening landscape is seen reflected in trembling waters, Tennyson's favorite image of the moment's half-presence:

(Ricks 354)

> Willows whiten, aspens quiver,
> Little breezes dusk and shiver
> Through the wave that runs for ever
> By the island in the river.

Tennyson is noting how windstruck willows turn up the paler undersides of their narrow leaves, how aspens quake even on apparently windless days, how little winds darken their paths along the water. But the phenomenal accuracy is, as usual, at least half in the service of dissolution. The scene shimmers with falling dipodic rhythm and transience. It seems almost nervous—in the whitening of the willows there are uninsistent but irrepressible suggestions of snow or shock or instantaneous aging, and "whiten," "quiver," and "shiver" are all words that go well with fear. Held before us by anxious incantation, the landscape is infused with the familiar Tennysonian desynchronizations of time and process:

(ll. 19–23)

> By the margin, willow-veiled,
> Slide the heavy barges trailed
> By slow horses; and unhailed,
> The shallop flitteth silken-sailed
>   Skimming down to Camelot.

There is an ambiguous border here—which is "veiled," the barges or the margin? On this dimmed boundary of the self, seemingly public objects begin to flow in private and paradoxical time as Tennyson slips into one of his nearly always winning meditations on frictionlessness. "Slide the heavy barges" balances ease and effort, fluidity and resistance, as does "trailed / By slow horses." There is one kind of time for heavy matter, another for gliding thought. The flitting "shallop," with its short-voweled falling rhythm, skims the river as lightly as its sounds touch the high front of the mouth, and then vanishes, stage right, into the horizon of dream.

This poem, however, repeatedly imagines potential onlookers and, finally, love looks in fiercely:

> A bow-shot from her bower-eaves,
> He rode between the barley sheaves,
> The sun came dazzling through the leaves,
> And flamed upon the brazen greaves
>   Of bold Sir Lancelot.
> A red-cross knight for ever kneeled
> To a lady in his shield,
> That sparkled on the yellow field,
>   Beside remote Shalott.
>
>   . . . . .
>
> All in the blue unclouded weather
> Thick-jewelled shone the saddle-leather,
> The helmet and the helmet-feather
> Burned like one burning flame together,
>   As he rode down to Camelot.

(ll. 73–81, 91–95)

"He" drops without antecedent and the poem thrusts us from a dim room into the blinding glare of midday, all sharp edges and impinging light. The language takes on a razorlike glide of *e*'s, *v*'s, *z*'s and a burden of heavier consonants. There is claustral pressure; detail presses and points.

This kind of moment is not uncommon in Tennyson. The space of absent presence collapses under strong sun—in "Mariana in the South," "glaring sand and inlets bright" function as the "blinding wall" of the present—which is so natural an adversary to Tennyson's "grateful gloom" (Ricks 403) that it can hardly be called a symbol. "Thought," he says, "wells not freely from the mind's recess / When the sharp sunlight occupies the sense" (Ricks 268).

His senses easily overloaded, Tennyson was extraordinarily sensitive to the pressure of light, which takes him away from himself until the twilight returns. "When the outer lights are darkened, / The memory's vision hath a keener edge" (Ricks 302). Memory, like a star, fades in the dawn. Of course, Tennyson means by memory not only the traces of particular events, but, as in "Ode to Memory," something very like desire, release into the soul's fluidity—"Visit my low desire . . . Thou dewy dawn of memory" (Ricks, p. 211). More generally, Tennyson often images the pressure of the present in terms of closeness to the head and associates it with both madness and death:

(Ricks 700)

Come not, when I am dead,
    To drop thy foolish tears upon my grave,
To trample round my fallen head.

(Ricks 1086)

Dead, long dead,
Long dead!
And my heart is a handful of dust,
And the wheels go over my head.

The Lady of Shalott's love for Lancelot is equally momentous, and equally threatening. Its oppressive light is a discovery of the hard limits of body, self, and mortality. She is suddenly stranded in the present, a pure object she can finally give a name to: "And round about the prow she wrote / *The Lady of Shalott.*" Dying down the river in a pure Tennysonian fade-out, she becomes paradoxically invulnerable, a fantasy of poetic power. The Lady of Shalott lives in obscurity and dies of exposure, but only *we* know the hardest truth, which is that she has not existed at all. Just an arm's length from the storm of her mind, the calm object of her fatal obsession sees only what he sees:

But Lancelot mused a little space;
He said, "She has a lovely face;
God in his mercy lend her grace,
    The Lady of Shalott."

This brief discussion oversimplifies the issues, and perhaps makes the poet for whom they are issues at all seem tenuously connected to life. But the transition from immortality—being no one and everyone like the Lady of Shalott—to mortal individuality is the labor of more years than the twenty-odd Tennyson could lay claim to when he published the first version of this poem. These very choices and themes underlie many of the nineteenth century's greatest poems—"Tintern Abbey," the "Intimations" ode, and "The Eve of St. Agnes," among others—and they drive the careers of Browning and Yeats, poets whose engagement with life has seldom seemed suspect. The crisis of the Lady of Shalott should not be neutralized with the dead shorthand of "art vs. reality." It is about choices we never stop making or evading. In souls as in landscapes, particularity is death. But it is also love.

IV

The Tennysonian Flow

Time flowing in the middle of the night
The Mystic

WATER IS the element I love best of all the four" Tennyson once said (*AT Mem.* 1:49), and his discovery of this most frequent scenic equivalent of his poetic flow in "The Lotos-Eaters"—"a land of streams!"—is punctuated by exhilaration. Like Wordsworth, Tennyson aspired to the condition of a river. To speak is not merely to use flowing language, but to flow out with it: "Or else I had not dared to flow / In these words toward you" (Ricks 464). Under him, in him, around him is motion nearly without matter, memory almost without content. Even at the outset of his career the vision of fluidity is so comforting, so automatically meaningful, that it seems to him sufficient to climax a poem. Thus the end of "Midnight," from 1827:

The moaning pine-trees to the wild blast bending,
    Are pictured faintly through the chequered
        gloom;
The forests, half-way up the mountain climbing,
    Resound with crash of falling branches; quiver
        Their agèd mossy trunks: the startled doe
Leaps from her leafy lair: *the swelling river*
    Winds his broad stream majestic, deep, and slow.

(Ricks 112; my emphasis)

For the young Tennyson, as for Sir John Denham, whose "Coopers Hill" he is probably echoing—

O could I flow like thee, and make thy stream
My great example, as it is my theme!
Though deep, yet clear, though gentle, yet not dull,
Strong without rage, without ore-flowing full.

—the noble river, "majestic, deep, and slow" is not simply an image but a harmonious way of being. But in "Midnight," as in most of Tennyson's early work, such fluidity remains an image or aspiration rather than an achievement. The grateful invisibility of "pictured faintly" predicts later work, but "chequered gloom," turning gray areas into balanced black and white, is pure Pope and far from Tennyson's later and more spacious dimnesses. And the movement of the last four lines is, first, uncharacteristic, and second, wrong. The three consecutive steep enjambments are awkward, and they emphasize the risk of the two consecutive sixth syllable caesuras:

> quiver
> Their agèd mossy trunks: / / the startled doe
> Leaps from her leafy lair: / / the swelling river
> Winds his broad stream.

This is a rhymed stanza that wants to be blank verse. We have no "flow" but instead a gasping stop-start. Tennyson has not yet mastered the fluidity of movement that must underlie his vision of fluidity, and so, perhaps, has not yet completely seen it.

In "The Walk at Midnight," from about the same period, there is a similar conflict between the space and flow Tennyson desires and the techniques with which he attempts to enclose them:

> The whispering leaves, the gushing stream,
>   Where trembles the uncertain moon,
> Suit more the poet's pensive dream,
>   Than all the jarring notes of noon.

(Ricks 124)

These lines report on Tennyson's dim center, but they do not quite bring us there, though we recognize the unease with noon light, and the yearning toward a whispering, trembling, streaming landscape. The appearance of The Poet is regrettable, but there is a more important problem with syntax, not merely the syntax of a sentence but the syntax of a world. That is, the particulars embedded in this quatrain are too obviously Examples: The Leaves, The Stream, The Moon, each pushed into place with an obligatory and isolating present participle or adjective. Then, too, the quatrain's sing-song invokes not Tennysonian trance but the expectation of a clinching thought. The stanza never lets go, never lets us go. Its stiffness keeps poet and reader partially "out" of the poem. It remains a statement, never opening into an interior landscape.

Tennyson, like Wordsworth before him, was born neither emotionally nor technically into the nineteenth century. Like Wordsworth, he helped create the century and the sensibility he would inhabit. His discovery of his feelings was inextricably bound up with his discovery of the technical means to express them, for a poet must convey his vision first of all to himself. "Tintern Abbey," for example, finds a *poetic* current that Wordsworth feels is hardly extricable from the fluidity of his landscape or from the flow, "far more deeply interfused," of

(ll. 100–
102)
> A motion and a spirit, that impels
> All thinking things, all objects of all thought,
> And rolls through all things.

Since Wordsworth, more patient than his successor, tends to develop in the course of a poem the mood Tennyson normally presupposes, the opening paragraph of his great meditation acknowledges a dramatic tension Tennyson perhaps detected when he complained about its four uses of "again." In 1798 Wordsworth returns to a vista of the Wye valley after an absence of five years:

(my
emphasis)
> Five years have past; five summers, with the length
> Of five long winters! and *again* I hear
> These waters, rolling from their mountain-springs
> With a soft, inland murmur.—Once *again*
> Do I behold these steep and lofty cliffs,
> That on a wild secluded scene impress
> Thoughts of more deep seclusion; and connect
> The landscape with the quiet of the sky.
> The day is come when I *again* repose
> Here, under this dark sycamore, and view
> These plots of cottage-ground, these orchard-tufts,
> Which at this season, with their unripe fruits,
> Are clad in one green hue, and lose themselves
> 'Mid groves and copses. Once *again* I see
> These hedge-rows, hardly hedge-rows, little lines

Of sportive wood run wild: these pastoral farms,
Green to the very door; and wreaths of smoke
Sent up, in silence, from among the trees!
With some uncertain notice, as might seem
Of vagrant dwellers in the houseless woods,
Or of some Hermit's cave, where by his fire
The Hermit sits alone.

As another poet of "the eternal landscape of the past" (Ricks 903), Tennyson naturally expressed "profound admiration" for "Tintern Abbey" (*AT Mem.* 2:70) and his objection to the "again's," though based on a misunderstanding of Wordsworth's conduct of a poem, is emotionally valid. Returning to a former haunt, Tennyson himself felt "The same, but not the same" (Ricks 938). So the repeated "again" may indeed protest too much—nothing is ever again. Wordsworth appropriates a landscape that resists him and asserts a unity of mind he does not yet feel. Past and present are uncomfortably at odds; he is alienated from his own life.

Wordsworth's unease is visible in the scene itself, for the opening of "Tintern Abbey" is a good example of the reading of landscape practiced by The Wanderer in *The Excursion:*

(1:160–62)   Even in their fixed and steady lineaments
He traced an ebbing and a flowing mind,
Expression ever varying!

The romantic reciprocity of mind and nature is often best tracked in such imagery of "ebb and flow," and, indeed, Wordsworth's tremor of identity is reproduced in the Wye valley landscape, which alternately focuses and blurs as his sense of alienation strengthens and weakens. The isolation of the steep cliffs recalls "more deep seclusion," which, however, seems to disappear into the large "quiet of the sky." The sense of separation crystallizes again ("here, under this dark sycamore"), but the orchards blend "in one green hue" and "lose themselves," as he, following, loses himself. The hedgerows rise up, but rename themselves ("hardly hedge-rows, little lines"), run wild, and cease to be boundaries. Grass overwhelms the farms in green unity, but wisps of unlocated loneliness rise "in silence, from among the trees," and what the poet finally extracts from the vastness of the landscape and the ambiguity of his mood is an image of solitude "where by his fire / The Hermit sits alone." The rhetoric says "I am here *again*. I am one self." But the landscape is already telling the poet what he will later tell us—that the self is unstable, both one and many, that our borders harden and fade, that we are simultaneously alone and at one with our world.

In the course of the poem these tensions are quieted, and it is significant that the first stage of the resolution is triggered by an assimilation of the past. Turning away from the recalcitrant present of the landscape, Wordsworth *remembers* it—in fact, with a double distance, he *remembers remembering* it. This is poetic justice, but it may not be realism. The memory of remembering that the poem takes for granted is actually relatively rare. In fact, memory seems largely transparent to itself. One normally remembers the process of remembering only when it has been externalized—when two people have done it together, or when one person has written it down. That both externalizations are relevant to this poem may explain something about the friendliness of its solitude, but the more obvious point is that Wordsworth is, like Tennyson in "Far-Far-Away," folding a moment of isolation deeply into the flow of time. He sees and remembers, he remembers remembering, he imagines the present as "life and food / For future years," and, turning to his sister Dorothy, he foresees her remembrance of him. The present no longer teeters precariously at the end of time.

Wordsworth undergoes something like a Tennysonian fade-out. The remembered remembering dissolves him. His borders are inundated by

>   that blessed mood,
> In which the burden of the mystery,
> In which the heavy and the weary weight
> Of all this unintelligible world,
> Is lightened:—that serene and blessed mood,
> In which the affections gently lead us on,—
> Until, the breath of this corporeal frame
> And even the motion of our human blood
> Almost suspended, we are laid asleep

(ll. 37–49)

> In body, and become a living soul:
> While with an eye made quiet by the power
> Of harmony, and the deep power of joy,
> We see into the life of things.

The upwelling of Wordsworth's melancholy joy is virtually indistinguishable from the slowly flowing, falling, pooling sentences that characterize the blank verse he redeemed from eighteenth-century stiffness. The lines are so understressed (averaging fewer than four strongly accented syllables each) that they seem only half conscious of the iambic requirement they slip under rather than confront. Rhythm becomes subliminal, hypnotic. Broken across feminine caesuras (that is, following an unstressed syllable), often involving a weak second foot—a Wordsworthian rhythmic signature—the lines pause, fade, and almost as an afterthought pick up their beat:

> Is lightened̆: / /—thăt serene and blessed mood . . .

> In bodў, / / ănd become a living soul . . .

> Of harmŏnў, / / and the deep power of joy . . .

With its settling (rather than steep or sharp) enjambments, the passage seems to drift, rather than drop, from line to line:

> we are laid asleep
>
> In body

   It lulls us, further, with repetitions of words ("blessed mood," "power"), and syntax,

		that
In which		of
In which		and
Of		
	that	and
In which		
		of
And		of
In body		and
Of	and	of
		of

and with the gentle, rhythmically independent roll of polysyllables—"Of all this unintelligible world"—that almost, as so often in
Wordsworth, seems to think *for* him.

A half dozen stylistic features, therefore, work together to
draw the reader into the trancelike suspension the poem describes,
and describes as the mood of poetry and vision. In this state of
lowered tension, the very boundaries between words seem to disappear in the way romantic poets of fluidity are so fond of describing:

(Words-
worth,
"Resolution
and Inde-
pendence")

The old Man still stood talking by my side;
But now his voice to me was like a stream
Scarce heard; nor word from word could I divide.

(Keats,
Endymion)

                          she linked
Her charming syllables, till indistinct
Their music came to my o'er-sweetened soul.

(Tennyson,
"The
Lover's
Tale," Ricks
326)

Falling in whispers on the sense, addressed
More to the inward than the outward ear,
As rain of the midsummer midnight soft,
Scarce-heard.

Words dim and slip soothingly under consciousness. One recalls "And beauty born of murmuring sound / Shall pass into her
face" and the "cannot choose but hear" and "cannot choose but feel"
that echo through Wordsworth and Coleridge. Pater, indeed, says
Wordsworth's rhythms have a "sedative" quality, and in so characterizing them he is echoing Wordsworth's own Preface to *Lyrical
Ballads*. The very movement of Wordsworth's poems has the feature of "unlimited continuity" that Northrop Frye takes as characteristic of romantic poetry. Wordsworth aspires to the breeze, the
stream—to ideals of flow. It is not that he rearranges his style to
"imitate" a particular mood, theme, or aspect of a landscape at any
given moment in his poem, but that he is trying to incorporate in
the poem the comprehensiveness and the mystery of the moment
before words. "Now this is very profound, what rhythm is,"
Virginia Woolf once said, "and goes far deeper than words. A sight,
an emotion, creates this wave in the mind, long before it makes

words to fit it." Writers are likely to think of poetic flow as anterior, and to describe composition as words rising to fill music already there. Both Wordsworth and Tennyson are fascinated by flowing water; both find it an appropriate metaphor for the kind of poetry they wish to write; style and theme *are* profoundly related, but not necessarily (though occasionally) in the sense of moment-by-moment imitation or onomatopoeia. Rather, a poet's *characteristic* (but by no means inescapable) flow arises from the same deep bias of the psyche—a sense of how experience passes, how the mind works, or simply what is comfortable—from which characteristic themes and images also arise.[1]

Wordsworth discovered a flow or voice that makes the even more extreme dissolutions of such poets as Tennyson possible. The separation of the self from the drift of its experience, the swift eternity of the mind's time, is Tennyson's constant fascination. It can surface as an explicit theme, as in "Mariana" or "Tithonus," or it can appear in individual images. But the quintessentially "Tennysonian" is hardly isolable, and seems to be part of the very movement of poems. It is bound up with the enormously complex interaction of rhythm, juncture, pitch, pausing, sound patterning, syntax, and lineation that produces what we easily recognize (but only with tremendous difficulty describe): a poet's idiosyncratic voice, or, at an even more instinctual level, his typical "flow."

The characterization of the flow of verse is so fraught with difficulties, so completely dependent on the vaguest and most subjective impressions of readers, that it would be foolhardy to begin without acknowledging the problems involved. Take for example what might seem the most basic aspect of poetic flow—its "speed":

(Browning, "Rabbi Ben Ezra")

Irks care the crop-full bird? Frets doubt the maw-
    crammed beast?

Tennyson, "Tithonus")

    I wither slowly in thine arms,
Here at the quiet limit of the world,
A white-haired shadow roaming like a dream
The ever-silent spaces of the East.

In his survey of nineteenth-century prosody, Saintsbury seems constantly tempted to assess poets in terms of the speed of their verse. Tennyson is seen, generally, as a languorous poet, Browning, generally, as a rapid one. Perhaps an "average reader" comparing these two samples would confirm that judgment, perhaps not. Scientists timing a series of "average performances" might find it to be "objectively" true or false. In either case the innocent reader might well remain unconvinced, for the subjective definition of poetry as "slow" or "fast" is inevitably based on several potentially conflicting psychological and poetic factors, and is probably unrelated in any important way to what we could learn about the reading of lines from a stopwatch.

Browning's line above might seem quicker than Tennyson's simply because of the momentum superimposed by the rising intonation of the interrogative, or because we cannot help perceiving the energy and ebullience of the speaker as a kind of speed. Then, too, Browning has a syntactical speed related, if distantly, to the rapidity of thought Donald Davie describes in Pope:

> *"The thriving plants ignoble broomsticks made,*
> *Now sweep those Alleys they were born to shade."*

> *Here too, in this iambic verse, we get an impression of rapidity, but of a quite different sort. This is rapid because it expresses so much in so short a time. The rapidity of Byron is a rapid movement of the lips and tongue; Pope's rapidity is a rapid movement of the mind. Pope's rapidity we perceive by empathy; Byron's we do not.*[2]

Browning is not here quite so mentally active as Pope (though it is well to recall that Swinburne's denial of Browning's obscurity cites something very like Davie's rapidity of mind as the source of his difficulty for early readers).[3] But a prosier version of Browning's line might read, "Are birds with full crops fretted with cares? Are beasts with their maws crammed fretted by doubts?" We sense the poem's compression or short-circuiting of language as a swiftness of thought.

Taking these factors together, a reader might well judge Browning's line to be rapid, but he would implicitly devalue at least two factors that tend to impede it. First, the extreme compression also creates intellectual difficulty, even laboriousness, that some readers might perceive as slowness. Second, in "Irks cáre the crop-full bird" the initial spondee and the difficult precision of the mouth's transition between the consonants of *irks–care* and *crop–full* create rhythmic tensions that translate psychologically into effort— again slowness. This last effect is purely physical, rooted in the anatomy of the mouth. And yet no trained reader would find that the tension disappeared upon mental recitation. Read silently, poetry retains a real physicality. The movement of a poem remains even then a dreamlike movement of the body.

Rhythmic tension is produced by the failure of the actual rhythm of a line to match exactly the expected beat. The reader's adjustments are various and extremely subtle. Take, for example, a stanza from Hardy:

("Before
Life and
After")

> A time there was—as one may guess
> And as, indeed, earth's testimonies tell—
> Before the birth of consciousness,
> When all went well.

Jean Brooks suggests that metrical tension forces us to read the last line as four strong, nearly equal stresses: "Whén all wént wéll."[4] Certainly the last three syllables bear some stress. Had Hardy written "When all was well," the line would reduce more easily to a less tense iambic: When all was well. But something in the change of "was" to "went" (perhaps the shortening of the vowel and the difficulty of the mouth's transition between the final *t* of "went" and the initial *w* of "well") forces more stress on "went" *retroactively*. In this tense environment, we space out *all* the words, something like when–all–went–well, thus retroactively raising the stress, if only slightly, on the alliterating "when." Whatever the actual mechanism, the phenomenon of retroactivity in metrical tension is common, as are retroactive phenomena in language generally. The implication is that the mind in some way divides when reading poetry. We must read a line whole (as in speed reading) with a sense of the overall stress pattern matched against expectation. We must, at the same time, move through the line syllable-by-syllable, physically *saying* it. The "whole line" reading becomes relatively more important in lines of high tension where the mind and tongue have more adjustments to make. In low tension poetry, like Tennyson's or Wordsworth's, we can proceed in a more relaxed and unwary fashion, syllable by syllable, confident that the poem will "carry" us. This may account for the feeling in reading Tennyson's verse that we are on the edge of the arriving moment, somehow "in" an experience or in time. Whether his lines are slow or fast (and Saintsbury commends him at one point for his extraordinary "variety of speeds"),[5] they submerge us in a shorter (that is, rhythmically nonretroactive) present in which we are not required to foresee and control the succession of moments. The lines, like the life Tennyson characteristically describes, flow by without our assistance and almost without touching.

In Tennyson's lines from "Tithonus," as in Browning's from "Rabbi Ben Ezra," the reader's judgment of speed depends on several conflicting factors. Tithonus, as a character, is far less energetic than the Rabbi. He even insists that time moves slowly: "I wither slowly in thine arms." But even this beautiful evocation of languor encourages us to see happening before us a process imperceptible in real time. Tithonus becomes a visibly fading light rather than a gradually aging man. How does this sort into slow and fast? The long-voweled spondees of "fár-fólded" and "white-háired shadow" moan audibly and are perhaps read slowly, but these very lines accelerate into short vowels and fourth-foot pyrrhics (which in most contexts impart a kind of "skim" to the line) before blurring into the expansive vowels of the line-endings: "Here at the quiet limĭt ŏf the world," "The ever-silent spacĕs ŏf the East." Finally, the passage's stepwise ascent into abstraction—the movement from the metaphor "shadow" to "like a dream" (a simile that thrusts off the original figure like the second stage of a rocket) to the even vaguer "silent spaces"—might be felt as a kind of acceleration: as the passage gathers momentum, the gravity of the concrete dissipates, and the world, as so often in Tennyson, dissolves.

The "speed" of a line is therefore complex, and only one of its components (and by no means the most important one) can be measured with a stopwatch. The lines of any poet are likely to seem slow in some ways, fast in others, as time in "Mariana" is both slow and fast. Perhaps what is in the end most significant is Saintsbury's *impulse* to measure the velocity of poetry. A Victorian himself, he senses that nineteenth-century poetry is in some new way an experience we move within, and that its momentum is a way of feeling and organizing time.

A poet's typical flow or sound is, again, extraordinarily difficult to isolate. Is "The moan of doves in immemorial elms, / And murmuring of innumerable bees" a tour de force, or is it only a slight exaggeration of the Tennysonian voice that can tell us something useful about his method? Data processing might provide an answer—but would we analyze all his poems, or only those we had already decided sounded truly Tennysonian? The polysyllables here do not seem entirely characteristic, but they are used to a typical end—a sense of unimpeded flow. So, too, the restriction of the consonants. Would a syllable by syllable statistical study reveal that Tennyson in general favors slightly what here he favors strongly— the gentler, more sliding tensions of liquids and nasals, as opposed to hard stops? Hopkins would perhaps have thought so—he chose a passage from "Enoch Arden" as *too* Tennysonian, and his choice was informed, one suspects, not just by its ornateness but by its exaggeratedly Tennysonian sound:

> The mountain wooded to the peak, the lawns
> The winding glades high up like ways to Heaven,
> The slender coco's drooping crown of plumes,
> The lightning flash of insect and of bird,
> The lustre of the long convolvuluses
> That coiled around the stately stems, and ran
> Even to the limit of the land, the glows
> And glories of the broad belt of the world,
> All these he saw.

(Ricks 1143–44)

In "The lustre of the long convolvuluses" Tennyson is rolling *l*'s almost moistly on his tongue, and he is in some ways close to Wordsworth's "Whose dwelling is the light of setting suns," a line he rated as the second most musical in English. His top choice,

Milton's "Of Abbana and Pharphar, lucid streams," may also be distantly audible in this passage.[6] In both the Tennyson and the Milton the boundaries between sounds and words are oddly disturbed and blurred. A little inattention would turn either into something other than English. The vowels of "the glows / And glories of the broad belt of the world" are, in a fashion common in Tennyson, almost too spacious for the line. Their length attenuates the rhythm—Patmore once pointed out that one can beat time better with a drum than with a bell—and it seems left to the *reader* to restrain them.[7] The line acquires something more like a waveform than a roughness and is slowed without the jammed consonants which, prized in Browning ("irks care"), are relatively rare here. Then, too, the frequency of disyllabic words is high and so, consequently, is the proportion of falling rhythm. The lines become reluctant with hardly any reduction (perhaps with an increase) in smoothness. Tennyson has managed myriad restraints without tension, textures without sharpness. For all their artistry, though, Hopkins is right to find the lines "Parnassian," merely typical. They are seen or heard rather than imagined—and in lists. The eyes and ears are forced into a little too much heartless work.

Whatever the methodological difficulties of isolating its essentials, one of the factors in the "Tennysonian sound" must be his idiosyncratic handling of rhythm, though it is a factor not entirely independent of those just touched on. Tennyson chided Patmore for his attempt to assign inherent moods to various English measures (*AT Mem.* 1:469–70), but though forms and meters have no innate voice, the poets who use them *do*. The voice, like any personality, can appear in many moods, or vary, or evolve, but it is nevertheless true that more good poets end in monotony than in utter confusion.

Poets use most of the possible rhythmic variations possible within the bounds of metricality quite frequently, so that slightly irregular lines are far more common than perfectly regular ones. But they have typical *patterns* of substitution that can help characterize their individual voices. The variations among poets are rather subtle, and individual poets vary from form to form and throughout their careers. Scansion, which tracks these variations, is of course somewhat subjective, but more limiting than its sub-

jectivity is its coarseness. Lines that scan identically may have
vastly different sounds and movements. Some large aspects of the
Tennysonian rhythmic flow may, however, be characterized. At
the risk of seeming to imply more scientific accuracy than is appropriate, I give, in tabular form, the substitution pattern for one
Tennyson poem.

Metrical Substitution in "Tithonus"
Pentameter Line (by foot)

First			Second			Third			Fourth			Fifth		
T	S	P	T	S	P	T	S	P	T	S	P	T	S	P
11	5.3	0	0	13	20	0	5.3	20	1.3	5.3	29	0	5.3	1.3

Note: Numbers are rates per hundred lines.
T = trochaic
S = spondaic
P = pyrrhic

These figures, of course, mean very little without a sense of
what is normal. Tennyson's rate of more than one deviation per line
is not abnormal, nor is his paucity of noninitial trochees (the only
one in the poem is deployed for a special effect—the erection of a
city in "While Ilion like a mist róse ĭnto towers"), though these
would be slightly more frequent in Shakespeare or Browning or
any "rougher" poet.

Nor is the comparative abundance of initial trochees unusual.
Like Wordsworth in "Tintern Abbey," Tennyson is in fact quite *low*
here, partly because the first-foot trochee is associated (statistically,
not inevitably) with the initialization of thoughts and can be less
frequent in poets who either favor extended sentences or wish, in
the interests of continuity, to de-emphasize the breaks between
them. Initial trochees are much *more* frequent, for example, in Pope,
who works in strongly marked two-line units. There are twenty-
odd (about twice Tennyson's rate) in the first 100 lines of *Essay on*

Criticism. Almost three quarters of them are in the *opening* line of a couplet, and almost all the couplets with an initial trochee in the second line also have one in the first.

An abnormally curious scanner would find other similarities between "Tithonus" and "Tintern Abbey." Perhaps the most important phenomenon revealed by the table is the excess of pyrrhic feet over spondaic. There is a compensatory mechanism, whether in the English language or in the minds of poets, which tends to even out the number of stresses and slacks in the pentameter line. A line with a fourth-foot pyrrhic, for example, is more likely than an average line to have a third- or fifth-foot spondee. Stresses and slacks, therefore, tend to balance at five. This principle is often (even usually) violated in individual lines—it is only visible as a statistical tendency. Poets, in my experience, tend to have a slight excess of pyrrhic over spondaic feet. They are, that is, understressed, but to widely varying degrees. In Pope's *Essay on Criticism*, for example, there is a fairly good balance in the first 100 lines, perhaps 10 excess pyrrhic feet, about the same rate as in Shakespeare's sonnets. In Wordsworth's "Tintern Abbey," the understressing is vastly more conspicuous—about 50 per 100 lines—and the figure for Tennyson's "Tithonus" is comparable (36). Part of this difference is attributable to the differing dynamics of blank and rhymed verse, but both Tennyson and Wordsworth are low-tension poets in all forms. We feel this in the murmuring, flowing, gliding quality of their lines, in the dimming of attention, in our "wait" for stress, in the sense that the rhythm runs on without us and ahead of us.

This understressing constitutes a basic and important feature of Tennyson's blank verse, and a basic and important similarity with Wordsworth, but their convergence in this and other technical characteristic should not be allowed to obscure their difference in flow. Wordsworthian blank verse is more frequently enjambed. It tends to roll slowly from one often feminine and/or nonmedial caesura over the line break to another. Its greater deliberateness is associated with a higher frequency of unrolling polysyllables than is usual in Tennyson. Tennyson's lines, less strongly and frequently enjambed, seem, as noted above, to trail away.

Tears, idle tears, I know not what they mean,
Tears from the depth of some divine despair
(Ricks 784)   Rise in the heart, and gather to the eyes,
In looking on the happy Autumn-fields,
And thinking of the days that are no more.

Here, weak enjambment isolates the lines, which tend to skim through their second halves and then blur as they dissipate their momentum in the right margin, often in a moaning terminal vowel. The aim of "typical" Tennysonian lines is dissolution, and in this they are more radical than Wordsworth. Tennyson can be Wordsworthian, but typically, as in the lines just quoted, he is nearly bodiless.

The table of metrical substitutions in "Tithonus" might be used to make one other point about Tennyson's flow. Clearly, Tennyson's favorite substitutions in this poem are second-, third-, and fourth-foot pyrrhics. The second-foot pyrrhic has been discussed earlier in this chapter in relation to Wordsworth. The fourth-foot pyrrhic is not an uncommon substitution—it occurs once every eight or nine lines in Shakespeare's sonnets and Pope's *Essay on Criticism,* and at an unusually high rate of once every five lines in "Tintern Abbey." But in "Tithonus" it is present in nearly 30 percent of the lines, and it occurs with special frequency near the emotional climaxes of the poem. It seems to cause, or at least underlie, the late-line glide, the fading and trailing, that Tennyson finds so comfortable, so right, in blank verse:

The vapours weep their burthen to the ground

Consumes: I wither slowly in thine arms

Here at the quiet limit of the world

A white-haired shadow roaming like a dream

The ever-silent spaces of the East

Thy cheek begins to redden through the gloom

Yet hold me not for ever in thine East

Release me, and restore me to the ground

In what has been considered the standard account of English meter, Halle and Keyser find the pyrrhic to be the least tense of the possible irregularities[8]. This is at once too bold and not bold enough. On one hand, pyrrhics can be heavier or lighter, slower or faster, depending on their position in the line, their location in relation to pauses, the rhythmic pattern of surrounding syllables, etc. Used with a seventh-syllable caesura, as Wordsworth often uses it— "Thoughts of more deep seclusion; / / and connect"—the fourth-foot pyrrhic can sag and slow. On the other hand, it would not seem unreasonable to surmise that at least *some* of the Tennysonian examples above are *less* tense (because of increased speed and decreased stress density) than the equivalent *regular* lines.

Whether as sign or cause, the fourth-foot pyrrhic is intimately associated with the Tennysonian fade-out. About third-foot pyrrhics one has to be even more careful. They can contribute somewhat to the glide of the poem—"And beat the twilight into flakes of fire"—but their effect is smaller and more problematic. The effect of all rhythmic variations is heavily context-dependent. Fourth-foot pyrrhics will often glide or skim, and second-foot pyrrhics frequently sag. A third-foot pyrrhic, poised in the middle of the line, can do either, depending even more sensitively than the others on context. Tennyson, more often than not, makes it skim. Pope, in contrast, likes to use it in conjunction with a fifth-syllable caesura to poise and balance his couplets without the more conspicuous shock of masculine fourth and sixth syllable caesuras—

Appear in Writing / / or in Judging ill . . .

To tire our Patience, / / than mislead our Sense . . .

and he once insisted that only the fifth-syllable caesura could be used in several consecutive lines without becoming monotonous.[9]

Finally, it should be pointed out—though carefully, given the general confusion about the distinctions among metered verse, free verse, and prose—that lowered stress density is, practically by definition, a feature of prose. The difference between verse (free and otherwise) and prose is in part, as Charles O. Hartman points out in his excellent *Free Verse,* a convention of attention. A poem typed out as a prose paragraph will seem to have fewer significant stresses—and even the simplest poem so treated will seem suffocatingly ornate as it loses the subtle impulse of verse lineation. Conversely, as Hartman notes, lineating prose, or even scanning it in its original paragraphic form, will increase its stress density: "To scan prose is in itself a misleading technique. It requires of the prosodist, and creates in the reader, a kind and degree of attention that demonstrate the impossibility of distinguishing clearly between poetry and prose. As we read the sentence with the attention poetry demands, it becomes poetry; yet it never ceases to be prose. . . . Either technique—scanning prose or turning it into verse—has the specific effect of increasing the density of accents."[10]

Wordsworth has been called—inaccurately with regard to rhythm—prosy; Tennyson has not, and for good reason. And yet his blank verse can share with prose a conceptual if not a literal speed: in its lowest-tension forms, it has high momentum, if not high velocity. It does not change emotional direction easily. It is effortless, relatively unresisted by the more familiar forms of metrical tension or rough-hewn sound. Whether slow or fast, it seems always to be ahead, preparing a frictionless way, drawing the reader along. It exhibits some of the touchless passing more common in prose of certain types—one thinks of Woolf's temptation to call her novels "elegies." Whatever one calls this property of Tennyson's special version of iambic verse—effortlessness, glide, fade, dimness, unreality—it becomes an inescapable feature of the Tennysonian world.

Rhythm is almost a character in Tennyson's poetry, and character is a rhythm. The speakers of Browning's dramatic monologues are given tricks of speech, habits of mind, strategies of evasion, theories of art—and the strong flavor of personality. Tennyson is less interested in our differences. Working near dissolution, death, desire, where we are least particularized and most alike, his poems slip into the repetition of the fewer and more general words necessary to trace the faintness of existence. Tennyson's characters, insofar as they are not all the same, are differentiated not by idiosyncratic ideas or the arcana of personality but through variations in their personal rhythms. Each is known primarily by his experience of the flow of time.

Tennyson, consequently, is a poet of situation rather than of character. This is true even in "St. Simeon Stylites," perhaps his most sharply etched portrait, and the one that has struck observers as an exception to the Tennysonian rule. Thus R. H. Horne in *A New Spirit of the Age,* in 1844: "Certainly Tennyson is not all dramatic. . . . he only selects a peculiar class of characters—those in whom it shall not be requisite to dispossess himself of beauty (Stylites being the only exception). . . . His characters, as we have said before, are generalizations or abstractions; they pass before the imagination, and often into the very centre of the heart and all its emotions; they do not stand forth conspicuous in bone or muscle, nor in solidity, nor roundness, nor substantial identity."[11]

Unlike Browning, Tennyson cannot revel patiently in the unbeautiful, the resistant Other. Whatever curiosity he feels—and he is not a curious poet—is quickly overwhelmed by disapproval. The figure of Stylites, consequently, turns grotesque, sacrifices its independence, and becomes the object of Tennyson's most significant satire. But sympathy of *situation* remains, and it is easy to see how "Stylites" could have become the basis of a lyric monologue like "Tithonus" or "Ulysses."

Tennyson's speakers are usually at an end, either near death or at a point where they choose to regard their real lives as past. Stylites is no exception. "My end draws nigh; / I hope my end draws nigh," he says, like a parody of the exiles in Tennyson's juvenilia or a revision of *In Memoriam*'s "Is this the end? Is this the end?" (sect. 12). His pillar is the literalization of Tennysonian distance, and though his altitude is somewhat less than that of Tithonus, it still imposes dimness: "I scarce can hear the people hum." He almost seems to mock the stance of the Victorian age's preeminent mourner with "Show me the man hath suffered more than I." Like Tennyson, he feels himself at odds with time, and there is something perverse in the whole texture of his life—his "But I die here / Today, and whole years long, a life of death" recalls "Perdidi Diem," "I have never *lived* a day, but daily die" (Ricks 269). And finally, for Stylites as for Tithonus, Ulysses, and Tennyson himself, life has somehow failed to accumulate:

> I think that I have borne as much as this—
> Or else I dream—and for so long a time.
> . . . . .
> then they prate
> Of penances I cannot have gone through,
> Perplexing me with lies; and oft I fall,
> Maybe for months, in such blind lethargies.

(Ricks 546–47)

The years, dim and unparticularized, are more loss than life. Thirty blend into the ghost of one.

In contrast, Tennyson gazes in the "lady poems" at figures whose attraction is that they have found more satisfying ways to move through time. Marion's concern for the commonplace is an instinctive grasp of flow that makes time perceptible, particular, comprehensible. The fluid confidence of Eleanor becomes the foil for Tennyson's existential awkwardness, his desynchronization:

> For in thee
> Is nothing sudden, nothing single;
> Like two streams of incense free
> From one censer in one shrine,
> Thought and motion mingle.

(Ricks 368)

"How can we know the dancer from the dance?" Both Tennyson and Yeats knew the answer, and it is a measure of their temporal dispossession that they must imagine creatures of perfect flow like Marion, or like Rosalind, for whom

> the slope and stream of life,
> The life before, the life behind,
> In the ear, from far and near,
> Chimeth musically clear.

(Ricks 440)

In Tennyson's *Princess,* too, we can hear some of Yeats's admiration for aristocratic courtesy and custom, which both poets image as naturalness of timing—"Like creatures native unto gracious act /

And in their own clear element, they moved." The perfect grace of
dancers tempts us to imagine that they move in an element slightly
more viscous than air, one in which motion and resistance, expression and restraint are perfectly balanced. Water, perhaps—familiar
enough in Tennyson—but in Tennyson the medium is also, and
always, time. These figures of flow link particular moments in a
continuous stream. They are the pole of Tennyson's imagination
that might be called "patience" in order to distinguish it from his
more familiar (Ulysses, Tithonus, Stylites) virtue, "endurance."
Patience is what Tennyson himself seems to have lacked, and he
attributes it primarily to souls more public and less elegiac than his
own. "Endurance" he found closer to home. He admired it less,
loved it more, and discovered it in all speakers who are his surro-
gates.

These competing senses of self and flow often underlie the
strikingly counterpointed movements of Tennyson's blank verse,
one extreme of which is represented by this passage from "The
Coming of Arthur:"

> And so there grew great tracts of wilderness,
> Wherein the beast was ever more and more,
> But man was less and less, till Arthur came.
> For first Aurelius lived and fought and died,
> And after him King Uther fought and died,
> But either failed to make the kingdom one.
> And after these King Arthur for a space,
> And through the puissance of his Table Round,
> Drew all their petty princedoms under him,
> Their king and head, and made a realm, and reigned.

(Ricks 1470)

Ruskin once complained of "increased quietness of style" (*AT
Mem.* 1:452) in the *Idylls* and this is perhaps part of what he meant.
The rhythm and syntax are, first of all, less varied than Tennyson's
best. The elegiac *and,* repeated a dozen times, insists on the ease and
rapidity of connection and levels all grammatical hierarchy. With
weak internal pauses, the lines skim. Weakly enjambed, they float
free. History, character, and feeling are dimmed in the rush. Lives,

acts, eras dissolve in breathless speed. The lines wait for nothing, but they endure all.

Tennyson's other, very different blank verse movement is rarer, and is often matched with his aspirations toward the antiself of patience. This movement is heard, for example, in "Oenone," in the speeches of Hera and Athena:

> Self-reverence, self-knowledge, self-control,
> These three alone lead life to sovereign power.
> Yet not for power (power of herself
> Would come uncalled for) but to live by law,
> Acting the law we live by without fear;
> And, because right is right, to follow right
> Were wisdom in the scorn of consequence.

(Athena, Ricks 392–93)

Withheld, half-swallowed, reticent, the very moment of this verse speaks of what *In Memoriam* calls "the faith that comes of self-control," a solidity almost exactly antithetical to Tennyson's shifting, dissolving poetic center. The lines have a much greater "backward lean" than those from the *Idylls*. They are parenthetical in a way that Tennyson's normally more straight-ahead movement seldom allows, and the articulation of polysyllables is deliberate, weighty. With stronger caesuras and a more ponderous, less trailing kind of enjambment, the passage attains the dignified laboriousness sometimes evoked when Tennyson touches on the antiself of patience.

Patience and endurance are also the choices in "Ulysses," which is an argument of styles—both of writing and of living—that reflects Tennyson's paradoxical experience of time:

> It little profits that an idle king,
> By this still hearth, among these barren crags,
> Matched with an agèd wife, I mete and dole
> Unequal laws unto a savage race,
> That hoard, and sleep, and feed, and know not me.

(Ricks 561–62)

This sounds much more like Athena than like the narrator of "The Coming of Arthur." Ulysses (like his author, who has just lost

Arthur Hallam and hope) is imprisoned in a jagged, unalterable present. The passage, with its uncharacteristically emphatic stresses, its accumulation of subordination and qualification, its feeling of compression, and the roughness of its terms of condescension, has an un-Tennysonian sharpness that, as in "Stylites," he finds appropriate to anger, an emotion his poems usually dim. With its employment of rhythms and words that both poet and reader sense as "outside" Tennyson, the passage takes on a kind of Browningesque patience that allows resistance to become a part of beauty. This is not Tennyson's usual virtue, and its true representative in the poem is not Ulysses but Telemachus, whom he strives to admire.

Like his poet in the aftermath of Hallam's death, Ulysses has lost his past, so that his "I am a part of all that I have met" is less a Promethean assertion than a desperate wish that finds sustained expression in *In Memoriam*. As life vanishes from beneath him, Ulysses tries to recapture it with gestures so large that they dissolve as much as they encompass: "I will drink / Life to the lees," he says,

> I am become a name;
> For always roaming with a hungry heart
> Much have I seen and known; cities of men
> And manners, climates, councils, governments.

(Ricks 562)

We might detect something unconvinced in Ulysses' autobiography. Ricks calls it "plumped amplitude."[12] Far from Tennyson's "base rhythm," this is uncharacteristically impeded verse, and its deliberation is, half-consciously, frustration. Ulysses/Tennyson is only half there. Attempting patient engagement, he achieves something closer to summary, for even as it lingers with the antiself of patience, the poem is eager to launch into the longer straight-ahead phrases and gliding rhythms of Tennysonian endurance—"to follow knowledge like a sinking star / Beyond the utmost bound of human thought." Ulysses vanishes into his own horizon.

But his acceleration is brought up short. When Ulysses describes his unfamiliar son, lines fall with uncharacteristic heaviness one into the other, stall and laboriously restart, and we sense in the patiently accumulating sentence a delay almost ominous:

> This is my son, mine own Telemachus,
> To whom I leave the sceptre and the isle—
>
> (Ricks 564)   Well-loved of me, discerning to fulfil
> This labour, by slow prudence to make mild
> A rugged people, and through soft degrees
> Subdue them to the useful and the good.

Tennyson's praise of his antiself evokes rhythms and diction reminiscent of the humbler productions of Wordsworth. Underneath these frustrations is visible his yearning to be himself again. The poem is anxious to accelerate and it does so, paradoxically, by collecting the details of a more languorous Tennysonian mood. The solid earth dissolves in ghostly voices and Ulysses is drawn into the vast echoing twilight, the larger unity whose Tennysonian metaphor is death:

>   my purpose holds
> To sail beyond the sunset, and the baths
>
> (Ricks 565)   Of all the western stars, until I die.
> It may be that the gulfs will wash us down:
> It may be we shall touch the Happy Isles,
> And see the great Achilles, whom we knew.

The heroism of Ulysses, "to strive, to seek, to find, and not to yield," is the heroism of endurance and of "wild unrest." It is infinitives without objects, power unqualified by application. Its reach is not toward the intractable present, but toward the future, and, in what is surely the poem's most touching line, toward the past of "the great Achilles," the lost Arthur Hallam. In the end, Tennyson is thinking through two rhythms, two ways of living in time.

V

Repetition and Resolution

A link among the days

                                                    In Memoriam

PEOPLE DO not consider that every human being is a vanful of human beings, of those who have gone before him, and of those who form part of his life" (*AT Mem.* 1:323n). Tennyson was intimate with the multiplicity of the self, but unlike Browning he did not distinguish its voices sharply. Less "patient," less sure of his border with the world and with others, he chooses not to inhabit each aspect of the self in turn but to record, with a higher generality and a finer dimness, the flowing and passing of all. Perhaps because he feels virginal—untouched, unshaped, unchanged by a life he has only dimly lived—Tennyson is easily dissolved by thoughts of what might have been and what may be. His other lives are never far from the surface, and their subterranean movements are darkly mirrored in the looming and fading of his encircling landscapes and in his recurrent sense of ghostliness:

> As when with downcast eyes we muse and brood,
> And ebb into a former life, or seem
> To lapse far back in some confusèd dream
> To states of mystical similitude;
> If one but speaks or hems or stirs his chair,
> Ever the wonder waxeth more and more,
> So that we say, "All this hath been before,
> All this hath been, I know not when or where."

(Ricks 459)

Déjà vu is a magical transparency that would seem to arise from a split in the mind. Tennyson is present in a room with Arthur Hallam. An "absent" or past part of the mind suddenly arrives on the scene of their conversation, finding that what it sees apparently for the first time is already stored in the memory of the part that was "there" from the beginning. Time folds. What is happening seems already to have happened. Something like this, involving a lag in the transfer of information between the two hemispheres of the brain, has in fact been proposed by neurophysiologists as an explanation of the common phenomenon. In any case, déjà vu would seem to be a special case of the Tennysonian pastness of the present. It is a repetition whose original is obscured, and, like all Tennysonian repetitions, it dims and shakes the self.

Something similar seems about to occur in the oddly Browningesque "Romney's Remorse." The dying painter speaks to his nurse:

Have I not met you somewhere long ago?
I am all but sure I have—in Kendal church—
O yes! I hired you for a season there,
And then we parted.

(Ricks 1418)

This, as it turns out, is not déjà vu. The "nurse" is in fact the wife Romney had abandoned fifty years before in the conviction that marriage was an obstacle to art. The life he failed to live returns to haunt him. Many shocks of "mystical similitude" might be found to spring from such unhappy origins did their trails not vanish as we traced them toward the unconscious. Tennyson, because he was a guilty soul, and because his failure to distinguish moments must have meant that more of them were lost to the vague unknown, was probably more vulnerable than most to the beckoning of lost originals. The unfinished past repeatedly imposes itself on his present, trying to end, but all he clearly knows of it is unfocused regret and objectless desire, or, as he himself put it, "immeasurable sadness" (Ricks 1227).

Tennyson's vague feelings of betrayal were constantly attaching themselves to rememberable acts. R. W. Rader, for example, has demonstrated that Tennyson was quite strongly drawn to Rosa Baring, who jilted him for a richer suitor, immediately before, and perhaps during the early stages of, his courtship of Emily Sellwood, who eventually became his wife.[1] To an outsider, the affair looks trivial. Though wounded, Tennyson apparently inflicted no pain the easiest of situations, it would seem, to forget cleanly. Tennyson felt blessed by his eventual choice—"the peace of God entered into my life when I married her"[2]—and it is unlikely that he mourned Rosa, but in poems written up to fifty years later, the affair is still a source of anger, guilt, and regret. It seems clear that Tennyson's imagination reinvented her, that she refused to stay in the past because he feared she explained the present.

Rosa reappears as the heroine of "Locksley Hall" (probably written after his quasi engagement to Emily) and of *Maud* (written after his marriage). In both poems, the hero rages at "the madness of love," the flaws of women, and the corruption of civilization. It is usually said that their almost embarrassing anger proceeds from Tennyson's frustrations with rejection, poverty, and obscurity, but *Maud* at least belongs to a period when these emotions might well have subsided. One suspects that what kept them alive was Tennyson's guilt. He had perhaps come to recognize Rosa as unworthy of him ("I am shamed through all my nature to have loved so slight a thing," "Locksley Hall") and had failed perhaps (depending on how much the affairs overlapped) to recognize Emily immediately as his true life. In Tennyson's mind, the relatively casual episode becomes an alternate life that, running parallel to the course he actually took, seems constantly to dim and betray it. Rosa becomes a symbol of the troubling transparency and arbitrariness of the lived self.

The affair of 1834–36 is still on his mind in "Locksley Hall Sixty Years After" of 1886 where the dimming protagonist ("All the world is ghost to me") allows the ghosts of the two women (dead in the poem, but both actually living as he wrote) to meet. Finally, Emily (Edith) forgives him for Rosa (Amy): "Here today was Amy with me, while I wandered down the coast, / Near us Edith's holy shadow, smiling at the slighter ghost" (Ricks 1361).

In the meantime, however, and undoubtedly for reasons deeper than Rosa Baring, the strange division of lives and loyalties had come to propel a striking number of Tennyson's narratives. The triangle of Arthur, Guinevere, and Lancelot comes immediately to mind, but more touching is the love that might have been—Lancelot's wistful encounter with his own lost innocence in the youthful Elaine. Most directly to the point are the narratives that deal with less guilty but still regrettable divisions of loyalties and lives. The title of the "The Ring" (1889) refers not only to the symbol of matrimony but to the circularity of life and the simultaneity of lives. The speaker seems to be equally in love with two cousins—"one was fair, / And one was dark, and both were beautiful" (Ricks 1388)—or not in love at all. He marries the fair Miriam. After she dies in childbirth, he marries the dark Muriel, who mistreats him and his daughter, steals Miriam's ring, and is destroyed by spirits who protect it. In "The Sisters" (1880), the narrator wins the love of one twin sister, then changes his mind and marries the other, only to recognize that he has left the deeper love for the shallower. When both sisters die, he is left with twin daughters who bear their names:

> Now in this quiet of declining life,
> Through dreams by night and trances of the day,
> The sisters glide about me hand in hand,
> Both beautiful alike, nor can I tell
> One from the other, no, nor care to tell
> One from the other.

(Ricks 1298)

Even in context it is difficult to say whether these lines refer to present or past, to the living twin daughters or the memory of the dead twin sisters. Unable and unwilling to narrow himself, the narrator comprehends all possibilities, living like a ghost between two lives.

Tennyson's dissolution of the details that distinguish characters and moments is related to his tendency to repeat and to perceive in repetitions, and it has consequences for the kinds of poems he is suited to undertake. One could hardly imagine him writing *The Prelude,* an autobiographical narrative of "the growth of a poet's mind." Given his habitual generalizing and blending of past and present, it seems unlikely that he could have conveyed a very detailed notion of his evolution. His best long poem is no such Wordsworthian analysis but *In Memoriam,* seventeen years of sporadic repetition of a mood and a pain that time and long handling finally smooth. One doubts, indeed, that the many Wordsworthian shadings of joy, fear, and despondency were explicitly available to him. His moods are too strong and sudden to be carefully differentiated, much less narrated or explained—they are invoked. He writes not Wordsworth's "Five years have passed" followed by a paragraph of careful self-summoning, but, immediately, "Tears, idle tears, I know not what they mean." It is a good guess that Tennyson's scientific accuracy was for him a kind of attention set against his own nearly automatic distances. The price of failing to discriminate the present may ultimately have been that most Tennysonian sadness, the fear of having lived no life.

At issue here, at least obliquely, is faith. The poet whose cry was "O let the solid ground / Not fail beneath my feet" (Ricks 1060) was not one to trust easily in the domestic consolations of the moment. For Tennyson, faith begins with—is almost identical to—faith in the past, and *In Memoriam,* for all its faltering, is an exceptionally insightful and accurate record of a completed act of memory. In 1831 Tennyson's loved and hated father had died. It must have been the most wrenching and guilty of deaths, and there is no elegy. Hallam's death two years later was a relatively unambiguous and utterable tragedy, and, as Gerhard Joseph has demonstrated[3], it gradually changed the shape and direction of both Tennyson's fears and his poems. "Mariana," "The Hesperides," and "The Lady of Shalott" had been poems of encirclement, powered by vague dread. But the poems that follow Hallam's death—or were revised heavily between the 1832 and 1842 volumes—survey clearer losses from a greater distance. Tithonus gazes down from the heavens on our small planet—and on Tennyson's now distant past. Ulysses, too, looks back on a life that is no longer his and sees clearly what has been lost—"the great Achilles, whom we knew." Bedivere/ Tennyson of "The Epic" feints once, twice, and finally lets go of Excalibur and the memory of the two Arthurs. Even the sections added to "The Lotos-Eaters" look back—"Dear is the memory of our wedded lives"—or down, from the perspective of the indifferent gods. The past lies on the other side of a great gulf, and the poet who lived it is two people—"if I be he that watched"—or no one at all. He contemplates in his irreconcilable divisions a "confusion worse than death."

In Memoriam is Tennyson's drift toward reassembling a livable life, and it would be difficult to overemphasize how much his faith in that life depends on the reassimilation of the past. The God who threatens to die in the nineteenth century is the Rememberer, and it is his disappearance that the Wordsworthian spot of time, the Victorian elegiac mode, increased literary emphasis on the particularity of characters and privileged moments, and the century's flood of biography and autobiography all hedge against. Literature must remember what Heaven may not. Tennyson's elegy asserts his own life.

The evolutionary biases of nineteenth-century thought can intrude oddly here. Not just planets and their species, but societies, nations—and individual lives—evolve. Though evolution finds in history the best study of the causes of the present, it can be the secret enemy of the self's integrity, for it ultimately degrades the past. The past is superseded by the present, which, in turn, the future will soon displace. *In Memoriam* opens with a protest against this disruption of identity and a questioning of the compensations of "progress":

> I held it truth, with him who sings
> To one clear harp in divers tones,
> That men may rise on stepping-stones
> Of their dead selves to higher things.
>
> But who shall so forecast the years
> And find in loss a gain to match?
> Or reach a hand through time to catch
> The far-off interest of tears?

"Let love clasp grief lest both be drowned," Tennyson continues. Sorrow asserts the reality of the past, of love. Throughout the poem, therefore, Tennyson and Hallam in effect struggle to remember each other. Hallam, Tennyson senses, is evolving ever higher in the angelic sphere, where he may, like Tithonus, be forgetting his life on earth. But as James Kissane has wisely pointed out, Tennyson's fears that Hallam will forget him are "inversions of a more serious, 'actual' fear that the poet will forget Hallam"[4], that the past, love, identity, will cease, that there will be no "link among the days" (sect. 40). In the evolutionary context, Hallam as the future forgetting the present mirrors Tennyson in the present losing the past.

The faith of *In Memoriam* depends upon the merger of Hallam and Tennyson in memory. This is perfectly natural, indeed almost inevitable, but at the same time impossible to force, and difficult even to desire. Tennyson at first tries to deny the loss of Hallam as an individual—he deplores the idea that the submersion of personality in God is the final goal of the dead. Yet it is finally Hallam's loss of distinctness in memory, his inseparability from Tennyson himself, which assures the poet that neither of them will perish.

Even in the fictional structure of the poem, the change is gradual. Soon after an admission that in early sections of the poem would have seemed to Tennyson worse than fatal, "O last regret, regret can die!" (78), he turns to the final loss—and gain—of Hallam:

(sect. 85)
> Whatever way my days decline,
>   I felt and feel, though left alone,
>   His being working in mine own,
> The footsteps of his life in mine.

Tennyson knew, as Auden said, everything about melancholy, but his ideas on this and every subject are so unlike what we are used to thinking of as ideas—and so much more like emotions—that it is easy to underread him, to call him, as Auden also did, stupid. This section is not a dutiful cliché about the good influence of the noble departed one. It defines the subtle, real feeling that the young dead, their paths cut short, continue somehow, following in our footsteps, living our lives behind us. And it is this kind of unity—when the return of dislocating memory will no longer produce "confusion worse than death" (sect. 90—another of Tennyson's finely original insights on memory and loss)—for which the poet is reaching.

The turning point in the fiction of the elegy is the move from Somersby, Tennyson's childhood home (actually in 1837, four years after Hallam's death) depicted in sections 100–103. Here

Tennyson must let the past, finally, become the past, his ambivalence wonderfully expressed in a single line break—"I turn to go: my feet are *set* / To *leave*" (102)—and even more wonderfully in yet another of the poem's emotional discoveries, "I think once more he seems to die" (100).

As Tennyson leaves the site of his past, Hallam drops into a deeper past, dies again. But his loss is part of a gain. The deep fusion of souls that eventually results finds Hallam nowhere—but also everywhere: "Behold, I dream a dream of good, / And mingle all the world with thee" (sect. 129).

Prefigured by the vision of section 95, in which the lights of East and West, future and past, mix and "broaden into boundless day," section 130, the true climax of the poem, is profoundly Wordsworthian:

> Thy voice is on the rolling air;
>   I hear thee where the waters run;
>   Thou standest in the rising sun,
> And in the setting thou art fair.
>
> What art thou then? I cannot guess;
>   But though I seem in star and flower
>   To feel thee some diffusive power
> I do not therefore love thee less:
>
> My love involves the love before;
>   My love is vaster passion now;
>   Though mixed with God and Nature thou,
> I seem to love thee more and more.
>
> Far off thou art, but ever nigh;
>   I have thee still, and I rejoice;
>   I prosper, circled with thy voice;
> I shall not lose thee though I die.

Hallam's absorption into the very substrate of being is the Tennysonian faith, which is not at all to say that some of the poet's worst years were not ahead. Hallam becomes "vaster passion," God, Nature, the principle of flow, the continuity of time and the self. All this is vague, but vagueness is where Tennyson is most precise. We should not, in the large gestures of the language, lose sight of his essential emotional accuracy. As so often, he has successfully used smoke to find the shape of wind, and the result exceeds its Wordsworthian original in poignance, though it does not equal it in brooding power:

> And I have felt
> A presence that disturbs me with the joy
> Of elevated thoughts; a sense sublime
> Of something far more deeply interfused,
> Whose dwelling is the light of setting suns,
> And the round ocean and the living air,
> And the blue sky, and in the mind of man:
> A motion and a spirit, that impels
> All thinking things, all objects of all thought,
> And rolls through all things.

("Tintern Abbey," ll. 93–102)

This sense of a deeper and more deeply connected memory, relatively unspecific but more continuous and powerful in flow, may have a physiological analogue. Those who sustain brain damage can lose all memory of the past, and recall only events occurring after their accidents. Or they may lose the capacity to form new memories, and live only in the past. But often they retain both the deep past and the capacity to form new memories but lose all memory of the most recent three years, which seem to be the most vulnerable to disruption. This suggests the existence of a kind of interim past, the memories of which are physically different (in storage and retrieval) and rather fragile—they are also, as we know from everyday experience, relatively detailed and distinct. Of course, no scientific explanation is required for the poetic phenomenon. The point is merely that Tennyson is the most sensitive recorder and interpreter of the shift from one level of memory to another. Here, as elsewhere, we watch him watching himself feel. In some ways Tennyson is a poet of deep inarticulateness, but he is an *emotional* intelligence of the highest order.

Eventually, all but the most traumatic memories become less painful—and painful and pleasant memories alike become after a while the basis of the indefinable faith that we were, are, will be. The sense of continuity with the past, again, triggers faith in the future. *In Memoriam* is the example at hand, but Wordsworth's title "Intimations of Immortality from Recollections of Early Childhood" may in itself substitute for a paragraph here. Rossetti's déjà vu in "Sudden Light" similarly broadens into a sense of life after death. Conversely, his inability to reconcile the guiltily divided past loves of *The House of Life* makes him decidedly uneager to endure the confusion worse than death that their simultaneity in heaven might effect. Less divided, Tennyson can hope more sincerely to be swept up in one being "Until we close with all we loved, / And all we flow from, soul in soul" (sect. 131). The faith of the Victorian poets, when they can both believe it and wish for it, is that time is continuous and the self coheres.

Given the constant intrusions of his parallel lives and the inarticulate murmurings of the unresolved past, it is not surprising that Tennyson was more than ordinarily open to the idea of communication with the otherworld. The topic proposed for his first talk to the Cambridge Apostles was "Ghosts," though fear—not of the otherworld but of this one—kept him from delivering it. He slept in his dead father's bed, hoping to be visited by his spirit, and if he listened intently he could hear what he wanted to call the voices of the dead:

> The Ghost in Man, the Ghost that once was Man,
> But cannot wholly free itself from Man,
> Are calling to each other through a dawn
> Stranger than earth as ever seen.
>
> . . . . .
>
> No sudden heaven, nor sudden hell, for man,
> But through the Will of One who knows and rules—
> And utter knowledge is but utter love—
> Aeonian evolution, swift or slow,
> Through all the Spheres—an ever opening height,
> An ever lessening earth.

(Ricks 1384–85)

The theme is repeated from *In Memoriam*. There is no "sudden heaven, nor sudden hell" but a continuous evolution—and a widening distance—that links the progress of the rising dead to the recession of the past. Naturally, Tennyson would see it that way. The many ghosts—and the even more frequent ghostly existences—in his poetry have, it seems, less to do with the afterlife than with the paradoxes of pastness. They express the folding of time, as in "The Coach of Death," written when Tennyson was in his mid-teens:

> They see the light of their blest firesides,
> They hear each household voice:
> The whispered love of the fair young wives;
> And the laugh of their rose-lipped boys.

(Ricks 77)

The quatrain might be seen as a variation on the theme of déjà vu. A past self suddenly returns to the present—only to find that it has been pre-empted. The idea resonates through *In Memoriam,* where Tennyson is official enough to say he will not believe it:

> if they came who past away,
> Behold their brides in other hands;
> The hard heir strides about their lands,
> And will not yield them for a day.

(Sect. 110)

With heaven unreachable, and hell denied, with Tennyson's consent, by his friend F. D. Maurice, Tennyson's ghosts swarm up from something like Hades. There the dead subsist on fading memories and bodiless and powerless desires, much like many of his living speakers. Hades is the institutionalization of Victorian dimness and temporal dispossession. Swinburne finds it a pleasant, indeed exhilarating, resort in *Tristram of Lyonesse* ("A life less thick and palpable than ours"), "By the North Sea," "The Garden of Proserpine," and "The Triumph of Time" ("I wish we were dead together today"). In "The Blessed Damozel," Rossetti evokes the same half-life by blending heaven and earth.

In Tennyson one does not have to be literally dead to inhabit this underworld or underlife, for dispossession begins with the living, and death can be his metaphor for pastness and powerlessness. The hopeless detachment of the lotos-eaters is imaged as the distance between life and death: "if his fellow spake, / His voice was thin, as voices from the grave." Their pastness makes their return to the present as difficult as the resurrection of the dead:

> For surely now our household hearths are cold:
> Our sons inherit us: our looks are strange:
> And we should come like ghosts to trouble joy.

(Ricks 434)

. . . . .

There *is* confusion worse than death.

When Tennyson identifies with his ghost, he finds a vehicle for his feelings of dispossession. He may be longing for intensity, but just as often he finds his absence sadly fascinating. As an artist of death, he obtains strange riches by letting go of life, an experience Hardy, that other connoisseur of pastness, illuminates:

> *For my part, if there is any way of getting a melancholy satisfaction out of life it lies in dying, so to speak, before one is out of the flesh; by which I mean putting on the manners of ghosts, wandering in their haunts, and taking their views of surrounding things. To think of life as passing away is a sadness; to think of it as past is at least tolerable. Hence even when I enter a room to pay a simple morning call I have unconsciously the habit of regarding the scene as if I were a spectre not solid enough to influence my environment; only fit to behold and say, as another spectre said: "Peace be unto you!"*[5]

"Enoch Arden" provides a striking example of the paradoxical passivity and power of the man inhabiting Hades-on-earth. Presumed dead at sea, Enoch returns after a decade to find his house empty. He imagines his wife "dead or dead to me," and learns that she has married his best friend and that his children remember no other father. He gazes through their window on a warm domestic scene and experiences that ultimate transparency of the present—his life going on without him. Turning away, almost ashamed ("softly like a thief") he vows "not to tell her, never to let her know," thereby, like the long-suffering heroes of so many Victorian novels (Hardy's not least among them) sacrificing not his life (though that ends soon) but his identity, his very reality. There *is* confusion worse than death.

But that is not the whole story, for Enoch's moment of unimaginable helplessness gives him a strange strength:

> Then he, though Miriam Lane had told him all,
> Because things seen are mightier than things heard,
> (Ricks 1148)   Staggered and shook, holding the branch, and feared
> To send abroad a shrill and terrible cry,
> Which in one moment, like the blast of doom,
> Would shatter all the happiness of the hearth.

Though he refrains from using it, Enoch at this moment has
the destructive force of a god, of fate, of time itself. The ability to let
go of life is a source of unearthly power. Nor is this an isolated
instance. In "The Dying Swan," a very early piece, Tennyson hears
the swan's final song take "the soul / Of that waste place with joy /
Hidden in sorrow." "Prevailing in weakness," the swan's dirge is "a
carol free and bold . . . As when a mighty people rejoice" (Ricks,
231–32). The Lady of Shalott, also "bold" in dying, becomes a
terrible prophet. She looks

> down the river's dim expanse
> (Ricks 359–   Like some bold seër in a trance,
> 60)   Seeing all his own mischance—
> With a glassy countenance.

and as she dies toward Camelot, the amazed onlookers "crossed
themselves for fear."

Tennyson rarely spoke directly to the future, but his power
was in such dying, and when he felt his own end nearing, he wrote
"Merlin and the Gleam." In this, one of his very last poems, he turns
to poets of succeeding generations with oracular confidence, binding them with his own swan song:

> O young Mariner,
> You from the haven
> (Ricks 1413) Under the sea-cliff,
> You that are watching
> The gray Magician
> With eyes of wonder,

I am Merlin,
And *I* am dying,
I am Merlin
Who follow The Gleam.

This particular kind of authority is unusual in Tennyson. We are more likely to remember him as a poet of the dimness of life, as the recorder of the intrusions of the world and the upsurgings of the past. But it is well to remember the paradox these lines insist upon—that loss is knowledge, that powerlessness is power. The characterization of Tennyson as the architect of palaces of art is a vast oversimplification. To say that Tennyson's poetry is in flight from life is meaningless or at most only partially meaningful. Half of the truth is that our whole nature is to escape life because it is death. The other half, depicted more poignantly by Tennyson than by any other poet, is that life escapes *us*.

Part Two

ROSSETTI AND SWINBURNE

VI

Dante Gabriel Rossetti:
The House of Lives

Shall Time not still endow
One hour with life, and I and she
Slake in one kiss the thirst of memory?

The Stream's Secret

WHAT ROSSETTI'S introductory sonnet calls the "arduous fulness" of
The House of Life is intensity on the edge of dissolution. For Rossetti, as Pater says, existence "is a crisis at every moment," and his need
to form a "moment's monument" begins and ends in his Tennysonian sense of the shadowiness of life. Pater's assertion that in
Rossetti's work "the great affections of persons to each other . . .
formed the great undeniable reality in things, the solid resisting
substance" is a partial truth completed in Wilde's lament that "when
one looks back upon the life that was so vivid in its emotional
intensity . . . it all seems to be a dream and an illusion." In *The
House of Life,* memory alternately vanishes and appears with the
haunting intensity of the exhumed Elizabeth Siddal's "golden hair
undimmed in death" (no. 36).[1]

Rossetti's sense of the moment is clarified in "Eden Bower,"
his deeply personal and yet essentially Victorian version of the Fall.
Parted from Adam, the enraged Lilith begs her first lover, the
serpent, for his shape, and prophesies her temptation of Eve, the
expulsion from Eden and the murder of brother by brother. The
vengeful past, that is, destroys the eternal present, creating time and
loss. Like Rossetti, Adam (this time in a sonnet on Lilith) survives as
the prisoner of memory—"and round his heart one strangling
golden hair." (no. 78) The general relevance for Rossetti's life is
clear though specific application is unwise. By the time these poems

were written, Rossetti's true wife Eve might just as easily have seemed to be Jane Morris—or no one at all—as Elizabeth Siddal, and certainly Rossetti never quite identified Lilith. Fanny Cornforth sat for the original *Lady Lilith* (1868), but to please one of his well-heeled "victims of art," Rossetti replaced her head with that of Alexa Wilding in 1872–73. The description of "Adam's first wife" in *The House of Life* as "subtly of herself contemplative" (no. 78), though apparently written for Fanny, fits nearly any of Rossetti's dream women at least as well.

Neither in life nor in art could Rossetti keep loves separate. His poetry, like Tennyson's, derives its ghostliness from the blendings of memories and selves. The past like a palimpsest blurs the outlines of the present. "Meshed with half-remembrance hard to free" (no. 50), each moment is half unreal, half past. "The Present is and is not," says "The Cloud Confines," echoing Tennyson's "Mariana in the South," and the poet of *The House of Life* finds it impossible to tell whether his free-floating sorrow is "fresh storm" or "old rain the covert bears" (no. 68). Fredeman, noting that the poem "surveys the crises of his life," and that it is largely in the "retrospective mood," characterizes the *The House of Life* as "Rossetti's *In Memoriam*." It is indeed elegiac—and Tennysonian—not only in its attitude toward the past but in its sense of the present, its simultaneous perception of love and loss, what Pater called "the desire of beauty quickened by the sense of death." From Tennyson and even more from Keats, Rossetti learned that hidden deep in the sensuous moment is the fluidity of loss, the paradox that it is "rich to die." *The House of Life,* Pater concludes, is "a 'haunted' house."[2]

The elegiac interpenetration of past and present is visible in Rossetti's work early enough to confirm that it is the work of the psyche and the Zeitgeist only later seconded by amatory complications. With its perspective split between a lady stranded in heaven and her bereaved earthly lover, "The Blessed Damozel," for example, is a kind of double elegy that yearns for both an irretrievable past and a distant present. Seeking a source for the damozel's heavenly plaint, Ford settles on Keats's *Isabella* and the cry of the spirit of the dead Lorenzo, "I am a shadow now alas! alas! / Upon the skirts of human nature dwelling." This is exactly the emotion which Culler finds underlying Tennyson's "passion of the past," "not the passion . . . *for* the past, but the passion of the past itself, its yearning, its suffering, its desire to recover itself and be,"[3] and which appears later in Hardy's imploring armies of ghosts. But one also recognizes in it the plight of many of the *living* speakers of the most memorable Victorian poems. Tennyson's lotos-eaters liken their powerless detachment from the present to death—"Our sons inherit us, our looks are strange, / And we should come like ghosts to trouble joy." "The Blessed Damozel" examines this "confusion worse than death," the sense of being both in and out of life, both present and past. In its evocation of the ghostly isolation of immortality, the poem also recalls "Tithonus." Mariana, the Lady of Shalott, and the Hesperides are also immortal—at least they are divided profoundly between feelings of transience and of eternity. The "ten years" of this poem have been "scarce a day" for the damozel, but "ten years of years" for her lover. Rossetti, too, participates in the Tennysonian desynchronization of experience.

Both embodying and opposing the instability of the present and the ghostliness of the self is Rossetti's deployment of sensuous particulars. Like Browning and many of his speakers, Rossetti senses particulars as stabilizing, as a kind of grip or impedance. Take the opening stanza of "The Blessed Damozel":

> The blessed damozel leaned out
> > From the gold bar of Heaven;
> Her eyes were deeper than the depth
> > Of waters stilled at even;
> She had three lilies in her hand,
> > And the stars in her hair were seven.

(Lang 1)

McGann is surely correct in insisting that details such as those in the last two lines are "non-symbolic,"[4] and in this case their feint toward symbolism is also important. The form of a statement is filled by materials that resist translation. If they do not quite, as Christ would have it, assume the status of "physical objects,"[5] we do respond to what might be called their pseudospecificity as an interruption, however gentle, of the suface of the poem. The unexpected concentration and specificity, the invocation of the eye, which must be at least partially unsuccessful (one surely does not see exactly "seven" stars), is a kind of difficulty. The damozel is "stilled" by details. Indeed many of Rossetti's poetic devices—rhythmic, formal, imagistic—are in effect analogous to the flattening and *stiffening* of surfaces so evident in his paintings. Like the elaborately realized lily among the stark planes of *Ecce Ancilla Domini!* the flowers and stars of this stanza function as arresting incongruity. Insofar as Rossetti is a painterly poet or a literary painter he is often exploiting not so much the similarities of the visual and verbal arts as their partial incompatibility. Like the woodspurge with its stubbornly matter-of-fact "cup of three," nonsymbolic details can function as a kind of irreducible reticence against which a poem's feelings work and deepen.

A somewhat different effect is achieved in "My Sister's Sleep," where details open up space almost by driving a wedge into the imagination:

(Lang 5)

> Through the small room, with subtle sound
> Of flame, by vents the fireshine drove
> And reddened. In its dim alcove
> The mirror shed a clearness round.

Though this is the *In Memoriam* stanza used before *In Memoriam,* it has none of Tennyson's elegiac glide. Rossetti harnesses the visual to his syntax. The accumulation of prepositional phrases, the premature arrival of "by vents" and the consequent withholding of the verb "drove," the strategic line break and the unexpected run-on "and reddened" equate the effort of syntactical progress with the revelation of scene. Description becomes a mysterious action. Detail itself seems to push back the darkness and participate in the lengthening of a moment.

A third effect of particularity is evident in the knitting needles that "met lightly" in "My Sister's Sleep," or the sudden sweeping of a lute by the hem of a dress in "The Bride's Prelude," or again in "The Blessed Damozel":

(Lang 2)

And still she bowed herself and stooped
    Out of the circling charm;
Until her bosom must have made
    The bar she leaned on warm.

Probably a memory of Madeline's "warmed jewels" in "The Eve of
St. Agnes," this image derives its impact not from its stilling or
opening of a stanza but from the simple touching of two parts of the
scene—a warm body and a gold bar—at least one of which, we
discover in the shock of their contact, we have been thinking of as
an abstraction. The effect might be described as "closeness," certainly in the sense of "nearness," and almost (and elsewhere more
conspicuously) in the sense of "humidity." That Rossetti is able to
surprise readers over and over again with such "touches," suggests
that just as his painterly effects depend partly on the refusal of the
visual and verbal media to mix smoothly, so his use of "physical"
detail depends on the innate tendency of poetry to pull away from
the physical, and to be astonished at its own limited capabilities for
minuteness.

In all three cases, particularity can be said to have its own
shaping pressure or touch. Mediating between the fluidity and
solidity of moments, it is one among many stylistic means to the
counterflow or reticence or restraint that is developed in the poetry
of Browning, Christina Rossetti, Hardy, and the later Yeats.

These might be called typically Rossettian uses of detail, but
Rossetti is an oddly centerless poet. His voices range from the
suffocatingly ornate to the determinedly laconic, and he can sound
like nearly anyone. Tennyson, Browning, Swinburne are within
easy reach. "Even So" could be lost in Hardy's *Collected Poems* and
Poirier has pointed out that "The Woodspurge" could be mistaken
for Frost's.[6] Perhaps this adaptability is a clue to his success as a
translator. In any case, *The House of Life* is by another Rossetti. Its
"arduous fulness" is achieved largely without the use of the kinds of
particulars under discussion, and there is no attempt at the slightly
stiffened, homemade, quasi-medieval effect to which they normally contribute. Before examining the features of syntax, sound,
rhythm, and diction that lend to the sonnets their very different

texture, it might be well to take a look at a prominent exception to this dearth of particularity. The relative popularity of "Silent Noon" in an age that has not had much to say about *The House of Life* suggests that it is in some ways atypical:

> Your hands lie open in the long fresh grass,—
>   The finger-points look through like rosy blooms:
>   Your eyes smile peace. The pasture gleams and
>   glooms
> 'Neath billowing clouds that scatter and amass.
> All round our nest, far as the eye can pass,
>   Are golden kingcup-fields with silver edge
>   Where the cow-parsley skirts the hawthorn-hedge.
> 'T is visible silence, still as the hour-glass.
>
> Deep in the sun-searched growths the dragon-fly
> Hangs like a blue thread loosened from the sky:—
>   So this wing'd hour is dropt to us from above.
> Oh! clasp we to our hearts, for deathless dower,
> This close-companioned inarticulate hour
>   When twofold silence was the song of love.

(No. 19)

The dragon-fly, surely, lodges this poem in the mind, and in the anthologies. Here detail is performing all its expected functions by turns. It thickens the poem. The hyphenated words, especially, emphasize the naming function of language over its flow. Because they imply a difficulty in the match between language and something outside which it struggles to encompass, they enforce a different attention. Laid out almost across the grain of the expected sonnet flow, they are a "visible silence." But the Rossettian sonnet cannot bear the burden of all this specificity without a slight deformation. The "silver edge" of the particular slashes flow into stops and starts. "Silent Noon" is one of only ten sonnets in *The House of Life* consisting of more than five sentences. And in only one-third of the sonnets is there (as here) a sentence ending anywhere but at the end of a line. The details demand a kind of movement alien to the sequence. They seem to isolate themselves, push off from each other. This is less true when, in a fashion more typical of *The House of Life,* Rossetti unsays his details, reduces their solidity by yoking them to their opposites in lengthened oxymorons: clouds "scatter *and* amass," the pasture "gleams *and* glooms." These are less facts than motions. The "still fervour" (no. 21) of true oxymorons is common enough in the sonnets, but these extended versions render "The swift beat / And soft subsidence of the spirit's wing," (no. 21), both the insurgence and decay of a moment. In this way Rossetti achieves an arc of restraint without the resistance of particulars.

This bears directly on Rossetti's much-discussed pictorialism. The poet himself insisted, defensively, that his poems were "in no way the result of painters' tendencies" and declared himself free of "word painting" (*LR* 2:850). His sonnets bear him out in some obvious respects. Much, for example, has been made of the painterliness of his personifications, conspicuous if only because they hover densely near the beginning of the sequence:

> I marked all kindred Powers the heart finds fair:—
>> Truth, with awed lips; and Hope, with eyes upcast;
>> And Fame, whose loud wings fan the ashen Past
> To signal-fires, Oblivion's flight to scare;
> And Youth, with still some single golden hair
>> Unto his shoulder clinging, since the last
>> Embrace wherein two sweet arms held him fast;
> And Life, still wreathing flowers for Death to wear.

(No. 1)

> Love's throne was not with these; but far above
>> All passionate wind of welcome and farewell
> He sat in breathless bowers they dream not of;
>> Though Truth foreknow Love's heart, and Hope
>>> foretell,
>> And Fame be for Love's sake desirable,
> And Youth be dear, and Life be sweet to Love.

Truth and Hope so depicted Rossetti could have found in countless paintings or in his painterly imagination, but the immediate inspiration for the language is just as likely to have been work such as Browning's "Pictor Ignotus," which he perhaps included in his admiration of "*Lippo Lippi* and the others of his art-poems, which seem to me perfection" (*LR* 1:277) soon after the publication of *Men and Women*. In any case, such allegorizing in a painter would of course be called "literary." The poem's best line, "All passionate wind of welcome and farewell," is effective precisely because it suddenly accelerates out of the visual, and not all the personifications are anything like concrete. The effect of the poem, in fact, depends on the shift from the easily visualizable figures of the octave to the less visible abstractions of line 12, and to those of lines 13–14, which hardly need to be capitalized at all, and which, as in "Youth be dear," describe not qualities of figures but our response to an idea. The movement from figures to general statement is felt as an elegiac fade-out, and is essentially verbal.

The relations between poetry and painting are real, but not easy to define. Color, for example, is not even the same class of event in verse as on canvas, and a poet who uses much of it is likely to communicate not the hues he places momentarily before us but the strain he is placing on his medium. But there are ways in which poetry invites spatial metaphors more obviously appropriate to other arts, and many readers have been tempted toward them in describing the experience of reading *The House of Life*. The title, of course, has not only an astrological but an architectural sense, which Swinburne elaborated when he compared the individual sonnets to chambers. Later critics have found themselves concerned with the *size* of these chambers. Baum, for example, finds them occasionally "cramped for room, as if he had planned a large poem" while Harris seems to find them too large, inflated, and notes that "one gets accustomed very early to reducing the sonnets to conventional statements."[7] Though these views might seem irreconcilable, both respond to *pressure* within the poems, one calling it centripetal, the other centrifugal. And many have remarked the closeness of *The House of Life,* realized as fully with the driving emotions of the sonnets as with the details of heat and humidity in "The Bride's Prelude." The pressure, the closeness, are part of the "arduous fulness" Rossetti sets against vanishing, but fullness easily becomes tenuous, trembles on the edge of dissolution. This paradox is inherent in Rossetti's method, for his intensity is prolongation, the extension of the moment, as here quite literally in "Nuptial Sleep":

> At length their long kiss severed, with sweet smart:
>   And as the last slow sudden drops are shed
>   From sparkling eaves when all the storm has fled,
> So singly flagged the pulses of each heart.
> Their bosoms sundered, with the opening start
>   Of married flowers to either side outspread
>   From the knit stem; yet still their mouths, burnt red,
> Fawned on each other where they lay apart.
>
> Sleep sank them lower than the tide of dreams,
>   And their dreams watched them sink, and slid away.
> Slowly their souls swam up again, through gleams
>   Of watered light and dull drowned waifs of day;
> Till from some wonder of new woods and streams
>   He woke, and wondered more: for there she lay.

(No. 6a)

On the microscopic level, Rossetti's sense of prolongation appears in the second-by-second movements of his lines, with their clustered stresses and valleys of slacks: "At length their long kiss severed, with sweet smart: / And as the last slow sudden drops are shed." Vogel calls this "stress-height rhythm"[8] and one can agree with him that it is characteristically Rossettian without following him to the conclusion that it is in any way noniambic, or even very unusual. Nor is the Rossettian effect purely rhythmic—one could easily find examples of lines with identical scansions that do not sound at all Rossettian. But given the even and deliberate pace of Rossetti's sonnets, the deployment of this kind of rhythm in seemingly self-prolonging sentences—and in concert with rolling polysyllables, indulgent voweling, and an idiosyncratic management of the sound-transitions between words—turns the quick stroke of iambic into viscous undulation, "arduous fulness."

This exaggeration of undulation is also evident in Rossetti's choice of the Petrarchan *a b b a a b b a* octave and in his handling of the sonnet as a whole. His sonnets seldom argue, nor do they exhibit the Elizabethan fondness for balance and antithesis, nor do they accept the rhetorical fragmentation encouraged by the four divisions and seven rhymes of the Shakespearean form. They typically contain four or five rhymes and three sentences. Linear development is de-emphasized by the continuous recall which is the product of a net of rhymes and is further obscured by a characteristic word order almost atemporal. In shape, they are simpler and rounder. The octave summons, the sestet gradually releases. The whole is a full curve, the invocation and subsidence of a moment.

A good deal of the sense of prolongation in Rossetti's sonnets is the consequence of his long sentences, but their actual length is perhaps less important than the effort and expectation of their prolongation. The sentences in "Nuptial Sleep" are actually somewhat shorter than Rossetti's average. What is more significant is, first, that we feel their enjambment as part of the labor of extension—

> Their bosoms sundered with the opening start
> > Of married flowers to either side outspread
> From the knit stem

—and further that the extensions of the syntax seem to be dictated moment-by-moment, each phrase surging out of the last rather than drawn forward by a visible goal.

Rossetti's drive for prolongation and intensity is satisfied largely in his characteristically inwoven—but seldom tensely suspended—syntax. An example is his description of the sonnet as "Of its own arduous fulness reverent." Here, rhyme and rhythm could easily have survived a more "normal" word order, such as "Reverent / Of its own arduous fulness," but in folding the thought and withholding resolution, Rossetti thickens the sound of the line, and therefore increases the sense of effortful prolongation. The effect is partly rhythmic. The postponement of "reverent" turns the end of the line into *virtual* trochees and dactyls whose dawdling retroactively thickens the pronunciation of "arduous"—a reader is more likely to attempt to make iambic expectation fuse the disyllable *-uous* in Rossetti's line than in the alternate.

Rossetti may be conscious in these lines of striving to "imitate" fullness—and his "fullest" passages tend to be full of striving—but it might be more accurate to say that a preexisting tendency of his language has surfaced momentarily in self-description. This happens in all poets—it seems to happen with special frequency in Rossetti:

(No. 50)

> And now Love sang: but his was such a song,
>   So meshed with half-remembrance hard to free,
>   As souls disused in death's sterility
> May sing when the new birthday tarries long.

The weaving of the second line imitates its own meaning. Indeed, the whole quatrain is "meshed with half-remembrance." Because their relationship is not entirely clear until the period, we are free to connect thoughts "incorrectly," if momentarily, and we cannot wholly "free" them from the extra associations that crowd Rossetti's poetry. Despite the clarifying comma, for example, it is difficult not to read "hard to free as souls . . . in death," even though "such a song . . . as souls . . . may sing" is sanctioned. And it is even more difficult because this *incorrect* reading of lines 2–3 is extremely close to the *correct* reading of lines 3–4. Foreseeing and remembering, the lines are oddly unsequential and, consequently, oddly unresolved. In number 37, also a sonnet about old love haunting new, the case is similar, but no punctuation or grammatical antecedent, however hazy, forbids a whole series of "mistakes":

> "When that dead face, bowered in the furthest years,
>   Which once was all the life years held for thee,
>   Can now scarce bid the tides of memory
> Cast on thy soul a little spray of tears, —
> How canst thou gaze into these eyes of hers
>   Whom now thy heart delights in, and not see
>   Within each orb Love's philtred euphrasy
> Make them of buried troth remembrancers?"

The first quatrain begins in relatively simple ambiguity—the sentence is complex, but one knows what is missing (a verb), even though the subject "face" begins to dim with distance and increasing complexity of modification. But the confusions of then and now begin to cloud the syntax. We expect the *when* clause to introduce an action in the past or a general case—a *whenever.* "When to the sessions of sweet silent thought / I summon up remembrance of things past" goes Shakespeare's sonnet, "I sigh." It is *when–then.* Rossetti, oddly, has it *when–now.* What had seemed conditional abruptly becomes immediate and actual. And there is another slight dislocation as the long-sought object, "tides," is snatched away to be the subject of "cast." In this we feel the effort of prolongation. And of course the meaning of the line is ambiguous. The literal sense is that the memory of the dead love no longer has the power to make the poet weep. Somewhere in the mist, however, a spray of *flowers* is cast on the grave of Rossetti's dead soul. Who is dead and gone, and when? Continuing, we can only believe that "How canst thou gaze into these eyes of hers" refers to the old love who has been the subject of the previous sentence. But the next line, with another jarring "now," forces us back to the new love, into whose eyes we gaze only to find "buried troth," the past. In this quatrain, too, prolongation is palpable—the end of each line completes a thought, and could, in fact, be terminally punctuated. The very fact of continuation changes the meaning of the sentence behind us. This is always happening in Rossetti's poetry—it is only more obvious here.

These uncertainties of syntax have a cumulative effect on expectations. For one thing, despite the undisguised artifice of the poems and the number of off-rhymes, the reader *never* has the sense that syntax has been inverted for convenience in rhyming, though modern ears are sensitive to that distortion. This implies that Rossetti has broadened expectation to the extent that hardly any word order is heard as abnormal. Consequently, in reading a long sentence, we are headed into darkness, with only a weak idea of how the syntax will be resolved. Not only does this facilitate false connections, it means that Rossetti's sentences seldom close with the pleasure of fulfilled expectations, that almost audible satisfaction with which the Johnsonian period clicks shut. They do not conclude, or even reach an end. They lengthen, and finally reach *for* an end.

Rossetti always insisted that he was not a poet of single good

lines. Whether this is a cause or an effect of the poems' continuous
self-reconsideration is not clear, but it is true that Rossetti's lines
seem to have relatively little integrity, little separate existence and,
like Spenser's, they take a long time to become fixed in memory.
The existence of single words is also qualified in the Rossettian
syntax. The "snatching away" of nouns, and with them some of the
solidity of the poems, is repeated on a smaller scale by intricate
modification, the most obvious manifestation of which is the
bracketing of nouns with adjectives and verbals in phrases such as
"gracious fostering union garlanded," "triune loveliness divine,"
and "hollow faces burning white." Substantives are floated loose or
spread out. No noun seems wholly where it is or what it is. The air
is thick with fullness in solution.

On scales both large and small, the fullness and the dissolution
of *The House of Life* are in the richness of its ambiguities and its
alternative ways of seeing the same word ("O lovely and beloved,
O my love") or the same thing: "A glance like water brimming with
the sky / Or hyacinth-light where forest-shadows fall" (no. 31).
Both images are characteristically Rossettian, the first in its fullness
to satiety, the second in its solution of petals in light and shadow.
The "glance" is partially, even gratefully, lost in the redundancy of
simile.

Considered as syntax, the Rossettian hyphenations appear in a
different light. That "forest-shadows" clearly does not need a
hyphen, and that "hyacinth-light" may not, only emphasizes Rossetti's fondness for forcing words into close neighborhood, even
when their connection is not entirely effortless:

> Tell me, my heart,—what angel-greeted door
(No. 41)   Or threshold of wing-winnowed threshing-floor
> Hath guest fire-fledged as thine, whose lord is Love?

Most of Rossetti's compounds could be expressed without hyphens
in a prepositional phrase (e.g., "fledged with fire") and they are
consequently read as compressions or short-circuits—as if an intense feeling had arced across a gap in the language. In this passage a
whole series of verbs is frozen into compound adjectives. Such
words are thicknesses, partly because of their uneasy alignment

with the syntax, partly because they are often stress heights, partly because they are conceptually difficult. They are compressed; they contain unreleased action.

Compression implies crowding, and indeed readers unsympathetic to Rossetti's sonnets often seem to be *repelled*—not merely morally or aesthetically, but almost literally pushed out and away. Calling for unfamiliar forms of relaxation and tenacity, Rossetti's huge syntactical gestures and inexplicit connections, his swarming emotions and nearly desperate prolongation, can elicit resistance or reports of vagueness, disorder, closeness—an uncomfortable feeling of being buffeted and overinvoked. Nowhere is this more apparent than in reader responses to Rossetti's aspirations toward the condition of music. Rossetti's fondness for pure sound, however, is not very pure, and it does not produce nonsense—or when it does, locates it in a context limited enough that its shape as *gesture* is clear. One of the most extreme examples is "Through Death to Love":

> Like labour–laden moonclouds faint to flee
>   From winds that sweep the winter-bitten wold,
>   Like multiform circumfluence manifold
> Of night's flood-tide,—like terrors that agree
> Of hoarse-tongued fire and inarticulate sea. . .

(No. 41)

The polysyllabic complication of "multiform circumfluence manifold" is perhaps extreme, but its interweaving of *m*'s and *f*'s (in which the ear detects theme, variation, resolution) is a typical dissolution. Nor is this particular confluence of sound and meaning entirely coincidental, for polysyllables in Rossetti often in their very movement "mean" something like this—entanglement, confusion, unity in complexity. In Rossetti, polysyllabic roll is a form of poetic touch, of attention, and it parallels his complicated word order in effect: things interweave but do not quite disappear. "Absorption is not annihilation," as he said in another context. (*LR* 3:989–90) He seeks the furthest dissolution that can still be felt as fullness.

Confronting the "inarticulate" (surely in the precision of its articulation one of the poet's most articulate words), Rossetti lets sound carry him a little beyond paraphrasable meaning, but the direction of his disappearance is usually clear. He exploits sound not for nonsense but for two senses at once, even to the point of creating subliminal oxymorons in which the suggested meaning unsays the explicit:

(No. 4)

> How then should sound upon Life's darkening slope
> The ground-whirl of the perished leaves of Hope,
> The wind of Death's imperishable wing?

Rossetti's colors bleed; his words will not stay in place. It is nearly impossible in this context to hear "imperishable" solely as meaning "permanent, unending." It contains *perish,* its opposite, and is linked by assonance to the little cyclone of *whirl–wind–wing.* The energy of its first plosive, then breathy articulation is assimilated into an image of windy transience. This confusion of time and the things it acts on is inherent in Rossetti's elegiac vision. In "Last Fire," the apparent subject is timeless golden fruit:

(No. 30)

> This day at least was Summer's Paramour,
> Sun-coloured to the imperishable core
> With sweet well-being of love and full heart's ease.

Hidden within the literal meaning are all the elements—perish, heat, sweetness, color (noon or sunset?), and perhaps even a reminiscence of Keats's "fill all fruit with ripeness to the core," to suggest—even if Rossetti had not already taught us to assume the simultaneity of fullness and dissolution—rotting or at least very ripe fruit. Rossetti's idol had maintained that poetry should "surprise by a fine excess." In *The House of Life* the "fine excess" is swollen, caught at the edge of satiety by an even finer restraint, a restraint almost invisible because it apparently originates neither in the speaker nor in the "visible silence" of detail but in the very limits of utterance and feeling. Engorged, language becomes its own restraint.

Rossetti's fondness for dim and elaborately composed spaces suggests that agoraphobia is his aesthetic, if not his disease. The "closeness" that is his art and his cure accounts for the essentially claustrophobic failure of attention in some readers, and it is probably in this that Buchanan's famous charge of "fleshliness" (the wrong word for a legitimate response) begins. To this accusation,

Baum replies wonderfully, saying that the "hothouse atmosphere" of *The House of Life* originates not in "immorality" but in "excess of artistry." The equation of the emotionally claustral with literary artifice (also applicable to Tennyson's moments of ornateness) is vehement in remarks of Browning during his period of sea air, open spaces, and cold bathing. He complained to Isa Blagden that Rossetti's work was "*scented* with poetry," and to the poet himself griped, "I cannot enjoy the personifications. Love as a youth, encircling you with his arms and wings, gives me a turn."[9] Rossetti was not oblivious to the nature of his effects, though he sometimes misjudged their intensity, and his errors of taste are often necessities of the psyche. He seems to have *sought* artificiality, even a degree of preciosity, as a means of embodying his strongly colored passion.

Preciosity, to take the extreme case, is perceived in our (bored? embarrassed? fearful?) recoil from excessive artifice. It seems to translate easily into our ambivalence about "things overknown," a feeling of entrapment in the self. *The House of Life,* like most love poetry but more deliberately so, is rife with a solipsism from which the strangely tenacious Rossetti does not back away. Intensity is often isolating—Rossetti's uniqueness is in his desire and his ability to turn on himself, to endure his own closeness and the density of his passion.

Rossetti's obsession with women, for example, is in proportion to their own solipsism. In a letter describing *Lady Lilith,* he calls her mood "that self-absorption by whose strange fascination such natures draw others within their own circle." (*LR* 2:850) He often perceives such self-absorption in almost grotesquely self-reflexive terms, as in "her breast's secrets peered into her breast" (no. 10), or "the underlip / Sucked in, as if it strove to kiss itself," (*PR* 24) a line from "A Last Confession" which Doughty associates with Elizabeth Siddal but which could describe many of Rossetti's subjects.[10] In this poem, the speaker's love for his adopted daughter heats up and closes in with suggestions of incest:

> She was still
> (*PR* 23) A child; and yet that kiss was on my lips
> So hot all day where the smoke shut us in.

As Casteras puts it, Rossetti has an excited sense of "lovers as second selves or doubles," and love is "a curious symbiosis of passion and shared identity."[11] Here, as in *The House of Life,* the intuition of "one nearer kindred than life hinted of" (no. 15), though it is not literally incestuous, is more than casual. It invokes ambiguous closeness—of the beloved, of oneself, of passion. It investigates a passion not without desire but somehow beyond it, including its satiation.

In his discussion of sensuous particulars in Rossetti's shorter poems, McGann justly remarks that through them "phenomena . . . are restored to a kind of innocence,"[12] but this statement is less applicable to *The House of Life* and to the area of Rossetti's life it maps. Innocence means innocence of *us,* and freshness is in part the quality of being outside the self. In the sonnets, however, Rossetti's desire is, in its "arduous fulness," claustral and all-enclosing. There is no outside, no other. All the lives he sees are lives he has failed to live. He asks

> "The lost days of my life until to-day,
> >   What were they, could I see them on the street
> >   Lie as they fell?"

and answers himself:

> I do not see them here; but after death
> >   God knows I know the faces I shall see,
> Each one a murdered self, with low last breath.
> >   "I am thyself,—what has thou done to me?"
> "And I—and I—thyself," (lo! each one saith,)
> "And thou thyself to all eternity!"

(No. 86)

Perhaps because he cannot integrate his lost selves, Rossetti seems doomed to meet himself over and over. Rossetti's "Lost Days" are a "confusion worse than death." The afterlife he must imagine is the past he cannot face.

VII

Swinburne:
Purity and Pain

We had stood as the sure stars stand, and moved
As the moon moves, loving the world; and seen
Grief collapse as a thing disproved,
Death consume as a thing unclean.

The Triumph of Time

LESS A personality than, as he might have put it, a shoreline, Swinburne is visible only as the hypnotically shifting border of land and sea, solidity and fluidity, cold strength and smothering passion. Because he lacks the patience and—though it may seem strange to say this of a man so eccentric and explosive—the self-indulgence of his mentor Rossetti, Swinburne can dwell only briefly in the Rossettian closeness

> Covered with love as a covering tree,

(*PS* 1:40)
> . . . . .
> Filled from the heart to the lips with love,
> Held fast in his hands, clothed warm with his wings.

Though such swarming passions continuously inform his poetry, they are qualified, sometimes by enthusiastic wit, sometimes by poisonous guilt, and most often by that most remarkable aspect of Swinburne—his drive toward cold clarity, impossible innocence, superhuman strength, inhuman purity.

"The Leper" is an instructive example. The story of an apparent rapist and necrophiliac who imagines that intercourse with an at first unwilling and later dead leper is love "well seen of me and her" should be nearly unreadable. But "The Leper" is hardly even shocking. It is almost a critical venture in that it so consciously, almost self-consciously, exploits the voyeurism of Victorian poetry—its fondness for maidens dead, swooning, sleeping, or merely unaware—to discover its limits. But like Browning's "Porphyria's Lover" (from which, along with Morris's "The Wind," it clearly derives, and whose conclusion it echoes), "The Leper" transforms violence less with critical distance than with terrifying *innocence:*

> It may be all my love went wrong—
>   A scribe's work writ awry and blurred,
> Scrawled after the blind evensong—
>   Spoilt music with no perfect word.
>
> But surely I would fain have done
>   All things the best I could. Perchance
> Because I failed, came short of one,
>   She kept at heart that other man's.
>
> I am grown blind with all these things:
>   It may be now she hath in sight
> Some better knowledge; still there clings
>   The old question. Will not God do right?

(PS 1:134)

On its own terms—those of the clear confusions of a dream, "A scribe's work writ awry and blurred"—"The Leper" is not revolting but strangely poignant. In order to be repelled by the corruption and closeness seemingly inherent in the situation, one must step outside the speaker's hallucinatory detachment and deliberately—and with some difficulty—reliteralize the narrative. The residue of the poem as it demands to be read is not diseased flesh but delicacy, naiveté, chill purity:

> Nothing is better, I well know,
>   Than love; no amber in cold sea
> Or gathered berries under snow:
>   That is well seen of her and me.

(PS 1:130)

The Swinburnean poles of closeness and clean power exhibited by "The Leper" appear alternately and more typically in "Laus Veneris," Swinburne's version of the Tannhauser legend:

Inside the Horsel here the air is hot;
Right little peace one hath for it, God wot;
    The scented dusty daylight burns the air,
And my heart chokes me till I hear it not.

(*PS* 1:14–
15)

Behold, my Venus, my soul's body, lies
With my love laid upon her garment-wise,
    Feeling my love in all her limbs and hair
And shed between her eyelids through her eyes.

. . . . .

Ah yet would God this flesh of mine might be
Where air might wash and long leaves cover me,
    Where tides of grass break into foam of flowers,
Or where the wind's feet shine along the sea.

Virtually swamped with love, the second of these stanzas
would have made a worthy (and almost undetectable) addition to
The House of Life. But there may be a shade of almost boyish
comedy in the emphatic alliteration of *Horsel–here–hot* and the
rhyme *God wot,* and this distance predicts the more convincing
"would God." Smothered in this humid interior, the knight yearns
for the purity and high windy light of the seacoast, Swinburne's
truest element. Swinburne is more convincing than Tennyson or
Rossetti at both luridness and heroic freshness, though he can
hardly hold them apart, as here in "The Triumph of Time":

        Sea, that art clothed with the sun and the rain,
    Thy sweet hard kisses are strong like wine,
        Thy large embraces are keen like pain.
    Save me and hide me with all thy waves,
    Find me one grave of thy thousand graves,
(*PS* 1:48)   Those pure cold populous graves of thine
        Wrought without hand in a world without stain.

    I shall sleep, and move with the moving ships,
        Change as the winds change, veer in the tide;
    My lips will feast on the foam of thy lips,
        I shall rise with thy rising, with thee subside.

What is remarkable here is the near simultaneity of Swinburne's three intensest loves. One—the faintest—is guiltily painful, poisonous, insidiously damaging. The second, exhilarating, is vast, cold, impersonal, heroic—as clean as those "pure cold populous graves." The third, in the troughs of the waves, is rest, oblivion. All three are imaged in the sea, as they might, in another moment, all be imaged in a woman, for there are few fixed symbols in Swinburne. There are instead perceptions. The meaning of objects in his poetic landscape is determined by the hardness or softness of the love felt in them at any given moment—their balance of cruelty, tenderness, coldness, shame, purity, pain, passion.

The Hades of rest is an inevitable subdivision of Victorian consciousness, and it is especially important in Swinburne who, more strongly than any of his contemporaries, feels the Keatsian inseparability of pleasure and pain. As the most intense of the Victorian poets, he also exhibits the most intense longing to sleep and be done. In his various and without exception touching renderings, Hades is the image of the elegiac consciousness, an existence, in Browning's words for Andrea del Sarto, "all toned down":

> I wish we were dead together to-day,
>> Lost sight of, hidden away out of sight,
> Clasped and clothed in the cloven clay,
>> Out of the world's way, out of the light,
> Out of the ages of worldly weather,
> Forgotten of all men altogether,
> As the world's first dead, taken wholly away,
>> Made one with death, filled full of the night.
>
> How we should slumber, how we should sleep,
>> Far in the dark with the dreams and the dews!
> And dreaming, grow to each other, and weep,
>> Laugh low, live softly, murmur and muse.

(*PS* 1:43)

"As the world's first dead"—the image is at once stunning and almost touchingly possessive, both faded and fresh. Hades, where "subtler natures taste in air less dense / A life less thick and palpable than ours" (*PS* 4:13), is the dimness of life, the only refuge from

Swinburne's round of furious and painful loves. Elsewhere, pain is inextricable from intensity, inextricable also from clarity, purity, strength. This bears directly on the well-known but often only half-read "Hymn to Proserpine." It is not merely that its pagan speaker resists Christian immortality in his desire for the oblivion of sleep, for he laments not only Proserpine, queen of Hades, but Apollo, "a bitter God to follow, a beautiful God to behold." The new regime denies not only the possibility of eternal sleep, but, within life, denies intensity by separating pain and pleasure. When he exclaims "Thou hast conquered, O pale Galilean; the world has grown grey from thy breath," he regrets not only the new deathlessness but the accompanying new lifelessness.

Hardly anyone has failed to notice Swinburne's idiosyncratic rhythmic textures but the reports of readers are strangely contradictory. "Swinburne's most novel rhythms are those which are extremely speedy and those which are extremely languorous," says E. K. Brown, and Lionel Stevenson notes his "two distinctive"—and seemingly opposite—"effects, speed and emphasis." Saintsbury cites Swinburne's "impulse to quicken, to quick time," but his absolutely accurate statement that "the intricate and massive stanza of 'The Triumph of Time' swells and swings like a wave" seems to describe quite other qualities than speed.[1] The implied confusion about the velocity of Swinburne's verse should be reminiscent of the discussion of Tennysonian flow above, and leads to similar conclusions about Swinburne's desynchronized apprehension of time—that speed and languor are simultaneous, without contradiction, and without strain. Take the stanza of "A Forsaken Garden":

> In a coign of the cliff between lowland and highland,
>   At the sea-down's edge between windward and lee,
> Walled round with rocks as an inland island,
>   The ghost of a garden fronts the sea.
> A girdle of brushwood and thorn encloses
>   The steep square slope of the blossomless bed
> Where the weeds that grew green from the graves of its
>   roses
>   Now lie dead.

(*PS* 3:21)

Brown uses this stanza as an example of Swinburne at his most languorous and dirgelike, and one certainly knows what he means. But no matter how slowly the stanza is read, a complementary impression of speed will not disappear. This is partly a matter of the uneven pacing of lines composed of blends of duple and triple feet. The unstressed syllables of an anapest (of the cliff) are read quickly to make it equivalent in time to the disyllabic feet. Accordingly, slowness is felt not in isolation but as the restraint of a swiftness somehow inherent in the lines, a wavelike swell and fall.

Swinburne's mixture of double and triple feet results in a rhythmic undulation at once more exaggerated and more effortless than Rossetti's. The texture of the lines is unlike Rossetti's "arduous fulness," and even farther from Browning. Swinburne's counter-motions meet, like Tennyson's, without standard tension. We are conscious of changes in gravity, of acceleration and deceleration, moving up and down to go forward. Change is rapid, progress slow—the lines become their own restraint. This dovetails with the brooding, obsessive quality of Swinburne's emotions, and is supported by myriad habits of sound.

The alternation of masculine and feminine rhymes, sets up a second wavelike motion. The weakly rhymed lines seem to end only tentatively and are somehow not complete until the strong rhyme of the following line. Consequently, the motions of the lines cross as if—to push Saintsbury's wave metaphor—they were in-rushing and subsiding waves. (What is in question here, of course, is not an accurate "depiction" of the ocean, but the Swinburnean swell and fall of emotion that led him to feel his strange and exhilarating kinship with the sea in the first place). Then, too, in "the weeds that grew green from the graves of its roses," each element—*weeds–grew–green–graves–roses*—repeats a previous sound, drops one, adds another, in a kind of relay that provides an illusion of momentum. In the end, the line returns figuratively to earth, but momentum, surviving the qualifications of meaning, surges on into the suddenly short line "Now lie dead." Too small to quite disperse the motion, the line is perceived in terms of *reticence,* which is, after all, the transfer of motion from reluctant words to willing reader. The reticence Hardy and Browning achieve with metrical roughness, understatement, or irony, Swinburne here produces with an almost imperceptible blend of motions. The effect is exaggerated and perhaps even more moving when the words in the short line are in themselves general and inconclusive:

(PS 3:21)

> So long have the grey bare walks lain guestless,
>   Through branches and briars if a man make way,
> He shall find no life but the sea-wind's, restless
>   Night and day.

The motion that swells through this ambiguous closure, that of endless ending, is inescapably Swinburnean.

But lest the Swinburnean tone seem inherent in the bare outline of a rhythmic pattern rather than in his special adaptations, it should be pointed out, on one hand, that Hardy, a vastly different poet, uses similar blends of double and triple feet—arranged, syllabified, and paused differently—and, on the other, that this logaoedic rhythm has in general been used for comic verse. In his superlative study of poetic rhythm, Derek Attridge summarizes the difficulties of triple rhythms:

> *Duple rhythms are much commoner than triple in the English literary tradition, and it is worth asking why this should be so. . . . One feature of English speech [is] the tendency towards an alternation of stronger and weaker stresses; verse in duple metre embodies this tendency as its basic rhythmic principle, and is therefore able to draw on the full resources of the spoken language, accommodating polysyllables and stretches of monosyllables with relative ease. Triple metres, on the other hand, have to work against this tendency in order to create an alternative rhythmic pattern, which can tolerate certain words only by suppressing their natural stress contours. Moreover, duple verse matches the two rhythmic principles of English, the stress-timed rhythm and the syllabic rhythm, by providing one syllable for a rhythmic peak and one for a trough; triple verse, on the other hand, favours stress-timing, both in its implied equivalence of one strong to two weak syllables, and in its overriding of the alternations of the language. This alliance with the stronger, and probably more fundamental,*

rhythmic principle produces a prominent rhythm that tends to simplify the contours of speech. A strong triple rhythm will often force a bad poet (or even tempt a good one) to subordinate semantic and syntactic choices to metrical choices, producing verse which is more gesture than expression.[2]

"Gesture" has its obvious dangers, but is alien neither to Swinburne's aspirations to the condition of music, nor to his virtually symphonic mode of thinking, nor to his preference for emotion that has not yet quite specified itself in words. And his meter, for all its limitations, turns out to have other advantages. In triple or mixed meters, the stress pattern, as Attridge notes, must be strongly marked. The differential—difference in value between stressed and unstressed syllables—of such lines is high. And it is relatively rigidly enforced—we are less likely to hear several degrees of stress among the stressed syllables. This evenness of emphasis counteracts some of the dipody native to the tetrameter but potential even in the pentameter, as in the Tennyson line "The woods decay, the woods decay and fall." Swinburne's stresses, in contrast, tend to retain one high value throughout the line—"I have put my days and dreams out of mind"—and the effect, though potentially wearying, is more often that of an enforced monotone, a strong restraint. This is true especially when the line is heavily monosyllabic. And despite one's aftermemory of a certain ornateness in Swinburne's poems (this is the residuum of the heavy patterning of sound and rhythm, and the blurring of individual words, not the actual quality of the diction) he is in fact among the most monosyllabic poets in the language. Rosenberg justly praises him as the master of "the bleak beauty of little words."[3]

Swinburne, indeed, learned to put this fierce monotone, with its suggestion of awful stoicism, even into the strictly duple blank verse of *Atalanta;*

(PS 4:275)

> Night, a black hound, follows the white fawn day,
> Swifter than dreams the white flown feet of sleep;
> Will ye pray back the night with any prayers?
> And though the spring put back a little while

Winter, and snows that plague all men for sin,
And the iron time of cursing, yet I know
Spring shall be ruined with the rain, and storm
Eat up like fire the ashen autumn days.

The verse, in its severe deliberation, is almost reversed. It favors initial trochees after breaks which, despite their steepness, carry forward little momentum, and its most conspicuous caesuras are early—they devour momentum. With its monosyllabic drag, its tendency to bridge over the normal positions for the medial caesural sag, and its evenness of stressing, the passage hints at the ferocious restraint, the terrible dismissal of love by Althaea, that will make *Atalanta in Calydon* the greatest of the Victorian verse dramas.

In stichic verse, moreover, unconfined by the stanza or by Rossettian agoraphobia, Swinburne can push his paradoxical method—microscopic restraint of macroscopic abundance—to its extreme:

                                        yea, she felt
Through her own soul the sovereign morning melt
And all the sacred passion of the sun;
And as the young clouds flamed and were undone
About him coming, touched and burnt away
In rosy ruin and yellow spoil of day,
The sweet veil of her body and corporal sense
Felt the dawn also cleave it, and incense
With light from inward and with effluent heat
(PS 4:30–
31)   The kindling soul through fleshly hands and feet.
And as the august great blossom of the dawn
Burst, and the full sun scarce from sea withdrawn
Seemed on the fiery water a flower afloat,
So as a fire the mighty morning smote
Throughout her, and incensed with the influent hour
Her whole soul's one great mystical red flower
Burst, and the bud of her sweet spirit broke
Rose-fashion, and the strong spring at a stroke
Thrilled, and was cloven, and from the full sheath came

The whole rose of the woman red as flame:
And all her Mayday blood as from a swoon
Flushed, and May rose up in her and was June.

This is two sentences, but it is almost one line—at least one hardly
pauses to notice the couplet rhymes. End-stopped couplets will
arrange themselves along a medial axis, almost slowing down to
avoid their rhymes, but Swinburne's never pause. Each phrase
seems to leap out from the farthest exhausted reach of the last.
Something like escape velocity is quickly reached. Freed from the
gravity of syntax, words begin to bleed into what Rosenberg—
characterizing Swinburne generally, but with particular relevance
for the pictorial qualities of this passage—calls "a single Turnerian
chord of color."[4] We are, as Rossetti might well have said but as
Swinburne actually did, "enmeshed in multitudinous unity" (3:33).

In this passage, as generally in Swinburne and Rossetti, it is
difficult to distinguish actor from object. It is nearly impossible to
know which of the myriad lights, heats, and colors radiate from the
sun and which from the awakened soul of Iseult. There is a remarkable fusion of self and world, flesh and light—the whole has the
intense, vague color of strong sun driving through closed eyelids.
The syntax supports these ambiguities. Like Rossetti, Swinburne
snatches away the solidity of long-sought grammatical objects by
making them subjects, and the distinction is further blurred by his
fondness for linking both active and passive verbs to a single subject
as in "Thrilled, and was cloven" or "flamed and were undone." The
setting of metaphor within metaphor similarly confuses the tenor-
vehicle distinction so that all of the sensuous qualities of both
belong to the moment described, and we forget that some are
imported from outside through the agency of a half-dozen similes.
Mind and reality are reduced to that line of turbulence which is their
meeting. This kind of dissolution of the border between self and
world is a constant in Swinburne's poetry, and has been described in
different ways by his best readers. Rosenberg, for example, sees
Swinburne as the poet "not of natural objects but of natural energies, less of things seen than of forces felt." McGann says that "like
Shelley and Mallarmé" Swinburne "strives to render not the thing

but the effect it produces." T. S. Eliot remarks that though a "bad poet dwells partly in a world of objects and partly in a world of words, only a genius could dwell so completely and consistently among words as Swinburne."[5] These assessments differ mainly in degree, and could be ordered according to the extent that they interiorize poetic reality—from "forces felt," the most external, to "effects," to "words," the most internal. Along these same lines, Browning intolerantly but predictably found Swinburne's style "a fuzz of words." He called it "florid impotence," echoing Pope's description of Sporus in "Epistle to Dr. Arbuthnot," and he tried his hand at it: "the *minimum* of thought and idea in the *maximum* of words and phraseology. Nothing is said and done with, left to stand alone and trust for its effect in its own worth. What a way of writing is that wherein, wanting to say that 'a man is sad,' you express it as, 'he looketh like to one, as one might say, who hath a sadness and is sad indeed, so that beholders think "How sad is he!"' "[6] Though this hardly approaches Swinburne's parody of Browning's "James Lee's Wife" in deadliness, Browning, despite his exasperation, hits on some truths: first, Swinburne's elegiac tone; second, his habit of looking at words in various contexts; finally his related habit of looking at minds, objects, and feelings from so many angles that they dissolve into the atmosphere of the poem. To a poet of otherness who dwindled into a poet of paraphrase, Swinburne's poetry of "prolonged mildly mixed metaphor" would have seemed obfuscatory and threatening in either half of his career, for it is precisely Swinburne's purpose to let "nothing stand on its own." McGann calls the stylistic features discussed above Swinburne's "techniques for suggesting the unity of existence," for their end is not clarity but the richness of the Rossettian oxymoronic vision.[7] A Swinburne poem takes all ways at once:

> Heart handfast in heart as they stood, "Look thither,"
> > Did he whisper? "look forth from the flowers to the
> > > sea;
> For the foam-flowers endure when the rose-blossoms
> > wither,
> > And men that love lightly may die—but we?"

(*PS* 3:22–23)

And the same wind sang and the same waves whitened,
    And or ever the garden's last petals were shed,
In the lips that had whispered, the eyes that had lightened
    Love was dead.

Or they loved their life through, and then went whither?
    And were one to the end—but what end who
        knows?
Love deep as the sea as a rose must wither,
    As the rose-red seaweed that mocks the rose.
Shall the dead take thought for the dead to love them?
    What love was ever as deep as a grave?
They are loveless now as the grass above them
        Or the wave.

The passage is full of equations, large and small. There is hardly a line that does not contain some leveling repetition of a word or phrase—"rose" occurs four times, forms of "love" seven. "The *same* wind sang and the *same* waves whitened." "Whither" is "wither." Lovers, by the grace of simile, are the same as the grass above them, and rose-red seaweed "mocks" the rose. Things are fused by their relation to a third term—foam and roses are equal because both bloom. Swinburne's double simile, "Love deep as the sea as a rose must wither" is covert synesthesia—as its tenor–vehicle relations blurs, qualities float free. For the duration of "deep as the sea as a rose," a flower has vast depths; for the time of "sea as a rose must wither," the odorous sea dies, and for the whole line love is invested with all the qualities flung out from the soundless collision of cold strength and delicate beauty. It is not merely that the mind is "fooled" by the sequence of the words, but that Swinburne has undermined sequence to the extent that any word in a stanza may brush lightly against any other, "swift to fasten and swift to sever." The passage is the height of Paterian musicality, and a critic with a certain kind of literalist bias might call it meaningless. It is both beautiful and moving, though what it says is not strictly what its words say.

The largest equation in the passage is that of the alternative fates of the lovers, and in it lies the evidence that the *or* which structures the poetry of Swinburne, Tennyson, and Rossetti signals loss as surely as it strives for unity. Doubling is not only connection but negation. Side by side, possibilities cancel each other. Both of Swinburne's stories disappear into time, and in their annihilation is his exhilaration. Like Tennyson a death-artist, Swinburne finds freedom and power at the dead center of loss.

In his dedicatory epistle to his collected works, and without quite saying that he is categorizing poems, Swinburne depicts two realms of the mind. One is the seacoast, which he describes in terms of *contrasts*—the "glory of cliff and crag" versus "the dreary beauty, inhuman if not unearthly in its desolation, of the innumerable creeks and inlets" (*PS* 1:xxii) or "the sand-encumbered tides" wearing at the beaches versus, further offshore, "the ineffable fascination of . . . translucent depths of water and divers-coloured banks of submarine foliage and flowerage" (1:xxiii). In this landscape, what Lang calls "Swinburne's bone-bred antitheses (unity and division, pleasure and pain, desire and restraint, growth and stasis, etc.)" (Lang 520) are both embodied and soothed. The second realm is unrelieved by such contrasts—and it is therefore, for Swinburne, unrelieving, an "oppression." It is "inland or woodland solitude— the splendid oppression of nature at noon which found utterance of old in words of such singular and everlasting significance as panic and nympholepsy" (*PS* 1:xxiii). Swinburne's preference for scenic, stylistic, and thematic borderlines, for what Rosenberg calls "the moment when anything shades into its opposite or contraries fuse," is very close to psychic necessity.[8] The shoreline, shifting and reshifting, is his mind in dynamic balance. When the undulant comforts of his landscape and rhythm are somehow thwarted or suspended, he writes near boredom and terror. In "Neap-Tide," for example, the disappearance of the shoreline (both the sea and the land are "far") becomes an image of perilously low energy and personal decline:

> Far off is the sea, and the land is afar:
>   The low banks reach at the sky,
>   Seen hence, and are heavenward high;
> Though light for the leap of a boy they are,
>   And the far sea late was nigh.

(*PS* 3:251)

"A Nympholept," with its "stress of sun" at noon, concerns another hour that refuses to pass. Stranded, Swinburne is eventually seized with panic in the original sense as his divisions cry out unsoothed. Postponed, his deepest necessities swell into the sense of "wrath scarce hushed and of imminent ill to be." "The Lake of Gaube" also begins in "strong compulsive silence of the sun," and its strange tensions must be released in a dive into a lake "Death-dark and delicious as death in the dream of a lover and dreamer."

The rarity in Tennyson and Swinburne of the glaring landscapes in which elegiac dissolution is thwarted hints at the dangers distanced by their normal styles. But part of the emotional complexity of Swinburne's poetry is that for him the drive toward dissolution is itself tainted and self-punishing. Loss becomes something internal and continuing, a hemorrhage of the spirit, not merely sadness but damage. Desire is a wasting disease. The very source of Swinburne's poetry is defiled, and the muse, as the hymns to Lucrezia Borgia suggest, can be as much poisoner as healer.

In this originates Swinburne's counterimpulse: to drive beyond elegiac dissolution to an antiself of cold clarity, strength, indifference, and restraint. This half of Swinburne normally finds its image in the sea, or in women with the indifferent strength of the sea. But these imagined purities, even in the moment of their imagining, are soiled with self and self-loathing. Nonhuman indifference becomes inhuman cruelty. Cold clarity becomes pain. "The Triumph of Time" swells with both the elegiac flux Swinburne's poetry most gratefully inhabits and his always ambivalent desire to engage its heroic antithesis. Swinburne seeks his image of otherness in the Yeatsian Lady of Pain:

> And still, through the sound and the straining stream,
> Through the coil and chafe, they gleam in a dream,
> The bright fine lips so cruelly curled,
>   And strange swift eyes where the soul sits free.

(*PS* 1:45)

> Free, without pity, withheld from woe,
>   Ignorant; fair as the eyes are fair.
> Would I have you change now, change at a blow,
>   Startled and stricken, awake and aware?
> Yea, if I could, would I have you see

My very love of you filling me,
And know my soul to the quick, as I know
    The likeness and look of your throat and hair?

Like the ocean, she is free, pitiless, strong, without tenderness, even without sentience. Her quality is, in a phrase Yeats used for the sea but meant for Maud Gonne, "murderous innocence." Like Yeats, Swinburne pursues his other self through love of his opposite. "Ignorant," as so often in Yeats, marks her pure otherness— if she were capable of understanding Swinburne's love, she would lose the purity of her indifference and no longer be the thing he loves. One may well find masochism in such an arrangement, but then one will also have to find it in Tennyson and Yeats. Nor is it very far from the perceptual disciplines of Hopkins's "stress" and "instress." That is, Swinburne's masochism is in one aspect a painfully high amplification of the normal need of humans in general, and of Victorian poets in particular, to love something that is not themselves, to find, beyond the dimmings of the self, a beauty that is strange and fresh and hard. Pater, as usual, is the best analyst of the Pre-Raphaelite tendency, here in the essay on Morris:

> The colouring is intricate and delirious, as of "scarlet lilies." The influence of summer is like a poison in one's blood, with a sudden bewildered sickening of life and all things. . . . A passion of which the outlets are sealed, begets a tension of nerve, in which the sensible world comes to one with a reinforced brilliancy and relief—all redness is turned into blood, all water into tears. Hence a wild, convulsed sensuousness in the poetry of the Middle Age, in which the things of nature begin to play a strange, delirious part. Of the things of nature the mediaeval mind had a deep sense; but its sense of them was not objective, no real escape to the world without us. The aspects and motions of nature only reinforced its prevailing mood, and were in conspiracy with one's own brain against one. A single sentiment invaded the world; everything was infused with a motive drawn from the soul.[9]

The combination of absolute self-enclosure and feverish intensity is more characteristic of Pre-Raphaelite medievalism than of the Middle Ages. Bloom finds Pater here "hinting that sadomasochistic yearnings and the anxiety of being a late representative of the tradition are closely related" and that "the heightened intensity of Morris and Rossetti (and of Pater)"—and of Swinburne—"compensates for a destructively excessive sexual self-consciousness."[10] Swinburne's poetry is a straining within a dream. If it is trying to escape the pain of whatever "reality" is, it is also trying to escape from the unreality of our *automatic* escape, our imprisonment in ourselves. Pain and intensity are not only what it flees but also a part of its return, a part of its clarity.

Swinburne is a poet of macroscopic abundance and microscopic restraint, a poet of vast passion in search of heroic silence. Often severely beautiful as dew on steel, his language is narrowed to invoke a world of clarity, purity, and violence. Surely no work depends more on the inherent deliberateness of monosyllables. *Cold, break, swift, strong, glad, keen, wild, sharp, clear* are Swinburne's words. And yet his momentary restraints are continually overwhelmed by the swing and swell of his undulant, expanding mood. Admitting that Swinburne's language is "not like the language of bad poetry, dead," T. S. Eliot calls it limited because it is not like "the language which is more important to us . . . which is struggling to digest new objects, new groups of objects, new feelings, new aspects."[11] There is at least a half-truth visible here since Eliot's purpose is a not very surprising contrast with Conrad and Joyce, but reservations must be registered, since the implication of "important" is that Swinburne is somehow less "realistic," less relevant.

Molly Bloom's monologue at the end of *Ulysses*, for example, is a portrayal of the state of awareness slightly below the rationally discursive but above that of emotions. This tributary of the literary stream of consciousness flows from that mood in which we are divided into speaker and listener and, with a kind of insomniac fervor, explain ourselves to ourselves, but surely no one thinks it is somehow "essentially" or "really" thought. This state, because it is (though barely) articulate, we can remember, and thus it seems in retrospect to occupy more of our lives than it actually does, but

Joyce is showing us as we function during only a small part of the day. And even then his monologue is more verbal than the mind. He must constantly invent linguistic devices to approximate both thoughts and discontinuities that, in the mind, never reach words.

Swinburne's meditations in "The Triumph of Time," are apparently more literary and coherent, and they are certainly—determinedly—less "new" in Eliot's sense, but they are in at least one way more fundamental. He, too, is concerned with repetitive explanations and self-dramatizations, but his fewer, older, dimmer words ride on rhythmic and syntactical patterns that deprive them of their objectivity. They body forth the deeper emotional ebb and surge that, brought a little further into consciousness, might eventually attach itself to more particular self-explanations and drive the Browningesque or even the Joycean monologue. Swinburne's is a vaguer intuition—it may be essentially nonverbal. But only a narrowly enthusiastic definition of realism would deny its reality.

Secondly, one must qualify Eliot's remark about the "digestion" of experience. There is constant digestion in Swinburne and Rossetti and Tennyson, constant dissolution. What Eliot misses is the *effort* of digestion—what sometimes fails is the resistance, the particularity of the Victorian world. In this regard, the cruelty and pain Swinburne often sees as the cause of his failures are essential to his self-denying quest—they are part of his attempt to discover resistance. His apostrophe to Sade, "You are only a very serious St. Simeon Stylites in an inverted position,"[12] asserts the quasi asceticism of his fascination. For Swinburne, pain is almost an antielegiac sensuousness. But it, too, fails to clear the dimness, for like all Swinburne's contraries it is blurred—by pleasure, by fear, by guilt—so that it becomes poisonous, damaging, impure, full of the shameful taint of self. As with his "broken blossom" or his "green reeds shattered," Swinburne seems able to discover the hardness of things only in its failure. A passage from "Anactoria" encapsulates both the direction and dissolution of his quest:

> Him would I reach, him smite, him desecrate,
> Pierce the cold lips of God with human breath,
> And mix his immortality with death.

(PS 1:69)

Both worship and hatred make Gods human, and the pathetic fallacy in Swinburne is the pathetic fatality. Once tainted with humanity, with self, even a cruel, insentient God dissolves helplessly in the elegiac flux.

There are other directions. Swinburne's genius for self-abasement was exceeded only (but greatly) by his inhuman power, and he threw himself at the feet of Mazzini, like Tennyson before him and Yeats after attempting the antiself of the public poet. The goddess of liberty engaged him deeply, but not painfully, not often poetically. Liberty is perhaps not the ideal subject for a man who was highest, best, even most free, in the shackles of his own obsessions, and one of the few successful poems in his Italian era is "Hertha," which with its hypnotic chant and its philosophical fusion of actor and object recalls Emerson's "Brahma" and the erotic closeness of his own earlier work:

(PS 2:74)   Love or unlove me,
                 Unknow me or know,
             I am that which unloves me and loves; I am stricken,
                 and I am the blow.

The most interesting of Swinburne's tendencies, however, evolves from his early fascination with sterility, and specifically with the "barren mother," the "mother maid," that sea which in Swinburne's various moods is nature, Sade, trance, Mary Gordon, Sappho, passion, utter insentience, freedom, pain. Browning had also discovered the desert seacoast and also knew as a great advantage its absence of easy pleasure and intrusive humanity:

    Well—and you know, and not since this one year,
    The quiet seaside country? So do I:
    Who like it, in a manner, just because
    Nothing is prominently likeable
    To vulgar eye without a soul behind.

For Browning, here in *Red Cotton Night-Cap Country,* it was the background, and antithesis, for a story of grotesque passion. It was Swinburne's *mind,* a symbolic landscape so long and fervently inhabited that it had subsided into nature and into second nature.

The barren strength of the coast becomes the very sensibility of
"On the Cliffs," "Neap-Tide," "Evening on the Broads," and the
endlessly fascinating "By the North Sea," a virtual encyclopedia of
Swinburne:

> A land that is lonelier than ruin;
>   A sea that is stranger than death:
> Far fields that a rose never blew in,
>   Wan waste where the winds lack breath;
> Waste endless and boundless and flowerless
>   But of marsh-blossoms fruitless as free:
> Where earth lies exhausted, as powerless
>   To strive with the sea.

(*PS* 5:85)

"Stranger than death," past "ruin," this landscape stretches
beyond the elegiac flux, out of the range of the self. In waste and
exhaustion, Swinburne begins to find the otherness, the strangeness, he seeks. It is perverse to say that "Swinburne projects an
inner sense of desolation on to the Suffolk landscape" when the
poem, on the contrary, swells with the exhilaration, wonder, and
grateful peace that only abundant energy would find in such neutral
tones:

> Miles, and miles, and miles of desolation!
>   Leagues on leagues on leagues without a change!
> Sign or token of some eldest nation
>   Here would make the strange land not so strange.
> Time-forgotten, yea since time's creation,
>   Seem these borders where the sea-birds range.

(*PS* 5:93)

> Slowly, gladly, full of peace and wonder
>   Grows his heart who journeys here alone.
> Earth and all its thoughts of earth sink under
>   Deep as deep in water sinks a stone.
> Hardly knows it if the rollers thunder,
>   Hardly whence the lonely wind is blown.

"Desolation" is not used here as an objective correlative. Rather the
purity of barrenness balances the relentlessly elegiac pathetic fallacy—"Sign or token of some eldest nation / Here would make the

strange land not so strange." It does not *express* Swinburne; it cleanses him with its momentary *refusals* to express him.

But this poem about divine barrenness, inhuman purity, is also full of defilement, pervaded, as David Riede points out, by Swinburne's eroticism.[13] For the sea can also be Dolores: "For the heart of the waters is cruel, / And the kisses are dire of their lips" (*PS* 5:91), and Swinburne senses his irresistible humanization of the other— "the hunger that moans in her passion" (*PS* 5:87)—as a desecration:

The grime of her greed is upon her,
    The sign of her deed is her soil;
As the earth's is her own dishonour,
    And corruption the crown of her toil:
She hath spoiled and devoured, and her honour
Is this, to be shamed by her spoil.

(*PS* 5:102)

Meeting himself, Swinburne recoils from his own closeness. Life-giving antitheses appear, are contaminated, dissolve, are cleansed, reappear. In the climactic passage, he presides over what must be described in Swinburnean terms as a final cleanliness. He watches with terrible joy as the ocean saps a graveyard. Here, even the "effort of digestion" is apparent in the sinew of the verse:

Naked, shamed, cast out of consecration,
    Corpse and coffin, yea the very graves,
Scoffed at, scattered, shaken from their station,
    Spurned and scourged of wind and sea like slaves,
Desolate beyond man's desolation,
    Shrink and sink into the waste of waves.

Tombs, with bare white piteous bones protruded,
    Shroudless, down the loose collapsing banks,
Crumble, from their constant place detruded,
    That the sea devours and gives not thanks.
Graves where hope and prayer and sorrow brooded
    Gape and slide and perish, ranks on ranks.

(*PS* 5:107)

Rows on rows and line by line they crumble,
    They that thought for all time through to be.
Scarce a stone whereon a child might stumble

> Breaks the grim field paced alone of me.
> Earth, and man, and all their gods wax humble
> Here, where Time brings pasture to the sea.

Even the metaphorical possibility of rest is seemingly denied, but the action, predictably, contains its opposite. Swinburne overwhelms the last human outpost—our sense of shock and shame—and, as in "A Forsaken Garden," presides with ecstasy over the sea's painful destruction of the future possibility of pain. Erosion is the fleeting moment lengthened and magnified, time made visible and palpable, and it is the mode of Swinburne's poetry. With surge and countersurge, it accomplishes its slow, almost undetectable changes. It is variations on the theme of variation. Like the seabird he imagined himself, like the wind indistinguishable from the bird, Swinburne is full of an energy that "satiety never may stifle."

"Gape and slide and perish." Perhaps it is not surprising that Eliot recalled the poet dwelling "completely . . . among words" when he ruminated, in "Burnt Norton," on their shiftiness:

> Words strain,
> Crack, and sometimes break, under the burden,
> Under the tension, slip, slide, perish.

But even in *The Waste Land,* where there are notes for such things, Eliot acknowledges no Victorian debts. So we are still vaguely under the impression that Chaucer is behind "April is the cruelest month," though Arnold's "The Buried Life" and Tennyson's "Is it, then, regret for buried time / That keenlier in sweet April wakes?" (*In Memoriam* 116) stand virtually in front of it. Nor is there, among the barely credible *Quellenforschung* of those notes any indication that "mixing / Memory and desire" might be somewhat similar to Swinburne's "as mist with sea / Mixed, or as memory with desire." (*PS* 1:156) No deception is of course implied. Poets can more easily articulate their gratitude to those they wish to become than their identity with those they already are. For Eliot, as for Yeats, Victorian poetry is the barely audible music under consciousness, a music not less but more important for being unacknowledgable.

Part Three

YEATS

VIII

Into the Twilight

I have grown nothing, knowing all.

Fergus and the Druid

YEATS IS not diminishing, but he is receding. By now he is closer in time to his Pre-Raphaelite predecessors, and even to their Victorian originals, than he is to us. It has been nearly fifty years since his death in 1939. Fifty years before that, when Browning died in 1889, Yeats was already in his mid-twenties and solidly enough entrenched in the literary establishment to express for the *Boston Pilot* his reservations about the poet whose world "was simply a great boarding house in which people come and go in a confused kind of way. The clatter and chatter to him was life, was joy itself. Sometimes the noise and restlessness got too much into his poetry, and the expression became confused and the verse splintered and broken."[1]

Browning is doing service here as the urban division of the Victorian Age—the boardinghouse tumult is more reminiscent of a Dickensian dinner than of *Men and Women*. He also stands in for the realism so despised by a poet who (early and late, Victorian and modern) dreaded the dilution of his poetry with merely "interesting" character and circumstance: "The old art, if it [had] gone to its logical conclusion, would have led to the creation of one single type of man, and one single type of woman, in whom would have been concentrated, however, by a kind of deification, the capacity for all energy and all passion. . . . The new art creates innumerable types, but in each of these types the capacity for passion has almost disappeared before some habit of body or mind" (*WBY Mem.* 188).

"All energy . . . all passion"—the *all* defines both the ambition and the dimness of Yeats's early poetry. It was against similar vague immensities in himself that Browning had originally set the self-limitations of the dramatic monologue, but if Browning's mask seemed a prism, Yeats's own, when he at last found he needed one, was a burning glass. Though the differences between an advanced Victorian and a conservative modern might in theory be small, the gap here is large enough. There is, indeed, great respect—asked, at sixty-five, which Victorian poet he admired most, Yeats replied as if the obvious answer might not be obvious: "Browning, of course, and if I live another ten years I shall admire Tennyson again" (*I & R* 2:203). But with admiration came risk. At about the same time, embarked on a course of rereading, Yeats called Browning a "dangerous influence" (*LY* 759). Even so, he was an influence easily or at least effectively fended off, for only in "The Gift of Harun Al-Rashid," saturated with "Karshish," is Browning's voice strongly audible. Comparing the two poems, one of Browning's finest with one of Yeats's oddest, seems unfair to Yeats, but it would show, among other things, how few his voices really are and how little his mainline poems are concerned with the merely "conversational." Yeatsian simplicity is not mimetic but reinvented. He tended to see the veerings and sputterings of Browning's dramatic monologues as an artificial spontaneity perhaps more appropriate to a dutiful conversationalist at that Victorian boardinghouse than to great poetry. A different critic might have found Browning's affectations of casualness to be a kind of generosity, but Yeats knew best how to protect his own solitary intensity.

The early Yeats, at least, could have been expected to enlist in Tennyson's cause, but he is often unable to see him as anything but the versifier of scientific truth and popular morality. He seems to have had little sense of Tennyson as a conduit between Keats and Rossetti, two poets for whom he had at least intermittent respect. Even when he allows Tennyson to be a lyric poet, he finds great distance between them. Reviewing the posthumous *Death of Œnone and Other Poems* in 1892, he faults Tennyson for "mere scene-painting" and characterizes him as the product of a late (and lyrical) hour of the world: "Modern writers . . . have been heavily handicapped by being born in a lyrical age, and thereby compelled for the most part to break up their inspiration into many glints and glimmers. . . . A hundred years hence their work will seem to lack largeness and simplicity." (*UP* 1:251)

When it suited his mood, Yeats himself could be quite content to sit out in the deepening twilight of the Decadence, but what he perceived as Ireland's backwardness would save him from the resultant fragmentation. Though it was growing late in Europe, local literature was still in its Epic Age. From his earliest years through *A Vision,* Yeats had a way of spreading himself through the possibilities of history. He could help turn out the lights, but there was also still the chance to be Ireland's "first" poet. Looking back, and down, at Tennyson, Yeats could be both past and future.

To many of Yeats's contemporaries, Tennyson and Browning must still have seemed, as indeed they seemed to each other, polar opposites, but Yeats, taking the long view of recent history, finds them essentially similar. Implicit in his assessments of both poets is distaste for an art too heavily invested in what Arnold had called "the world's multitudinousness." The multitudinousness could be scenic or psychological. In either case it led to submersion in mere circumstance. In the "new art" of Tennyson and Browning and their successors, "passion" dwindles into the realist's "vitality," a term Yeats always employed for literature's second-best energies. Personality warps into character. Desire becomes satire. There is a strong critical bias here, but it turns out to be at least as much antimodern as anti-Victorian. Decades later, examining an even newer art, Yeats was to accuse Eliot, Pound, and their confreres of the same enervation and fragmentation he found in the poetry and painting of their nineteenth-century predecessors.

Yeats's acquaintance with the generation of Victorians following Tennyson and Browning was more direct, but his criticism of their work, if often more intimate, was not ultimately less severe. He met Hopkins several times in his father's studio, but dismissed his poetry as freakish. In 1912 he visited Max Gate to present Thomas Hardy with the gold medal of the Royal Society of Literature, but his selection of Hardy for the *Oxford Book of Modern Verse* surely indicates indifference to the poetry. Swinburne's death in 1909, long after the blaze of his first books, ended what at least the

Irish poet saw as an informal competition for the title of chief poet in the language.

Yeats's letters of the eighties and early nineties are full of meetings with William Morris, whom he visited to dine, talk, and, apparently without much success, learn French. Morris remained for him "the happiest of the poets" (*E&I* 53), a creature of inexplicable "spontaneity and joy" (*A* 95) and, even after his intense admiration for the poetry had subsided, something of an idol: "If some angel offered me the choice, I would choose to live his life, poetry and all, rather than my own or any other man's" (*A* 95).

At Morris's, Yeats was surrounded by the painting—and even more thoroughly by the memory—of Dante Gabriel Rossetti, whom his father had already taught him to revere: "I was a romantic, my head full of the mysterious women of Rossetti and those hesitating faces in the art of Burne-Jones which seemed always anxious for some Alastor at the end of a long journey" (*WBY Mem.* 33).

Yeats's poetic imagination eventually moved beyond Pre-Raphaelitism. His poems, though in many ways conservative, are in just as many ways harmonious with the aims of his younger and more revolutionary contemporaries, but his visual imagination was less advanced. Never wholly reconciled either to impressionism or cubism, he never lost his attraction to Rossetti, who "filled so many faces . . . with an infinite love . . . a perfected love" (*E&I* 150). The Pre-Raphaelite "wonderful, sad, happy people, moving through the scenery of my dreams" (*E&I* 346) walked out into the scenery of his early poems. As the "traditional images most moving to young men while the adventure of uncommitted life can still change all to romance" (*E&I* 347), they were at once the very incarnation of always new-seeming youth and a part of the Tennysonian legacy. For Yeats and the "tragic generation," Rossetti was "a subconscious influence, and perhaps the most powerful of all" (*A* 201). Though they "looked consciously to Pater for [their] philosophy" (*A* 201), and though that influence should not be underestimated, the Pater in Yeats's mind is hardly distinct from Rossetti. Yeats chose to begin *The Oxford Book of Modern Verse* with a relineated version of Pater's Lady of the Rocks passage. But the "Mona Lisa" described there is, as David Riede has suggested, as much Rossettian as Leonard-esque.[2]

Rossetti the poet, indeed, is granted a pivotal place in "The Autumn of the Body," Yeats's myth of the evolution of nineteenth-century literature:

> *The poetry which found its expression in the poems of writers like Browning and Tennyson . . . pushed its limits as far as possible, and tried to absorb into itself the science and politics, the philosophy and morality of its time; but a new poetry, which is always contracting its limits, has grown up under the shadow of the old. Rossetti began it, but was too much of a painter in his poetry to follow it with a perfect devotion; and it became a movement when . . . Mr. Bridges . . . elaborated a rhythm too delicate for any but an almost bodiless emotion and repeated over and over the most ancient notes of poetry and none but these. . . . I see, indeed, in the arts of every country those faint lights and faint colours and faint outlines and faint energies which many call "the decadence," and which I, because I believe that the arts lie dreaming of things to come, prefer to call the autumn of the body. (E&I 190–91)*

The denunciation of the "extra-poetic" concerns of Tennyson and Browning—and Arnold and Swinburne—is a formula in Yeats's literary journalism. From the nineties onward, his essays and reviews are littered with deprecating references to their "criticism of life" (*UP* 2:91), their "psychology, science, moral fervour" (*E&I* 495), their "politics, theology, science, all that zeal and eloquence Swinburne and Tennyson found so intoxicating after the passion of their youth had sunk" (*E&I* 349). Though Yeats himself almost from the beginning found it necessary to violate the dim purity of his early work with analogously extrapoetic concerns (nationalistic, occult, and philosophical), later readers are likely to agree with him that they could unbalance the poetry of the major Victorians. And yet the "faint lights and faint colours and faint outlines" that here promote Rossetti to revolutionary status are equally characteristic of Tennyson, in whom they serve partly, as in early Yeats, to dissolve the encroaching multiplicity Yeats so feared. Yeats habitually speaks of his Victorian predecessors as if he had never read Tennyson's 1842 volume, or *Men and Women,* or the first *Poems and Ballads,* the works that formed his sensibility both directly and through Rossetti and Morris. The decline of Tennyson (and the omnipresence of weak imitators) had temporarily made the best Tennysonian poetry indistinguishable from the worst, but even apart from this retroactive and nearly inevitable downgrading, the omission is not inexplicable. Yeats is, first of all, concerned to see the Decadence as a revolution rather than as a late elaboration of a century-long trend, a twilight of a twilight. It is distressing for any young man, poet or not, to have to realize how much of youth, whose main self-recommendation is freshness and originality, was invented by those already dead. By ignoring the older Victorians, Yeats brings the source of revolution as close as his father's studio or Morris's Rossetti-haunted dining room. In redesigning the course of literary history, Yeats's criticism, always curiously proleptic, is making the future safe for a kind of poetry he already knew how to write.

Whatever the blind spots of his criticism, Yeats's early *poetry* converses with Tennyson's not in its laureateship but in its autumnal youth. Direct echoes, though not the most important indications of influence, are frequent enough, if miscellaneous. In the Arcadian play *The Island of Statues,* one of Yeats's first published works, Mariana's "clinking latch" perhaps sounds again as a "creaking gate" (*V. Ed.* 646). The dimness of the early Yeatsian landscape is equated, in the Tennysonian manner, with its pastness: "like old men's eyes the stars are pale" (V645). And Colin's love song

(*V. Ed.* 647)

>And thy neck's a poisèd lily;
>See, I tell they beauties o'er,
>As within a cellar chilly
>Some old miser tells his store

pillages Tennyson's "A spirit haunts the year's last hours" for diction, rhyme, and for its sad, ambiguously heavy-light touch:

(Ricks 215)

>Heavily hangs the broad sunflower
>   Over its grave i' the earth so chilly;
>Heavily hangs the hollyhock,
>   Heavily hangs the tiger-lily.

These possible echoes, selected from just the first scene, are perhaps less revealing than the second act's appropriation of lulled islanders murmuring around a fire, a Tennysonian image that seems to have been particularly powerful for the young Yeats. *The Wanderings of Oisin,* completed just after *The Island of Statues* and published in 1889, is thronged with lotos-eaters. Book 3, the Island of Forgetfulness, is a bedroom suburb of lotos-land, though echoes of Tennyson's poem are perhaps clearest in Book 1:

> Some danced like shadows on the mountains,
> Some wandered ever hand in hand;
> Or sat in dreams on the pale strand,
> Each forehead like an obscure star
> Bent down above each hookèd knee,
> And sang, and with a dreamy gaze
> Watched where the sun in a saffron blaze
> Was slumbering half in the sea-ways;
> And, as they sang, the painted birds
> Kept time with their bright wings and feet;
> Like drops of honey came their words,
> But fainter than a young lamb's bleat.

(*CP* 361–62)

The most noticeable similarities are, of course, the situation, the mood, and the languor. But with the exception of the not entirely fortunate "painted birds" (things are often "painted" in early Yeats—this is a dutiful loading of the scene, pictorialism with only half a heart), there is hardly a word or image that is not paralleled dimly in "The Lotos-Eaters." Tennyson's "yellow sand," "amber light," and "yellow lotos-dust" are probably finding their way into the sun's yellow (and dusty?) "saffron blaze." Tennyson's "slumbrous sheet of foam" is perhaps behind "slumbering half in the sea-ways." The characteristic Tennysonian imaging of distance from life as faintness of sound ("and if his fellow spake / His voice was thin, as voices from the grave") returns in "Like drops of honey came their words, / But fainter than a young lamb's bleat." Tennyson's dim and dimming oxymoron "*dark* faces *pale* against the rosy flame" is echoed distantly by "Each forehead like an *obscure star.*" And Yeats is indebted to the Victorian for the rhythmic background to dreamy languor not only generally but in specific auditory memories. Here, for example, the use of a combination of moaning terminal *a*'s and a second-syllable caesura for the drop into trance may be more than coincidence:

("Lotos-
Eaters")

but whoso did receive of them
And taste, / / to him the gushing of the wave
Far, far away did seem to mourn and rave.

(*Oisin*)

Bent down above each hookèd knee,
And sang, / / and with a dreamy gaze
Watched where the sun in saffron blaze
Was slumbering.

The scene as a whole is a rearrangement of the properties of "The Lotos-Eaters," and Yeats is most successful where he trans-lates Tennyson specifically, least successful in lines such as "Some dance like shadows on the mountains, / Some wandered ever hand in hand," where he is not imitating the Tennysonian poem but remembering, vaguely, what it is like to be inside one. Such lines presume, rather than re-create, the Tennysonian world, and in them Yeats seems (like most young—or minor—poets) more reader than writer.

Soon after the publication of *The Island of Statues,* Yeats la-mented in a letter to the poet Katharine Tynan that his poetry was "almost all a flight into fairyland from the real world, and a sum-mons to that flight . . . not the poetry of insight and knowledge, but of longing and complaint" (*LKT* 47). Though "fairyland" is too dismissive and "real" is problematic, Yeats locates the source of his attraction to such poems as "The Lotos-Eaters" in their elegiac perspective and in their creation of a world apart. His criticism of his own work is, if too severe, essentially accurate, and applies to more of it than is specifically "about" islands and bowers. As in Tennyson, these latter are simply a resonant metaphor for the entranced distance inherent in the very style and stance of the poetry. Again predictive in his criticism, Yeats defines and deplores this sense of the poems as a space, or "region" (the term is from Keats) before he is able to move beyond it:

(*LKT* 82–83; my emphasis)

My ideas of a poem have greatly changed since I wrote the "Island." "Oisin" is an incident or series of incidents; the "Island of Statues" a region. There is a thicket between three roads, some distance from any of them, in the midst of Howth. I used to spend a great deal of time in that small thicket when at Howth. The other day I turned up a poem in broken metre, written long ago about it. *The thicket gave me my first thought of what a long poem should be. I thought of it as a region into which one should wander from the cares of Life.* The characters were to be no more real than the shadows that people the Howth thicket. Their mission was to lessen the solitude without destroying its peace.

Oisin is not, in fact, much less of a "region" than the *Island*. Despite its gestures toward heroic "incident," *Oisin*'s plot is subordinated to atmosphere—the mood of elegiac distance that is the substrate of the "regionality" of Yeats's nineteenth-century poetry. Even on the island where "God is joy and joy is God" (*CP* 359) the chief pastime is a sadly fascinated contemplation of mortality:

> The hare grows old as she plays in the sun
> And gazes around her with eyes of brightness;
> Before the swift things that she dreamed of were done
> She limps along in an aged whiteness.
>
> . . . . .

(*CP* 362)

> And the kingfisher turns to a ball of dust,
> And the roof falls in of his tunnelled house
> And the love-dew dims our eyes till the day
> When God shall come from the sea with a sigh
> And bid the stars drop down from the sky,
> And the moon like a pale rose wither away.

Oisin is "the saddest harp in all the world," and Aengus, the presiding deity,

(*CP* 357)

>   dreams, from sun to sun,
> A Druid dream of the end of days
> When the stars are to wane and the world be done.

There *is,* after all, muted "joy" here. Perhaps "pleasure" is a better word, "pleasure" in the Keatsian sense, blended with faint pain. But in this ostensibly joyous and timeless world, love, the hare, the kingfisher, the stars, the moon dissolve with the touchless speed of Tennyson's "Man comes and tills the field and lies beneath." The very syntax is full of passing: nine of the twenty lines begin with an *and* that seems to let them go even as it introduces them. The island is an elegy for itself, a phenomenon Yeats clarifies in a 1904 essay: "When the tide of life sinks low there are pictures, as in the *Ode on a Grecian Urn* and in Virgil at the plucking of the Golden Bough. The pictures make us sorrowful. We share the poet's separation from what he describes. It is life in the mirror, and our desire for it is as the desire of the lost souls for God" (*Expl.* 163).

Pictorialism, anathema to Yeats in theory (and in Keats, Tennyson, and Rossetti) before he quite eschewed it in practice, is not precisely equivalent to "regionality." Visual detail is only more obvious, not necessarily more important, than sound, syntax, and rhythm in the constitution of a world apart. Yeats's point, particularly valid in the Tennysonian context, is that the true subject of such detail is the falling away of detail: what he feels in "pictures" is his "separation" from them, loss. The Tennysonian undersong of his worlds apart is the vanishing of the world, and their Edenic happiness is inextricable from sadness.

That "optimism" and "happiness" are so often urgent categories for the young makes it all the more interesting that young poets are so often exclusively and artificially sad. The melancholy joy of Yeats's islands probably serves to release gradually the pressure of anxieties Yeats cannot or will not distinguish clearly. It has a kind of protective anonymity: it is the emotion of the dissolution of emotions. Yeats was recognizing this, and perhaps diagnosing himself, when he found in the poems of his friend Arthur Symons "not passion, but passion's evanescent beauty" and ventured that their "charm and defect" was that "their pleasure in the life of sensation is not . . . the robust pleasure of the man of the world, but the shadowy delight of the artist" (*UP* 1:374). This 1895 review defends *London Nights* against the charge of immorality, and it is also defending Yeats—against that capitalized Experience about which he was so ambivalent. Symons was at this point much more a man of the world than Yeats, but his experience is to no avail because he is not enough of an artist to avoid seeming like one. The criticism happens to be accurate, but it was written because it was necessary.

The distance in poetic sadness is both a protection and a deep bafflement, but it may also be the first inkling of emotional autonomy, the ability to feel deeply without being swept away. This is perhaps the real freedom of the thicket of Howth, as Yeats hints in an early stanza so infused with the rhythm and diction of Rossetti and Swinburne that we need not look further for the source of its insight:

> Two spirit things a man hath for his friends:
> *Sorrow that gives for guerdon liberty,*
> And joy, the touching of whose finger lends
> To lightest of light things all sanctity.

(*V. Ed.* 686; my emphasis)

Yeats could have found "the bliss of being sad" in *The House of Life* (no. 84) or in Tennyson's death artistry. Loss is loss; but it is also freedom from the world, and power.

It would be odd indeed if these deep ambivalences did not shadow Yeats's loves. Seen through the haze of distance and the blur of recession, the women in his early poetry are as dim as any in Tennyson and Rossetti. He calls them "spacious loves" (*V. Ed.* 42n) in the first version of *Oisin,* and the implication is clear. Sad desire is one of those regions in which the soul blurs gratefully, losing its boundaries. "Our souls / Are love, and a continual farewell" (*CP* 15). Love is loss, vanishing is beauty, desire is dimness and flow—

> When I hold
> A woman in my arms, she sinks away
> as though the waters had flowed up between.

(*V. Ed.* 749)

The embrace of lovers is a disappearance:

> The love I know is hidden in these hands
> That I would mix with yours, and in this hair
> That I would shed like twilight over you.

(*V. Ed.* 765)

Yeats could have found these imagistic planks nearly anywhere in his Victorian reading. In this kind of love, selves "mix" (the word is inescapably Swinburnean) in the Tennysonian twilight of (Rossettian) "loosened hair." He could have found the whole house in Browning's "Pauline":

> eyes,
> And loosened hair and breathing lips and arms
> Drawing me to thee—these build up a screen
> To shut me in with thee.

The actual source is perhaps less important than the image's *familiarity:* Yeats is losing himself as much in *poetry* as in desire. Hair, at any rate, becomes the dim fabric of his erotic worlds apart. Less the tendrilous phenomenon of daily experience than a kind of personal twilight, it is repeatedly imagined as secret, spacious, blurred: "mingling hair" (*CP* 10), "drowned in her long dim hair" (*CP* 55), "hiding hair" (*CP* 58), "dim heavy hair" (*CP* 64). All these are most likely derived from Rossetti. "Her fall'n hair at last shed round my face" and "Beneath her sheltering hair" from "The Stream's Secret," and "Shadowed by her hair" from *The House of Life* are just a few of many possible originals. This Pre-Raphaelite hair recalls the "woven shade" (*CP* 43) which is Yeats's analogous dimness of landscape, "woven" as so often in Shelley and Rossetti, marking the point where vaguely troubling complexity surrenders to comforting blur. Hair seems at times to be the very fiber of space—certainly "Who Goes with Fergus?" turns interstellar distances, by means of "dishevelled," into ethereal hair:

(*CP* 43)
> For Fergus rules the brazen cars,
> And rules the shadows of the wood,
> And the white breast of the dim sea
> And all dishevelled wandering stars.

Similarly, in *The Shadowy Waters,* we are encouraged to be lost in hair that is itself lost in the Tennysonian horizon at the world's end:

(*V. Ed.* 768)
> My love shakes out her hair upon the streams
> Where the world ends, or runs from wind to wind
> And eddy to eddy.

Yeats is here delighting in the opening of dimnesses within dimnesses, an infinite recession for which there is also Rossettian precedent:

> I looked and saw your eyes
> In the shadow of your hair.

(PR 321)   . . . . .

> I looked and saw your heart
> In the shadow of your eyes.

Yeats, too, often sees—or unsees—eyes as "passion-dimmed" (*CP* 60) or "dream-dimmed" (*CP* 64) in a way that implicates both the seeing and the seen. Eyelids are "cloud-pale" (*CP* 64) or "heavy with the sleep / Men have named Beauty" (*CP* 67). Intensity and dimness are equated. Beauty is "sleep," the subsidence of the self. Tennyson's lotos-eaters, with their "half-shut eyes" were "falling asleep in a half dream." The Yeatsian beloved is commanded to be like them:

(CP 65)
> Half close your eyelids, loosen your hair,
> And dream about the great and their pride.

(CP 60)
> Beloved, let your eyes half close, and your heart beat
> Over my heart, and your hair fall over my breast.

Yeats may well have been influenced by the rapt Rossetti portraits of Elizabeth Siddal and others. In any case, such poems, like those portraits, instruct the onlooker in the kind of desire they are intended to inspire and receive. We do not, of course, literally "half-close" our eyes—the dimness of the poems and the paintings has in a way already done that for us—but we allow whatever loosening and blurring of attention that physical act corresponds to. "Love is less kind than the grey twilight" (*CP* 57) Yeats says, but in this poetry they are nearly the same, and to read it is to be half-lost in the Tennysonian dimness.

The action of Yeats's early lyric poetry is, over and over, release. Rhythm, he says, dissolves the will. A poem is a trance, a *gaze*, the mind going dim: "The purpose of rhythm, it has always seemed to me, is to prolong the moment of contemplation, the moment when we are both asleep and awake . . . to keep us in that state of perhaps real trance, in which the mind liberated from the pressure of the will is unfolded in symbols" (*E&I* 159). The idea of rhythm Yeats elaborates here (in 1900) is not equally relevant to all poetry, and is far more useful in discussing his early volumes than his later work. "He Wishes His Beloved Were Dead," for example, is one of Yeats's many contributions to that nineteenth-century subgenre, the poem of the dead lady. The title leads us to expect a curse, but its "wavering, meditative, organic rhythms . . . are the embodiment of the imagination, that neither desires nor hates, because it is done with time." Instead—dissolved, passionless—the imagination "only wishes to gaze" (*E&I* 163):

> Were you but lying cold and dead,
> And lights were paling out of the West,
> You would come hither, and bend your head,
> And I would lay my head on your breast;
> And you would murmur tender words,
> Forgiving me, because you were dead:
> Nor would you rise and hasten away,
> Though you have the will of the wild birds,
> But know your hair is bound and wound
> About the stars and moon and sun:
> O would, beloved, that you lay
> Under the dock-leaves in the ground,
> While lights were paling one by one.

(*CP* 70)

The early Yeatsian flow is more gliding, wavering, and attenuated than mere metrical regularity could account for. Anapests are employed for a Pre-Raphaelite late-line flutter perhaps even lighter than that provided by Tennyson's late pyrrhics. With its Tennysonian feeling of pursuit of (rather than accommodation to, or tension with) meter, the rhythm has a self-unfolding quality congruent with the regionality of the poem's emotions. It seems to demand the effortless continuation that the syntax with its elegiac *and—and—and* effortlessly provides. Nor do the words impede it: merely listing them out of context and in order of occurrence reveals how few their sounds are and how minimal the modulation between them: *were you, were, West, you would, hither, bend, head, would, head, your breast, you would murmur tender words,* and so on. So similar in sound, the words loosen and mingle. The voice fades, becomes a murmur heard through a wall, an uncertain depth. It is, Yeats might say, the verbal equivalent of a gaze.

The "landscape" of the poem is also dimmed and deepened. Lights are "paling out of the West." Hair is, again, interstellar space itself, "bound and wound / About the stars and moon and sun"— the *and*'s and the assonance miming, if not quite precisely "winding," then at least confusion. The last line of the poem originally read "While birds grew silent one by one," but this is both pictorially, and in its introduction of the unrepeated word *birds,* less dim than Yeats required. The final version, "While lights were paling one by one" is a more effective, because dimmer, version of the elegiac fade-out with which Yeats escaped his early poems. Consider the following endings:

(CP 14)	when we die our shades will rove,
	When eve has hushed the feathered ways,
	With vapoury footsole by the water's drowsy blaze.

(CP 15)	our souls
	Are love, and a continual farewell.

(CP 43)	And the white breast of the dim sea
	And all dishevelled wandering stars.

(CP 64)	drown their eyes with your hair,
	Or remembering hers they will find no other face fair
	Till all the valleys of the world have been withered away.

(CP 66)	"That drowsily drops faint leaves on him
	And the sweetness of desire,
	While time and the world are ebbing away
	In twilights of dew and of fire."

Dissolutions, twilights, mild apocalypses signal the end of the typical early Yeatsian poem, which is so full of ending from its very first word that, when its time comes, it subsides as gently as rippled waters. If Yeats's world apart is the loss of the world and his love is the loss of love, it might be said that the action of his poems is the release from the poem. Somehow, as these endings confirm, it is only half a step from their dim passage to no words at all.

"He Wishes His Beloved Were Dead" is also an emotion that is a release from emotion. Though the poem conspires to prevent both reader and poet from focusing on its dramatic situation, Yeats addressed it to Maud Gonne in 1898, following years of fruitless courtship and the kind of ambiguous (to Yeats) rejection that even the most serviceable suitor must have felt unjust. To express his rage would have been to disrupt an already unstable relationship and, perhaps more important, to approach admitting the self-destructiveness of his life-organizing quest. Instead, Yeats instinctively resorts to a strategy employed by hopeless lovers (especially Victorian ones) before and since. He dwarfs and dissolves his human resentments against the dimming backdrop of death. In this poem, difficult love is transformed into poignant sadness. Anger generalizes into tender regret. Love, again, is loss. The stance is a special case of the nineteenth-century convention W. D. Paden, in his discussion of Tennyson's juvenilia, calls the "mask of great age": "An adolescent writer who seeks to objectify his present emotions and his feelings towards the future usually speaks in terms of the past, and if the situation admits, of a vague and remote past. A feeling of guilt or a terror of wrongdoing often is phrased as remorse; the writer often speaks from a mask of great age."[3]

Though the mask of age was (and still is) a young poet's typical strategy, it is by no means restricted to adolescents. Tennyson, at twenty-four, used Tiresias, Tithonus, and Ulysses to speak for him in the crisis of Hallam's death, when he was neither adolescent nor as obsolete as they. Browning in numerous monologues, Hardy in general—"To think of life as passing away is a sadness; to think of it as past is at least tolerable"[4]—and Eliot don this mask. Janus-like, it looks both pastwards and ahead. Most directly, it expresses the poet's fear that life has vanished behind him. One does not have to be very old to feel that: the young, relatively unanchored, may be *more* susceptible than those whose longer pasts would apparently give them longer vistas to regret. Certainly Yeats at twenty-three was already numbering himself among the ghosts: "My life has been in my poems. To make them I have broken my life in a mortar as it were. I have brayed in it youth and fellowship, peace and worldly hopes. I have seen others enjoying while I stood alone with myself, commenting, commenting. I have buried my youth and raised over it a cairn—of clouds."[5]

But the mask of age also, as Paden says, embodies ambivalence about what is ahead. Overleaping the ambiguous present and the dreaded future, the poet looks back from a distance that turns both the painful and the unimaginable into sad loss. He adopts resignation as a precocious wisdom, dismissing experience before it is acquired. Yeats must often have found it necessary to repress his anger at living Maud; but for the dying, the passing, and the past, he could more easily express a less complicated tenderness. He can begin a curse with "When you are old and grey and full of sleep, / And nodding by the fire, take down this book" (*CP* 40), but in the end, love, the poet, the beloved, and all memory of anger will vanish into the sad Tennysonian horizon:

(*CP* 41)
> And bending down beside the glowing bars,
> Murmur, a little sadly, how Love fled
> And paced upon the mountains overhead
> And hid his face amid a crowd of stars.

The older Yeats worshiped "personality" in part because he had come to realize that the attenuated Victorianism of his early poems was a set of strategies for dissolving the self. Like Tennyson, he wrestles with the ongoing choice between particularity and dimness: "And when we love, if it be in the excitement of youth, do we not also, that the flood may find no stone to convulse, no wall to narrow it, exclude character or the signs of it by choosing that beauty which seems unearthly because the individual woman is lost amid the labyrinth of its lines as though life were trembling into stillness and silence, or at last folding itself away?" (*E&I* 243–44).

For the young, Yeats remembers, the greatest beauty is a beauty somehow generalized enough to receive an unfocused gaze. Perhaps it is perfect because instantly and wholly recognizable, in no way strange or resistant. But more than the image of the beloved is always in question. She is dim because the lover himself wishes to remain in the dimness. Her individuality would limit—particularize—him and his passion. Yeats's ambivalence toward experience, that is, arises from the Tennysonian choice between immortal anonymity and mortal individuality. Love is literally, as the "Lady of Shalott" has it, a life-and-death choice. Though part of Yeats tried to choose Maud's exteriority and his own future life—vaguely, he called her "noble"—for many years his deepest instinct was to dissolve her separateness into a dim region. Only gradually, when she is no longer possible for him, does her image sharpen to "beauty like a tightened bow," and eventually—cruelly—to "an old bellows full of angry wind." More particularized passion belongs to the late phase of Yeats's poetry, and is more likely to be inspired by friends, or lovers become friends, or even enemies (perhaps because they are all part of the made or chosen life) than by Maud Gonne (who seems to belong to a preexisting life, to have been chosen *for* him). In the meantime, however, not passion but its evanescence was Yeats's subject. Immortal in fluidity, the soul was simultaneously everything and nothing:

> I see my life go drifting like a river
> From change to change; I have been many things—
> A green drop in the surge, a gleam of light
> Upon a sword, a fir-tree on a hill,
> An old slave grinding at a heavy quern,
> A king sitting upon a chair of gold—
> And all these things were wonderful and great;
> But now I have grown nothing, knowing all.

(CP 33)

Yeats's early interests in Irish legend and occult studies probably reflect his ambivalence about "mortal individuality," and they embody the mingled fear of, and impatience for, the future that account for his attraction to the mask of age. Though Yeats recommended that modern writers go "back to their old legends . . . that they may not be lost in a world of mere shadow and dream" (*UP* 1:81), Eliot was surely correct in suggesting that the Celtic Twilight was "the pre-Raphaelite twilight"[6] in a nationalist disguise, and Graham Hough seconds him in saying that "the return to the legendary Irish past, whatever it may have felt like to Irishmen, is likely to be regarded by the literary historian as a late continuation of the medieval and archaising tendency that had pervaded English literature for more than a century."[7] In both his reworkings of Irish legend and his poems to Maud Gonne, Yeats strives to protect emotion from narrowing. The goal is heroism, passion. The result, often as not, is elegy. The poems wish that the world could be grasped wholly, and that the poet could therefore remain whole— though both he and the world must as a consequence live dimly. They convince Yeats that what he already knows and already is will suffice.

Yeats's energetic involvement with Madame Blavatsky, the Golden Dawn, and other such enterprises is often described as the result of his disillusionment with scientific materialism. So it seemed to Yeats in hindsight, but it might be noted that Yeats's dabblings in the occult have a definite experimentalist, even scientific, bias. This may be only to say that he aspired to magic rather than mysticism. Then, too, his initial interest was probably sparked by nothing so grand as a revolt against nineteenth-century thought, though perhaps he explained it that way even to himself. More likely he was acting out one of the paradoxes of youth—that its conscious and frustrating ignorance can be oddly simultaneous with a fear of "knowing all," probably itself a displacement of the fear of coming upon one's limits. Against this closing down of possibilities the unproven modes of knowledge hinted at by Yeats's occult studies perhaps protected him. Such interests also reflect Yeats's ambivalence about the inevitably slow realization of his identity and his poetry. Patient commitment to one's life, the gradual distillation of personal truth from pain and failure, may easily in the short run seem less attractive than the organized ascent to knowledge promised by occult ritual, which may, it is true, provide a way of predicting gains from real experience, and therefore of recognizing them more swiftly. So did Yeats's proleptic literary self-criticism. Perhaps we should not be surprised, therefore, that the vaguely magical and the schematically critical eventually merge in *A Vision,* which is a philosophy, a hobbyhorse, a laboratory, and perhaps above all a book of personal possibility.

Successes in the magical arena may also perhaps support the initiate in his sense of secret and unassailable worth before that worth can express itself in solid achievement, poetic or otherwise. And they reassure the poet when that achievement is threatened— Elizabeth Barrett Browning was not young when she took to séances, but one suspects that her passion for spiritualism was an unconscious attempt to outflank the rival poet in her own household, and it is difficult not to see Robert Browning's rage at the medium D. D. Home (whom he parodies as Mr. Sludge), and indeed at his wife, as his response to the threat that this short-cut to knowledge posed to the dignity of art and the patience of labor. Browning knew all about self-justifying myths of hoarded potential—his painters elaborate them obsessively[8]—but the young Yeats was not ready to discover that such myths, even when true, delude. Simultaneously immersing himself in the literary and legendary past on one hand, and, on the other, forcing the future with occult studies and the mask of age, Yeats vacillated between artificial innocence and premature age. He could not decide whether his life was unbegun or already over. He is himself a perfect example of the desynchronization of time from which so many of Tennyson's poetic characters suffer.

The anonymity of Yeats's early phase derives partly from his sense of being potentially many people, partly from his inexperience with his own character, and partly from fear of being a mortal individual. However much he may yearn to be his future self, he must feel experience as a limitation, and feel his crystallization as deeply connected with the ultimate limitation of death. Not, then, the "dying fall" that is a dispersion into the twilight, but the hard, personal fact of death. A poets' individuation must take him beyond the safe crepuscular pleasures of the poet-as-reader into the lonelier venture of being himself. He is likely to feel this necessary independence as a sacrifice of the universality—itself a metaphor for immortality—he acquires by living and speaking within the poetry of the past. Yeats's evasion of individuality perhaps condemned him to an extended stay in the twilight of life and art. But transformed into an insistence on the force of personality rather than the mere detail of character, on "passion" rather than "vitality," energy rather than elaboration, it preserved him from the various hyperparticularities of both Victorianism and modernism and made him the most conservative, and the greatest, of the twentieth-century poets.

IX

Discoveries of Restraint

If I sat down and thought for a year I would discover that but for certain syllabic limitations, a rejection or acceptance of certain elisions, I must wake or sleep.

A General Introduction for My Work

There aren't any rules. Thing is to cut a shape in time. Sounds that stop the flow.

EZRA POUND

IN 1910, distantly preparing for autobiography, Yeats was moved to say, "I have no sympathy with that mid-Victorian thought to which Tennyson gave his support, that a poet's life concerns nobody but himself." "His life," he continued, "is an experiment in living, and those who come after have a right to know it. Above all, it is necessary that the lyric poet's life be known, that we should understand that his poetry is no rootless flower."[1] Yeats's early poetry, its emotions generalized into anonymity, was in some danger of such pale flowering, but a newly distinct voice rather than biographical endnoting would finally root it. Paradoxically, his interest in biography is aroused just at the time he is beginning to regard his life as not quite his own. And, strangely, his sense of the special need for the true life of the lyric poet is imported directly from a master of obliqueness. Browning, himself investigating *im*personality (he was beginning *Men and Women*), had first urged the grounding of the lyric poet in his essay on Shelley: "He [the lyric or subjective, as opposed to objective, poet] is rather a seer, accordingly, than a fashioner, and what he produces will be less a work than an effluence. That effluence cannot be easily considered in abstraction from his personality,—being indeed the very radiance and aroma of that personality, projected from it but not separated."[2]

Along with Pater, Hallam's review of Tennyson, Shelley's

Defence, and Wilde's *Decay of Lying,* Browning's essay was a Yeats-ian critical touchstone. It would have absorbed him not only be-cause it brings one of his poets to bear on another but because it anticipates—for example in its critique of sincerity and its notions of what poetry must follow romanticism—many of the concerns of *A Vision.* Yeats accepted Browning's point about biography, but neither poet would have supposed a simple and direct connection between life and poetry. The poet who seems to have carried into later life his father's Paterian notion that the highest goal of individ-uals and cultures is the full expression of personality could also say, "All that is personal soon rots" (*E&I* 522). In such pronouncements "personal" means accidents of character and circumstance, and perhaps also those truths that mere sincerity, the "gentle sensitive mind" of "Ego Dominus Tuus," can see in its vague gaze down the well of the soul. But Yeats, like Browning, also needed the truths, the lives, that only the confrontation with otherness—"all that I have handled least, least looked upon"—can reveal in us. The location of this otherness—deeply interior or wholly exterior—probably needs to remain uncertain (Langbaum's phrase "exteri-ority of self" sums up the difficulty),[3] but Yeats knows that its strangeness, its chill, is what lends hardness and force to his poetry. Self-expression presumes self-estrangement. Expression is intricate with restraint.

Yeats's evolution required that he become, in the words of Browning's essay on Shelley, "substantive, projected from himself, and distinct." Though Yeats with his Shelleyan yearnings would never have accepted the limitations of the "objective poet" as de-fined by Browning—nor, for that matter, did Browning—and though their notions of "mask" are not identical, they are close in their sense that the independence of the poem as an artifact is proportional to the poet's self-detachment. Yeats's discovery of force is in part a re-creation in himself of the simplicity we normally see only in other people. And since for Yeats the surface of a poem was analogous to the border of a personality, there are strong parallels between the ways he attempts to shore up the weaknesses of his social self and what he does about the features of a poem's surface that control its relation to a reader.

Harder is a word that has been used to characterize Yeats's later poetry. It applies in several senses, which might be distinguished—though they must, ultimately, be rejoined. Emotionally, the poems are harder in that they are less dimly romantic, more restrained, less wavering. Colder, Yeats would say, though more passionate. They are harder as objects, too. With their adjustments in rhythm, syntax, and diction, they invoke clearer attention, present more definite surfaces. And in a sense involving both of these, the poems are harder as social acts: hard poets define harder readers.

Though it is easy to recognize the difference between "soft" (e.g., Tennysonian) and "hard" poetries, it may be worthwhile to recall the implications of this difference. Yeats's early poems, he would say, begin in a dim, incantatory dissolution of the will. In their passive receptivity they seem read rather than written, received rather than made. Spoken—almost—by and to no one, they are regions, and have in a sense neither authors nor readers but instead participants. Yeats's early rhythms "prolong the moment of contemplation" until it broadens into a gaze, a region. The reader will have a sense of blurred boundaries, of a kind of merger with the poem. He may imagine the poet undergoing a similar experience in writing it, and indeed Yeats's early theory of the musicality of poetry emphasizes the "binding" of poet and reader: "Have not poetry and music arisen, as it seems, out of the sounds the enchanters made to help their imagination to enchant, to charm, to bind with a spell themselves and the passers-by. . . . the musician or the poet charms and binds with a spell his own mind when he would enchant the mind of others" (*E&I* 43). Yeats's ideal poem, that is, magically dissolves the distinction between poet and reader, assumes them into "the seeming transitory mind made out of many minds" (*E&I* 43).

This describes adequately the tendency of Yeats's early work, but the less hypnotic middle and later poems are slightly more difficult of access. They discourage effortless mergers. The older Yeats, thinking of poems as forces rather than regions, deprecates "those outlines of lyric poetry that are blurred with desire and vague regret." And, in sentences that recall his personal difficulties with "undisciplined sympathy" and uncertain borders, he quite

specifically defines his problem as an undignified relationship between poetic and readerly selves: "deliberate beauty is like a woman
always desiring man's desire" (*E&I* 271). He criticizes Morris, a
stand-in for his earlier self, for his too easy reliance on this harmony
of poet and reader: "Modern literature, above all poetical literature,
is monotonous in its structure and effeminate in its continual insistence upon certain moments of strained lyricism. William Morris. . . . thought of himself as writing for the reader, who could
return to him again and again when the chosen mood had come,
and became monotonous, melancholy, too continuously lyrical in
his understanding of emotion and of life" (*Expl.* 220).

As the phrase "strained lyricism" implies, Yeats has found that
the identification of poet and reader seems ultimately to limit the
intensity of a poem. Dimness, though it can encompass the All, is
necessarily a dispersion. His later insistence that poet, reader, and
poem maintain dignified distances must therefore be seen as parallel
to his growing belief that passion is as much restraint as it is
lyricism: "We have all something within ourselves to batter down
and get our power from this fighting. I have never 'produced' a play
in verse without showing the actors that the passion of the verse
comes from the fact that the speakers are holding down violence or
madness—'down Hysterica passio'. All depends on the complete-
ness of the holding down, the stirring of the beast underneath. . . .
Without this conflict we have no passion, only sentiment and
thought" (*LDW* 94–95).

Yeats describes his discovery of restraint, and also, obliquely, a
response to Victorian poetry, for what he is attempting to "deepen"
behind restraint is the self-unfolding, self-releasing Tennysonian
flow. Or rather what that flow had come to—"sentiment and
thought" is exactly how Yeats would have defined the later work of
Tennyson and Browning and the weaknesses he most feared in
himself. Yeats's poems will become more personal, or more force-
ful, as they become more fierce in reticence.

The new Yeatsian strategies of "holding down" are clearest, if
not always most successful, in the revisions imposed by the older
poet on his earlier poems. "The Sorrow of Love" is given here first
in its 1895 version and then as it appears in *The Collected Poems* (most

of the revisions were undertaken for his 1925 collection *Early Poems and Stories*):

> The quarrel of the sparrows in the eaves,
> The full round moon *and* the star-laden sky,
> *And* the loud song of the ever-singing leaves,
> Had hid away earth's old *and* weary cry.

(*V. Ed.*
119–20n;
my
emphasis)

> *And* then you came with those red mournful lips,
> *And* with you came the whole of the world's tears,
> *And* all the sorrows of her labouring ships,
> *And* all the burden of her myriad years.

> *And* now the sparrows warring in the eaves,
> The curd-pale moon, the white stars in the sky,
> *And* the loud chaunting of the unquiet leaves,
> Are shaken with earth's old *and* weary cry.

> ——————

> The brawling of a sparrow in the eaves,
> The brilliant moon and all the milky sky,
> And all that famous harmony of leaves,
> Had blotted out man's image and his cry.

(CP 40)

> A girl arose that had red mournful lips
> And seemed the greatness of the world in tears,
> Doomed like Odysseus and the labouring ships
> And proud as Priam murdered with his peers;

> Arose, and on the instant clamorous eaves,
> A climbing moon upon an empty sky,
> And all that lamentation of the leaves,
> Could but compose man's image and his cry.

The subject is Maud Gonne. The changes are many, and of many kinds. Perhaps the most important in subtly altering our distance from the poem are syntactical. The early version, in beginning seven of its twelve lines with the elegiac *and,* emphasizes the continuity of flow and passing—"not passion but passion's evanescent beauty." Dramatic tension is completely subordinated to lovely monotone. Emotion is released almost before it is felt.

The revision, though not in the full-blown late Yeatsian manner, alters enough of the elegiac syntax to make an audible difference. There is slightly less emphasis on the self-prolonging
moment, the gaze, slightly more on the emotional discreteness of
lines and stanzas. The earlier version is hypnotic with syntactical
repetitions. The later Yeats, equally repetitious, uses repetition for
different ends, typified by

> A girl *arose* that had red mournful lips. . . .
> *Arose,* and on the instant clamorous eaves . . .

> ("Among
> School   a tale that she
> Children"   *Told* of a harsh reproof, or trivial event
> *CP* 213)   That changed some childish day to tragedy—
>   *Told,* and it seemed that our two natures blent
>   Into a sphere from youthful sympathy.

The repetitions of the early Yeats are dim, but those above enforce,
rather than dissolve, attention. They are a drop back followed by a
push off. Like a nicked record repeating itself and then suddenly
leaping forward, they express a small but dramatic schism in time.

In the 1925 version, too, the emotions become less generalized.
Yeats dispenses with some favorite dimnesses—"sorrow" and
"weary" virtually disappear from the poetry after "The Shadowy
Waters"—and with the self-referential "ever-singing" and "chaunt-
ing." But more severe restraints are imposed on the thirty-year-old
emotions. The "you," an address to an equal—and always, sub-
liminally, to the reader—becomes an older man's more indifferent
"a girl." The vastly elegiac generality of *all* in "all the sorrows" and
"all the burden" is transformed, closed down, in "all that famous
harmony of leaves," "all the milky sky," and "all that lamentation of
the leaves." In the last three, the *all,* rather than being a large
horizon in which the reader loses himself, takes on some of the tone
of "O, all *that.*" "All that famous harmony of leaves" implies "that
image I found so much more interesting long ago," and becomes a
kind of criticism of the younger man's feelings. It is less a gesture
toward the All than a half-amused and nearly impatient summary.

The diction of the 1925 version is given an abstract edge with "brilliant," "compose," "lamentation," "clamorous," and so on. Later Yeats is full of abstractions, which are often more polysyllabic and technical than these, and which often strike one less as abstractly vague than as astringent. They are indeed a part of Yeats's restraint of flow, his achieved reticence: "In dream poetry, in *Kubla Khan,* in *The Stream's Secret,* every line, every word, can carry its unanalysable, rich associations; but if we dramatise some possible singer or speaker we remember that he is moved by one thing at a time, certain words must be dull and numb. Here and there in correcting my early poems I have introduced such numbness and dullness, turned, for instance, 'the curd-pale moon' into the 'brilliant moon,' that all might seem, as it were, remembered with indifference, except some one vivid image" (*A* 291).

Yeats is explaining the mixed diction of his later work. In the "dream poems" he knew so well how to write, the All speaks to the All, and the diction must be harmonious lest the illusion and the tenuous unity collapse. But for the restrained, more distinct later Yeats, the wrong word is sometimes the right word. "Brilliant" enters Yeats's poetic vocabulary in "The Wild Swans at Coole." Far from being "deliberate beauty . . . always desiring man's desire," it is, in its disconnection from the reigning mood and diction of the poem (and of the nineteenth century), a kind of reticence—Yeats calls it "numbness and dullness." Rather than desiring us, it seems to block our access. Behind its resistance, its understatement, feeling builds slightly. The word, in making the scene seem "remembered with indifference," suggests again the separation of feeling and onlooking selves that Yeats thought necessary to distinctness of emotion.

Yeats, along with Hardy, is one of the pioneers of "wrong-word reticence," and he was very sensitive to its effects. In commenting on Lady Dorothy Wellesley's lines "The wild grey asses fleet / With stripe from head to tail, and moderate ears," Yeats says, "No poet of my generation would have written 'moderate' exactly there; the close of a long period, the ear expecting some poetic word checked, delighted to be so checked, by the precision of good prose" (*LDW* 26–27). Yeats would not, indeed, have written "moderate," but Lady Dorothy, in doing so, is carrying a

Yeatsian technique to its logical and un-Yeatsian conclusion. Here, and perhaps in Eliot and Auden, the Yeatsian reticence becomes compulsive qualification or deflation. Yeats's reticent abstractions restrain but deepen his romanticism. In the next generation's "checks" of feeling—more understated, consorting more with irony—Yeats might have felt restraint shading into underconfidence, the unease of romantics who cannot be what they are without being the victim of their own punch lines. Yeats saw this quality in most writers more "modern" than he. Eliot, Auden, and Joyce, he thought, had purchased their precision, wit, and topicality with an unacceptable diminution, and he regarded them as satirists ushering in a new Popean age.

For those in love with the very voice of the later Yeats, the newer and more reticent version of "The Sorrow of Love" provides premonitory excitement, and yet though Yeats's best poems depend on something like the hardened softness of this revision, it is difficult to say whether this particular grafting of one Yeats upon the other does not result in a certain incoherence. Yeats did not think so: "I have felt when re-writing every poem—'The Sorrow of Love' for instance—that by assuming a self of past years, as remote from that of today as some dramatic creation, I touched a stronger passion, a greater confidence than I possess, or ever did possess"[4]. One knows the feeling about old work: utter familiarity, utter strangeness, absolute inevitability. The encounter Yeats describes is not a little like his meeting with the "mysterious one" who will

> look most like me, being my double,
> And prove of all imaginable things
> The most unlike, being my anti-self.

(CP 159)

Yeats would prefer us to locate the antiself well outside the available self in "all that I have handled least, least looked upon" (*CP* 157), but it may be ultimately his *own* strangeness that he seeks, and certainly it is sometimes revealed to him in these foldings of time.

A poet handling anything so deeply remembered and deeply forgotten as an old poem can hardly be sure he is doing only what he thinks he is doing. The original "Sorrow of Love" has the beauties and the limitations of a late Pre-Raphaelite poem. The revision, charged with personal confidence, is full of poetic uncertainties. The lines about Odysseus and Troy have neither the poignance of Yeats's early poems to Maud Gonne nor the strength of his later forays into Trojan territory—they seem to have been written by some mid-rank Elizabethan sonneteer. The old dimness and the new astringency do not always sort well together. Yeats has perhaps explained too much of an inexplicable youth and, despite some striking cadences, "The Sorrow of Love" now seems less a harmonious poem than a stop on the way to *The Tower*.

The techniques of exclusion Yeats uses to "shut down" the regionality of "The Sorrow of Love" are not unique to that revision. In the 1892 version of "The Two Trees," Yeats describes Maud Gonne's heart with wings and Loves and flames and hair—though not with a movement—reminiscent of Rossetti:

> There, through bewildered branches, go
> Winged Loves borne on in gentle strife,
> Tossing and tossing to and fro
> (*V. Ed.*   The flaming circle of our life.
> 135n)   When looking on their shaken hair,
> And dreaming how they dance and dart,
> Thine eyes grow full of tender care:—
> Beloved gaze in thine own heart.

In the *Collected Poems* (most of the revisions were done for the 1929 *Selected Poems*) this appears as:

> There the Loves a circle go,
> The flaming circle of our days,
> Gyring, spiring to and fro
> (CP 48)   In those great ignorant leafy ways;
> Remembering all that shaken hair
> And how the wingèd sandals dart,
> Thine eyes grow full of tender care:
> Beloved, gaze in thine own heart.

Slightly embarrassed, this passage is willing to give itself completely to neither of its two Yeatses, but is nevertheless interesting for the direction of its revisions. "Gyring" and "spiring" seem imported from *A Vision* and perhaps incongruous in this Rossettian context—the kind of impatient half-thought that sometimes blemishes the later poems as well. And yet this may be a matter of perspective. Yeats knew, as most readers probably no longer do, that *gyre* was Rossetti's word—it occurs in sonnet 44 of *The House of Life* ("What unsunned gyres of waste eternity") and in "Rose Mary"—before it was Yeats's. And perhaps in Yeats's mind some kind of revision was necessary to keep "Tossing and tossing to and fro" from anticipating and weakening "Turning and turning in the widening gyre," the opening of "The Second Coming."

The dimness of "dreaming" is excised, as is the early Yeatsian gesture "dance." "Bewildered branches," typical in its invocation of intricacy lost in blur, becomes "those great ignorant leafy ways," halfway to the self-conscious indifference of "all *that* famous harmony of leaves"—both the initial images and the direction of transformation are similar. The mystery of dim bewilderment is dismissed, using "ignorant" partially as an almost literary-critical comment on Yeats's earlier poetic vanishings. "Ignorant" is, in addition, a marker of the Other in Yeats's poetry, as it is in Swinburne's, and it often does service in his half-admiring, wholly yearning dismissal of youth. Though ignorance is ignorance, it often suggests a senseless, unpredictable power that old men would best know how to use, if they still had it. Typically, it puts the past irretrievably behind him or allows beauty to be at once marvelous and somehow sublimely irrelevant:

(CP 260)   Bodily decrepitude is wisdom; young
             We loved each other and were ignorant.

                           the lines
             That young men, tossing on their beds,
(CP 139)   Rhymed out in love's despair
             To flatter beauty's ignorant ear.

(CP 144)   I would be—for no knowledge is worth a straw—
             Ignorant and wanton as the dawn.

Similarly, the Pre-Raphaelite dimness of "shaken hair" is criticized or distanced, becoming "all that shaken hair." As in "The

Sorrow of Love," dimness survives as a *category* but not as a *region*. It is a part of the self now forcibly past, now separate. Yeats judges it, he perhaps even responds to it (there is more than a little bittersweet in his rhetorical dismissals), but he does not *enter* it as fully, and neither does the reader.

A similar procedure is evident in the revisions of "A Dream of Death." The 1892 version reads:

> I dreamed that one had died in a strange place
> Near no accustomed hand,
> And they had nailed the boards above her face,
> The peasants of that land,
> And wondering, planted by her solitude

(*V. Ed.* 123n)

> A cypress and a yew.
> I came and wrote upon a cross of wood
> —Man had no more to do—
> "She was more beautiful than thy first love
> This lady by the trees,"
> And gazed upon the mournful stars above
> And heard the mournful breeze.

In the final version (many of the revisions first appear in the 1913 edition of *Poems*) it is:

> I dreamed that one had died in a strange place
> Near no accustomed hand;
> And they had nailed the boards above her face,
> The peasants of that land,
> Wondering to lay her in that solitude,
> And raised above her mound

(CP 42)

> A cross they had made out of two bits of wood,
> And planted cypress round;
> And left her to the indifferent stars above
> Until I carved these words:
> *She was more beautiful than thy first love,*
> *But now lies under boards.*

"Two bits of wood" adds, perhaps self-consciously, some of the hardness of particularity. More important (and more characteristic) is the alteration of "mournful stars" to "indifferent stars" as Yeats literally looks down on his old poem with new eyes. *Indifferent* helps confine emotion more specifically. It is both in meaning and in its abstract dullness a kind of reticence, in that we feel the sadness of the poem in spite of, against, the indifferences of the images and the poet—rather than through vague sympathy with a "mournful" landscape. The end of the first version, with its repetition of the elegiac *and* and of "mournful," becomes one of those early Yeatsian dim horizons, a fade-out. But the space of the poem is almost literally shut down by the revision: the view is covered with boards. We now comprehend the poem's motion and emotion not wholly though a merger with its regionality but also partly through exclusion from its surface, through its reticence.

Written in 1902 only a few months before Maud Gonne's marriage to Major John MacBride, "Adam's Curse" exhibits some of the insetting of past and present, and of old and new styles, that characterizes the revisions just discussed, but since Yeats is not using thirty years' hindsight to take advantage of an earlier self, its ironies are nearly invisible and its blend of manners is much more graceful. This may account for the peculiar place it has acquired in the Yeats canon. The poem is a summation of Yeats's early career. It speaks as the last of many poems of lastness, but despite pronounced tonal and imagistic affinities with *The Wind among the Reeds* it has seemed to many readers a prophecy of the Yeats to come:

> We sat together at one summer's end,
> That beautiful mild woman, your close friend,
> And you and I, and talked of poetry.
> I said: "A line will take us hours maybe;
> Yet if it does not seem a moment's thought,
> Our stitching and unstitching has been naught.
> Better go down upon your marrow-bones
> And scrub a kitchen pavement, or break stones
> Like an old pauper, in all kinds of weather;
> For to articulate sweet sounds together

(CP 78)

Is to work harder than all these, and yet
Be thought an idler by the noisy set
Of bankers, schoolmasters, and clergymen
The martyrs call the world."
                    And thereupon
That beautiful mild woman for whose sake
There's many a one shall find out all heartache
On finding that her voice is sweet and low
Replied: "To be born woman is to know—
Although they do not talk of it at school—
That we must labour to be beautiful."

With its "marrow-bones," "kitchen pavements," and "bank-ers," "Adam's Curse" has been cited as evidence for Yeats's advance in particularity, but these bits of the quotidian—after all, inversely romantic in that they are so obviously Examples of the Ordinary— could have appeared in plays from an even earlier stage of his career. Neither this kind of particularity nor its relations—sensuous den- sity, imagistic inventiveness, and so on—are very often crucial to Yeats's poetry, but it would not be inappropriate to find here a broadening in his sense of what materials and emotions are permis- sible in a poem, and a weakening of his generalizing "all." The fog lifts, we can make out individual faces and objects, but what stands out in highest relief is not the scene, or even the characters, but the voice.

"Adam's Curse" has often been heard as more "conversa- tional" than most early Yeats, but the term, though universally understood, is nevertheless slippery and misleading. We do hear someone "talking," but what we want to call "conversational" is not only, not even primarily, an accurate imitation of the syntax and diction of everyday speech—would anyone *say* this poem?—but a quality of *attention*. In the Yeatsian context, this means a restraint of the bodiless momentum that normally makes the early poems chant, glide, gaze, and turn "regional." "Adam's Curse" demands more in the way of syllable-by-syllable concentration than most of Yeats's previous work; however delicate, it is not quite hypnotic. Its slightly tensed surface firms the distance between poet and reader.

This translates into the sense of speaking-from and speaking-to that one is likely to characterize as "conversational" even when the words are not very similar to what is actually heard over a cup of coffee.

Some of the most important discoveries of "Adam's Curse," therefore, are rhythmic, and they are discoveries of reticence. The poem's momentum is finely but constantly restrained in a way that transforms attention. Relative to Yeats's early norm, the lines have what might be called a backward lean. The effect is similar to (though less exaggerated than) what would occur if each syllable were separated from its neighbor by a hyphen: "A-line-will-take-us-hours-may-be, / Yet-if-it-does-not-seem-a-mo-ment's-thought." In these lines, the slight tension has three sources. The first is the common phenomenon of monosyllabic drag, itself the product of both metrical expectation and the nature of the sound-transitions between words.

Second is metrical tension, most obviously the poising of the rhythmically ambiguous "maybe" in the all-important final foot— a rhythmic "Caution" sign that retroactively slows and tightens the whole line. "Máybe" is nearly impossible here—"máy-bé" is the forced reading. This rhythmic twist was imported from the alien metrical tradition of the old ballads via Keats ("O Soft embalmer of the still midnight"), Rossetti ("One flame-winged brought a white winged harp-player"), Morris, and Swinburne. In the middle of the Victorian period, even practitioners of high polish were looking back to Ruskinian Gothic for an aesthetic of counterflow and reticence, and their experiments with the rough-cut right margin were conspicuous enough to incite readers' noisy disgust. They seem, further, to have failed partially in their effect. For what was intended to texture and harden poems seems to have been perceived as yet another encroachment of the Victorian fluidity. "I hate the effeminacy of his school," Browning wrote, speculating that Rossetti used these "archaic accentuations to seem soft. . . . Swinburne started this with other like Belialisms,—witness his 'harp-player,'"[5] and Buchanan in the infamous "Fleshly School" found that the effect, which he ascribed to all Pre-Raphaelites, was "a cooing tenderness just bordering on a loving whistle." Yeats and

Pound, among others, would have to perfect the shaping of the line's end that develops in parallel with the control of the Victorian emotional fluidity. Though this particular line-end manipulation gives way to others in the Yeatsian rhythmic discipline, it is worth registering his interest in the aims of Pre-Raphaelite metrical experimentation.

Finally, reading these two lines after a random sample of prose one would find the mouth unnaturally restricted in movement—a disproportionate number of the consonants and vowels are formed close together near the front of the mouth, and greater than average muscular precision is necessary for their distinct enunciation.

These three factors combine to produce a steplike movement so common in the poem that one carries it forward into lines, such as the less monosyllabic third, where it might not otherwise be heard:

> A-line-will-take-us-hours-may-be;
> Yet-if-it-does-not-seem-a-mo-ment's-thought,
> Our-stitch-ing-and-un-stitch-ing-has-been-naught.

All these restraints are part muscular (having to do with the mouth) and part mental (having to do with rhythmic expectation), but they become for us, however vaguely, part of the speaker's personality. Rhythmic tension is read as psychological tension. The subtly impeded line becomes "restrained" or "reticent."

Two absences may be important here. The paucity of anapests in the poem thwarts Yeats's dreamier kind of momentum, and ultimately even its expectation. The second and less conspicuous absence is that of medial pauses in general and in particular the fourth-syllable caesura, the most common in English poetry. It occurs perhaps once in the first three paragraphs: "And you and I, / / and talked of poetry." Given our subliminal expectations—we often insert a pause after the fourth syllable of a line when neither punctuation nor sense strictly demand it—this caesura must be heard not merely as missing but as repressed. The potential sag after the fourth syllable is bridged with a series of tense monosyllables, as in both of the following lines—"I said: 'A line will take us hours maybe; / Yet if it does not seem a moment's thought"; or buried in

an unrolling polysyllable—"For to articulate sweet sounds together"; or overbalanced by equally strong pauses elsewhere—
"That beautiful / / mild / / woman, / / your close friend"; or simply
postponed till later in the line—"And scrub a kitchen pavement, / /
or break stones."

With their backward-leaning rhythms and their bridged or
delayed pauses, the lines of "Adam's Curse" are something like
tightropes over a ravine—each syllabic step must be attended to.
This linear reticence makes the pause at the end of the lines all the
more important, all the more noticeable, and serves to heighten our
sense of the lines' integrity even when they are relatively strongly
enjambed—"and yet / Be thought an idler by the noisy set." From
now on, Yeats will have the trick of running lines over without
letting them flow.

Achieved with slight difficulty, each Yeatsian line becomes
something more artifact, something less motion, and its end is
almost an edge. Yeats is, indeed, uncommonly active at the line's
end. Part of what will become the famous Yeatsian "tune" is a habit
of highlighting in some way the rhythm or cadence of the final
syllables of a pentameter line, especially the last three. This will
have several manifestations, all already audible in "Adam's Curse."
First, Yeats may end a line with a trisyllabic (or even longer)
word—other than Rossetti, few earlier poets deploy as many polysyllables as Yeats:

> And you and I, and talked of *poetry*

> For to articulate sweet sounds *together*

> Of bankers, schoolmasters, and *clergymen*

> The martyrs call the world. And *thereupon*

> That we must labour to be *beautiful*

Polysyllables compromise with rhythm in their own peculiar fashion. Coming at the end of slightly retarded lines, these trisyllables,
for a moment, seem to roll free, but they are soon brought under
control by the demands of meter. The necessity of slightly raising
the stress on the very last syllable to acknowledge the iambic gives

the lines an almost interrogative lilt. They become, at any rate, backward-leaning, tentative.

Another line-end manipulation that highlights the line's final three syllables is the seventh-syllable caesura (Wordsworthian, but deployed without Wordsworth's more trailing variety of enjambment): "And scrub a kitchen pavement, // or break stones."

Finally, Yeats may use various combinations of slight seventh-syllable caesuras, alliteration, fifth-foot spondees, or three terminal monosyllables to underline the final syllables:

That beautiful mild woman, *your close friend*

Our stitching and unstitching *has been naught*

That beautiful mild woman *for whose sake*

There's many a one shall find out *all heartache*

Though very different on the whole, all these lines tighten in their last three syllables. They seem bent on avoiding their ends, on backing into them. The tendency of rhymes to pull the whole line after them is subtly and intricately resisted. In the Yeatsian line, the satisfactions of conclusion are often withheld, postponed, qualified—and tensely lengthened. He ends neither with Pope's expensive click nor with Tennysonian trail or blur. Lines carry an ambiguous momentum. They seem to brake in their final syllables, pause tensely in the right-hand margin, spring slightly off the left. This barely perceptible "spring" probably results from the need to have simpler momentum restored after the mutings and repressions of the line-ends, and may be one cause of the slight sense of disconnection one feels in Yeats's later poetry. The restraint of individual lines makes the movement from one to another seem infinitesimally more dramatic. We hear their brake–pause–spring as feeling spoken against restraint, or as the sudden the veering of a thought.

To digress from digression, all these rhythmic features are heard, if anything more emphatically, in the pentameter of the later Yeats. Take "Among School Children," which will be considered in much greater detail in the final chapter:

I

I walk through the long schoolroom questioning;
A kind old nun in a white hood replies;
The children learn to cipher and to sing,
To study reading-books and history,
To cut and sew, be neat in everything
In the best modern way—the children's eyes
In momentary wonder stare upon
A sixty-year-old smiling public man.

(CP 212–
13)

2

I dream of a Ledaean body, bent
Above a sinking fire, a tale that she
Told of a harsh reproof, or trivial event
That changed some childish day to tragedy—
Told, and it seemed that our two natures blent
Into a sphere from youthful sympathy,
Or else, to alter Plato's parable,
Into the yolk and white of the one shell.

When Yeats, like his dancer, balances labor and grace to stay in touch with time, minute reticences of movement tense his arc of expression. Here, as in "Adam's Curse," this reluctance or backward lean may be approximated by continuous hyphenation: "I-walk-through-the-long-school-room-ques-tion-ing; / A kind-old-nun-in-a-white-hood-re-plies." As in "Adam's Curse" this is in part the effect of monosyllabic drag, but the point is not that Yeats is a monosyllabic poet. Later Yeats contains more than an average number of nonmonosyllables, and an unusual number of words of three or more syllables—these two stanzas contain nearly as many as the entire seventy-six lines of "Tithonus." What truly characterizes Yeats's poetry is an environment of slight, constant tension and a precision of rhythmic control that makes the constant shifting between trains of resistant monosyllables and self-unfolding polysyllables both highly conspicuous and emotionally significant. The two lines just quoted, for example, scuff monosyllabically (and tensely) along until they encounter a longer word—"replies," "questioning." Too late in the line for a wholehearted release, these provide a kind of skid, which, partially releasing tension, remains tentative. More forcefully, Yeats can burst a line by placing its major stress in an early polysyllable. "Time after time," says Hugh Kenner, "it is the abstract word, the polysyllable, that detonates":[6] "And send imagination forth"; "In momentary wonder."

In other rhythmic contexts, momentum can be entirely dissipated in a polysyllable that seems to trip all over itself, making the line seem half-said, reluctant: "There is a comfortable kind of old scarecrow." Polysyllables are part of the gravity that allows Yeats the grace of his dance.

As in "Adam's Curse," the caesura in these stanzas is often delayed or suppressed, ranging from the ninth syllable—"I dream of Ledaean body, / / bent"—all the way back to the first—"Told, / / and it seemed that our two natures blent."

What Yeats again avoids is the more conventional medial pause. He repeatedly bridges tensely—or rolls over—the expected fourth-syllable sag, giving into it only to mime the sing-song of the nun:

> The children learn / / to cipher and to sing,
> To study reading-books and history,
> To cut and sew, / / be neat in everything.

These lines rock and see-saw. The ideal Yeatsian line is more like a drawn bow.

Yeats's habitual feeling out of the cadence of the line-ending is also strongly in evidence. Most notable is his way of poising trisyllables just before the break:

> I walk through the long schoolroom *questioning*

> To study reading-books and *history,*
> To cut and sew, be neat in *everything*

> That changed some childish day to *tragedy*

> Into a sphere from youthful *sympathy*

There are also numerous instances of the complementary monosyllabic effect—the phantom triple emphasis at the end of the line:

Above a sinking fire, a *tale that she*

And wonder if she stood so *at that age*

For even daughters of the *swan can share*

There is a comfortable kind of *old scarecrow*

With rhythmic twists, alliteration, and the wedging together of
difficult syllables, these line endings are subtly firmed. Whether
hardened or softened, the Yeatsian line-ending tends to acquire a
definite, hanging pause. The transition from line to line thus involves a subliminal disconnection, and lines seem to come out of
the left margin with a small surge. Hidden restraints, again, focus
and amplify Yeats's power. In fact, Yeats is so various in his momentums that it sometimes seems he is using lines of different
lengths. In "Among School Children," this is true in effect only—
but in many of Yeats's greatest poems—"In Memory of Major
Robert Gregory," "Prayer for My Daughter," "The Tower," "A
Dialogue of Self and Soul"—four- and five-beat lines are regularly
contrasted.

"Adams' Curse," to return to the earlier Yeats, is entirely in
couplets, a form whose self-enclosure Yeats begins to favor as his
stoic middle phase gets under way. But the varying curves of
tension produced by his characteristic alternation of monosyllabic
tension with polysyllabic roll and by the long, complex, slowly
resolving sentences can limn the large expansions and contractions
of feeling. In Yeats's hands, the lines vary immensely in psychological duration and the pentameter couplet acquires all the flexibility of
the irregular ode stanza.

As many readers have noticed, the last two stanzas of "Adam's
Curse" seem to revert to Yeats's nineteenth century manner:

We sat grown quiet at the name of love;
We saw the last embers of daylight die,
And in the trembling blue-green of the sky
A moon, worn as if had been a shell
Washed by time's waters as they rose and fell
About the stars and broke in days and years.

I had a thought for no one's but your ears:
That you were beautiful, and that I strove

(CP 79)

To love you in the old high way of love;
That it had all seemed happy, and yet we'd grown
As weary-hearted as that hollow moon.

There *is* a good deal of weary Pre-Raphaelite beauty here, but few readers will be unmoved by the conclusion, and only those very anxious for the later Yeats will call it a failure. Nor is it a whole-hearted regression. Compared to the opening paragraphs, the final two do indeed exhibit slightly less linear integrity, slightly more reliance on the elegiac *and*. But though many aspects of the poem's tone and imagery are familiar, the rhythm is everywhere new, everywhere subtly underlain by Yeats's developing restraint. The fluidity that is an unexamined feature of the earlier poems is here *dramatized,* set against another, stiffer movement. Pictorially, the image of the moon engulfed in time's waters might seem to belong to *The Wind among the Reeds*. In context, and set to Yeats's newer music, it is another example of inset criticism. Surrounded by a new reticence, it evokes not the vast dimness of the early poems but that dimness as framed by a window. It is not an end in itself but rather a characteristic of a failed past. The life lived as if it were over is itself ending.

In Yeats, style and personality are so intertwined that his poems can be about art without ceasing to be about life. "Adam's Curse" equates poet and woman in their "labor to be beautiful" and to bring to birth, and it enacts its theme on the most fundamental level. All the poem's discoveries of reticence and restraint are in Yeats's mind an incorporation of labor into the movement of verse and the very flow of feeling. Yeats is newly implicated in "The Fascination of What's Difficult," and the difficulty implies a separation of poet and reader. When the poet labors, however gently, emotion deepens behind the effort of his utterance.

Yeats must have been aware that many of his acquaintances—AE and George Moore among them—thought he had completed his important work by 1895. With *The Wind among the Reeds* (1899), certainly, he had exhausted the vein of his early poetry. The books of his "middle period"—*In the Seven Woods* (1904), *The Green Helmet* (1910), and *Responsibilities* (1914)—impressive as they often are, may well have provided only dubious comfort. The unquestionable "Adam's Curse," from the first of these, is more a farewell to an old art than a direction he could pursue at the time. With long hindsight we can find in a dozen or so other fine poems predictions of the greater volumes that begin with *The Wild Swans at Coole,* but such vantage was probably only fitfully available to Yeats himself. His successes in the first decade or so of the century tend to be relatively short pieces in relatively slim volumes. Their new plain manner and often exhilarating stoicism are a considerable but sporadic achievement, and their heroic resistance of the temptations of late nineteenth-century verse could have foreshadowed either a revolution of style or the total abandonment of poetry. Yeats could not clearly have known which. What he saw as the long declines of Wordsworth, Tennyson, Swinburne, and Browning must have weighed heavily on his mind. In becoming himself, he had contracted visibly. One senses beneath the exaggerated conviction of the middle poems—"there's more enterprise / In walking naked"—that though Yeats was doing what he had to do, he could not be entirely sure his walk was not taking him into the desert. The self-transformation we now take for granted was protracted, agonized, and not at all inevitable.

The purest consequences of Yeats's evolution toward reticence are the hard, short, short-lined poems that are the strength of the middle volumes and the peripheral glory of the later ones. "To a Friend Whose Work Has Come to Nothing" embodies stylistically the stoic dignity it recommends:

> Now all the truth is out,
> Be secret and take defeat
> From any brazen throat,
> For how can you compete,
> Being honour bred, with one
> Who, were it proved he lies,
> Were neither shamed in his own
> Nor in his neighbours' eyes?
> Bred to a harder thing
> Than Triumph, turn away
> And like a laughing string

(CP 107)

> Whereon mad fingers play
> Amid a place of stone,
> Be secret and exult,
> Because of all things known
> That is most difficult.

This is a passionate poem, but it should be said immediately that its passion is inseparable from a fierce restraint. The short, tensed lines are inflected by their place in an expectant syntax, and squeezed off with rhymes reminiscent of the *difficult–colt–jolt–dolt–bolt* of "The Fascination of What's Difficult." They are never allowed to trail or fade elegiacally. Their beginnings, often spondaic or trochaic, seem cut from the same stone.

The poem is two long sentences struggling from a very small hole. There is a heightened tension between the parallelisms and simultaneities of thought and the sequence of language:

> how can you compete,
> Being honour bred, with one
> Who, were it proved he lies,
> Were neither shamed in his own
> Nor in his neighbours' eyes?

"How can someone honorable compete with a proven liar" would say most of this, but again none of it. The one-line version is linear, easier, and yet, with its verbals gone, less active. More to the point, the removal of the syntactical difficulties turns the lines into wishful aphorism. Without restraints, passion dwindles. In Yeats's sentence, the words seem under strain. One holds strongly to the memory of each line until its successor has concluded. To finish a line is to tuck a book into the bottom of an already high stack. Given its suspensions, a reader must bring to the poem not only an alert intellect but an almost physical sense of balance. Much more than in "Adam's Curse," labor, newly fascinating difficulty, is a part of the poem's very flow, and attention is transformed. We are consequently more aware of the separation of speaker and listener, and of the poem as intervening. Difficulty tells us the poem is not "all" of the poet, that he is held, or holding, back.

"To a Friend Whose Work Has Come to Nothing" recommends the virtues it embodies, urging a secrecy that is not mystery but restraint. Over and over, it moves us not by carrying us off, but by qualifying its own momentum. There is, for example, a tactical "stumble" in the two exhortations to secrecy: "Be secret and take defeat"; "Be secret and exult." One can almost hear these lines growing proudly silent, and the slight impedance that we translate into stoicism is in part caused by the transition from initially to terminally stressed disyllables. Keats brings this resource to bear on the wordless moment of wonder at the conclusion of "Chapman's Homer"—"Silent, upon a peak in Darien." Often clumsy even in pentameter lines, this transition could be even more audible in trimeter. But Yeats's ear has served him well, turning potential awkwardness into an asset. Similarly, the poem finally invokes us not with a sweep into the horizon but by stopping short. The concluding line, "That is most difficult," is exactly what it says. It remains partly stuck in the throat. Momentum, unresolved, is transferred to the reader. Even the on-one-foot rhyme—*exult/ difficult*—works this way. Though it perhaps avoids the glossiness of a conclusion too easily concluded, it is not an attempt to avoid the useful tensions of artifice. The weak rhyme is first of all a reticence, something half said, but it also forces us to do the other half of the saying by imperceptibly raising the stress on the final syllable of *difficult* to meet the expectations of rhyme and rhythm. In more Tennysonian lines, emotion is practically inseparable from poetic momentum. The continuous stylistic restraint of "To a Friend Whose Work Has Come to Nothing" is a different form of energy—in its tense *opposition* of feeling and flow, it is as much the arc of a dam as the reach of a river.

More passionate, more restrained, less dimly alluring, this is a new or at least an unused Yeats—a different poetic flow, a different poetic self. Harder, colder, sharper, we would say. "Unembarrassable," Yeats might add, for by this time he was thinking of the poems that ride on the self's dissolves as imploring, passive, weak. He had, as poets will, nearly identified the primary characteristic of his Victorian inheritance with the largest flaw he perceived in his youthful character, and he set out to remedy both at once.

Yeats took the title of a section of his autobiography "Hodos Chameliontos" from a study manual of the Golden Dawn[7], but he could also have been recalling Keats, whose famous characterization of the poet as a "camelion" who "has no Identity," who is "every thing and nothing," both the younger and the older Yeats could in their very different ways have assented to.[8] In practice, the full-hearted Keatsian empathy is different from the nearly bodiless fluidity in early Yeats—"And now I have grown nothing, knowing all"—and Tennyson. Perhaps exhibiting this vaguer empathy even as he attempts to dismiss it, Yeats often projects his dimness back into his romantic predecessor, describing him as if he were early Yeats, or Rossetti, the mentor of early Yeats: "Keats sang of a beauty so wholly preoccupied with itself that its very contemplation is a kind of lingering trance" (*E&I* 378).

Poets, like the rest of us, walk through peopled rooms, and the fluidity of the self can have a social as well as an imaginative component. In the same letter that defines the chameleon poet, Keats excuses himself, in terms that Yeats will echo, for a remark made in the fever of a party:

> It is a wretched thing to confess; but it is a very fact that not one word I ever utter can be taken for granted as an opinion growing out of my identical nature—how can it, when I have no nature? When I am in a room with People if I ever am free from speculating on creations of my own brain, then not myself goes home to myself: but the identity of every one in the room begins . . . to press upon me that, I am in a very little time an[ni]hilated not only among Men; it would be the same in a Nursery of children.[9]

Neither the partially whimsical questioning of the existence of a central self nor the sense of obliteration will be seen as terribly unusual, but it is interesting that both are a recurring themes in Yeats's journals as well: "I was always conscious of something helpless and perhaps even untrustworthy in myself; I could not hold to my opinions among people who would make light of them if I felt for those people any sympathy. I was always accusing myself of disloyalty to some absent friend. I had, it seemed, an incredible timidity. Sometimes this timidity became inexplicable, and [it is] still [in]explicable and painful to the memory" (*WBY Mem.* 33).

Keats would at least like to seem untroubled by his own shiftiness, but see Ricks's stimulating *Keats and Embarrassment.*[10] Yeats is clearly ashamed—and propelled, as a result, toward his opposite. "It is perhaps because nature made me a gregarious man, going hither and thither looking for conversation, and ready to deny from fear or favour his dearest conviction," he guesses, "that I love proud and lonely things" (*A* 115). That "proud and lonely things" could apply equally well to Maud Gonne or a tower is perhaps a revealing vagueness. Frustrated by his inability to hold identity, his convictions, his shape, he is constantly accusing himself of clumsiness, timidity, indiscretion, lack of self-possession. He tends to see his own weaknesses in terms of an instability of borders. He approaches others too easily, he thinks, with an insufficient sense of their—and his own—otherness: "I think I understand people easily and easily sympathize with all kinds of characters and all kinds of defects and easily forgive all kinds of defects and vices" (*LY* 345).

This sounds like a Keatsian generosity, but Yeats is concerned, too, with the limits of such limitlessness: "I have the defect of this quality" (*LY* 345). Synge and Lady Gregory "isolate themselves from all contagious opinions of poorer minds" (*WBY Mem.* 154–55), but he himself is unable to maintain a steady distance. The approaches he consequently allows later seem to him self-betrayals, in which "all my natural thoughts have been drowned by an undisciplined sympathy" (*Myth.* 325). Feeling his integrity sacrificed to "invasions of the soul," he swings to the other extreme, awkwardly restoring distance with "angry outbreaks which are pure folly" (*WBY Mem.* 154–55). Brooding over these failings, Yeats often imagines that a smaller, more instinctive, more constant anger might patrol and firm his personal borders: "I want you to understand that I have no instincts in personal life. . . . Above all, I have destroyed in myself, by analysis, instinctive indignation" (*WBY Mem.* 252).

Again, neither Yeats's clumsinesses, nor his reluctance to forgive them, nor his sense of them as self-betrayals, nor even his feeling shame as a torture—making a speech, he says, "I was ashamed until shame turned at last . . . into physical pain" (*Vision* 27)—will be perceived as terribly unusual. These are ordinary, if not universal, agonies. But poetry can rest on such ordinary agonies, and Yeats's repeated eloquence on the subject of embarrassment hints at its central importance for him. It is certainly more than a social inconvenience. He usually calls it, with revealing exaggeration, "remorse," or, less histrionically, "regret," as when he hints that it is in part responsible for the dimness of his early poetry, "those outlines of lyric poetry which are blurred by desire and vague regret" (*V. Ed.* 849). He keeps a mental file of hauntingly "shameful" acts and their witnesses that can be called up at any occasion: "Death of a friend. To describe how mixed with one's grief comes the thought that the witness of some foolish word or act one's own is gone" (*Expl.* 290).

These shameful memories can be the chief bar to reconciliation with one's life and with life in general, as in "A Dialogue of Self and Soul" or "Vacillation:"

(CP 246)
> Things said or done long years ago,
> Or things I did not do or say
> But thought that I might say or do,
> Weigh me down, and not a day
> But something is recalled,
> My conscience or my vanity appalled.

"The body calls it death, / The heart remorse" (*CP* 245), Yeats says, and the implication is that remorse, far from being an incidental pain, is a negation of being analogous to death: it threatens to dissolve the very architecture of the self. He would have assented to Keats's remark that "the most unhappy hours in our lives are those in which we recollect times past to our blushing—If we are immortal that must be the Hell."[11] Yeats's analysis of regret in the first draft of his autobiography (one of the many striking passages excluded from the overwritten and relatively bland final version) is even more penetrating:

> *The pain others give us passes away in their later kindness; the*
> *pain of one's own blunders, especially when they hurt one's vanity,*

never passes away. One's own acts are isolated and one act does not buy absolution for another. They are always present before a strangely abstract judgment. One is never a unity, a personality: to oneself, small acts of years ago are so painful in the memory that often one starts at the presence a little below "the threshold of consciousness" of a thought that remains unknown. It sheds a vague light like that of the moon before it rises, or after its setting. Vanity is so intimately associated with one's spiritual identity that the errors or what hurt it, above all if they came from it, are more painful in the memory than serious sins, and yet I do not think this means that one is very vain. The harm that one does to others is lost in changing events and passes away, and so is healed by time, unless it was very great.

(*WBY Mem.* 190–91)

The vague light of an embarrassment below the threshold of consciousness ("poetry . . . blurred with . . . vague regret"?) is familiar enough. Reading the more blushing passages of Keats and Tennyson one could almost believe that the vertigo of its rising is a main motive of the self's fluidity. But perhaps even more interesting is Yeats's equation of embarrassment and disunity of self. We forgive friends easily, he says, because they are a unity to us, and their kindnesses over time more than compensate for their minor cruelties. But we do not imagine ourselves as a unity. Our own blunders remain separate and free-floating—they may continue their accusations indefinitely. It is not merely that failure questions success, for the memories that retain the power to overbalance objectively much larger weights of kindness, achievement, and good intentions are inevitably memories not of mere mistakes but of self-betrayal, or at least they are seen that way. They are "dishonest" mistakes, and as such they challenge not only our competence but our very coherence as beings.

Much more than enough has already been written about the "mask" so important to Yeats at this stage of his career, but it might not be amiss to view it briefly from this angle. Yeats's mask is not really a poetic disguise. Its purpose is more to reveal than to hide, and more to organize than to reveal. Nor is it primarily a social defense, though the necessity of functioning in and writing for the public no doubt hastened it into being. When Yeats speaks of the mask as defending against the "terrors of judgment," he refers not to the disapproving crowd but to his harsher, more persistent internal judge. To "assume the mask of some other self" is to experience "a rebirth as something not oneself," and in so doing to escape the "infinite blinding beam" of self-judgment (*WBY Mem.* 191).

Blank unself-consciousness would at first seem to be the issue, but in practice Yeats wants a rather selective and specific unconsciousness. He wants to be able to regard himself as if he were another person, because other people, for all their horrendous faults, have advantages over us. They are, as Yeats says, far easier to forgive, because they are unities in *our* minds as we ourselves are not. They are simpler than we are, and therefore more certain. "When I look at others," Auden confirms, "I cannot see them making choices; I can only see what they do. . . . Compared with myself, that is, other people seem at once less free and stronger in character."[12]

Several aspects of Yeats's evolution after 1900 are propelled by his desire for this kind of otherness. Yeats's "Unity of Being" is an attempt to bring his whole self into focus—to be "all" without dispersion and dimness—but it is also related to his insistence on impersonality—it is partly an attempt to see in himself the strong coherence he automatically grants to others. Simplicity and strength. These are the qualities we tend to exaggerate in others, they are the qualities Yeats most wanted for his later poetry, and they are the features of the mask he defined, in *A Vision,* as proper to those of his own Phase 17: "simplification through intensity" (140). With intensity, the poet achieves a focus, a unity, that prevents the collapse into accuser and accused, or turns the internal accuser into a source of energy, a necessary antagonist. Certainly Yeats's sometimes troubling fascination with remorselessness—with the ignorant or the merely powerful—can be explained in these terms as a quite Swinburnean overcompensation for his own ungovernable fluidity. His difficult attempt to assimilate and forgive his whole history—"I am content to live it all again"—in "A Dialogue of Self and Soul" depends on extending to himself the mercy ("When such as I cast out remorse") he automatically grants to others.

Yeats found himself in the twentieth century with a self he regarded as weak and a poetic flow he could only see as weakening. His reformations of both self and poetry involved the exploitation of a hardness and coldness that had seemed to be beyond and outside them. His gathering of personal force is a history of intricate and minute self-estrangements. His passion is his restraint.

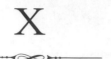

X

Yeatsian Shapes

the intellectual sweetness of those lines
That cut through time or cross it withershins.
                                    Coole Park, 1929

FROM HIS adolescence, Yeats had been fascinated by the temperature of emotions. He "persuaded" himself, he says, that he "had a passion for the dawn," (*A* 48) and years later, writing autobiography, he persuaded himself that this early impulse had returned to direct the evolution of his poetry after *The Wanderings of Oisin:* "I deliberately reshaped my style, deliberately sought out an impression as of cold light and tumbling clouds. I . . . became as emotional as possible but with an emotion I described to myself as cold" (*A* 48). The child Yeats may well have been father to the man. If so, this is another of those Yeatsian critical formulations that waited decades to take hold of his poetry. Though Yeats even at his most Pre-Raphaelite is free of Rossettian fever and humidity, and though his twilight has more ascetic clarity than Tennyson's, it is only with his middle volumes, and pieces such as "To a Friend Whose Work Has Come to Nothing" and "The Cold Heaven," that he achieves the "poem maybe as cold / And passionate as the dawn" (*CP* 146). The phrase, derived from one of his father's letters, finally settled in "The Fisherman," itself not a bad example of the genre.

In hardening the dimness of his early poetry, Yeats had denied more of himself and his past than he could continue to deny. Beginning with *The Wild Swans at Coole,* he opens himself again to elegiac dissolutions, but balances them with an achieved otherness. In that landmark volume, the past and its sadness return, but so "projected and distinct," so chilled, that the name of Lady Gregory's estate almost becomes a pun. In the title poem, especially, sadness is crystalline, artistic poise almost tactile, as if the words themselves rested on the tensed meniscus of the "brimming water among the stones":

> The trees are in their autumn beauty,
> The woodland paths are dry,
> Under the October twilight the water
> Mirrors a still sky;
> Upon the brimming water among the stones
> Are nine-and-fifty swans.
>
> The nineteenth autumn has come upon me
> Since I first made my count;
> I saw, before I had well finished,
> All suddenly mount
> And scatter wheeling in great broken rings
> Upon their clamorous wings.
>
> I have looked upon those brilliant creatures,
> And now my heart is sore.
> All's changed since I, hearing at twilight,
> The first time on this shore,
> The bell-beat of their wings above my head,
> Trod with a lighter tread.
>
> Unwearied still, lover by lover,
> They paddle in the cold
> Companionable streams or climb the air;
> Their hearts have not grown old;
> Passion or conquest, wander where they will,
> Attend upon them still.
>
> But now they drift on the still water,
> Mysterious, beautiful;
> Among what rushes will they build,
> By what lake's edge or pool
> Delight men's eyes when I awake some day
> To find they have flown away?

(*CP* 129–30)

This is one of Yeats's freest and most second-by-second rhythmic inventions. It is as if he needed to fend off more predictable momentums in order to keep his elegiac yearnings under control, his feelings precise. Though never cramped or cut off as in the middle poems, the lines here are restrained. They have less initial spring than is normal in Yeats—their labor, like that of the swans, is gentle but undeniable,

> Unwearied still, lover by lover,
> They paddle in the cold
> Companionable streams or climb the air.

No longer riding on a dissolving wave, Yeats's lines with moderate but detectable effort push back silence. The index of this new momentum is that Yeats can introduce extra unstressed syllables without allowing the poem to run. Where the loosened lines of "He Wishes His Beloved Were Dead" tend to skim—"Were you but lying cold and dead, / And lights were paling out of the West"—the later poem's backward-lean swallows anapests. They become more reluctant:

> Under the October twilight the water
> Mirrors a still sky.
> Upon the brimming water among the stones.

"The trees are in their autumn beauty / The woodland paths are dry." Yeats has the habit of sketchy or unconnected beginnings. His opening stanzas can be slow and inconspicuous summonings—summonings, it sometimes seems, of his own unmistakable voice, his syntax and rhythm. By the arrival of "Nine and fifty swans" we know we have been shown something. But what? The following stanza's "nineteen" is clearly the number of years since Yeats, in ill health and miserable over Maud Gonne (the subject this poem gets its strength from excluding), had first visited Coole to recuperate. "Nine and fifty," however, will not translate. For more than one reader, the impulse has been subtraction—1916 minus 1865—but Yeats was nowhere near fifty-nine. The impulse itself may show how firmly and quickly the swans have become associated with his life. If the number is more specifically meaningful, its meaning is not obvious, and in leaving it unexplained Yeats has left it to work as magic, which it does. His actual choice among many equally valid pseudospecificities seems to have been dictated by his ear. In the manuscripts he had tried out "five and forty," equivalent in tactical unmeaning but not in sound. His final choice bends a consonantal pattern around the hanging pause of the Yeatsian line break in fine but constant tension: "among the sto*n*es / Are *n*ine-and-fifty swa*n*s." It may be worth noting that even a small change—to "nine-and-*forty*—would have blurred the phrase. "Wa-te*r* / Mi*rr*or works the same way, and "Cold / Companionable streams" sums up over a line break the blend of distance and intimacy the poem achieves. "Companionable," itself unexpected, is a good example of the Yeats's ability to find out the tactile resistance of an abstract polysyllable and make its astringency a small obstacle that labor, with measured joy, overcomes. Like "brilliant" in "The Sorrow of Love" (and later in *this* poem) it works by being the right wrong word.

"Cold," more than an example, is the Yeatsian keynote. "To reverse the connotations of a homefelt word like *cold*," Kenner says, "to turn coldness into a bracing quality, neither the death of affect nor the absence of living warmth, would seem an impossible defiance."[1] Yeats did it, but he had a predecessor in Swinburne, a predecessor Dowson—"I would not alter thy cold eyes"—helped him keep in mind. Certainly "bitter," like "cold" associated with Yeats's tragic gaiety, is Swinburnean, and it is relayed by the Swinburnean lines of Dowson's "Villanelle of the Poet's Road" that Yeats so liked to quote:

> Unto us they belong,
> Us the bitter and the gay,
> Wine and woman and song.

"Let us go hence, somewhither strange and cold" had been Dowson's exhortation in "A Last Word," written near the turn of the century, but it was Yeats who survived to steer into the cold currents of modernism. The reach of those currents might be indicated by the fact that two poets so vastly different as Yeats and William Carlos Williams actually have a good deal of common purpose. Just as the new Yeatsian rhythms are tensed in order to exclude the trance and blur of Tennyson, so modernist experiments with syntax and form are designed to squeeze out the vague spaciousness of Victorian and Pre-Raphaelite poetry and to replace its fluid eroticism with a sharper, colder, drier desire. Williams illustrates this direction in "The Rose" from *Spring and All:*

> The rose is obsolete
> but each petal ends in
> an edge, the double facet
> cementing the grooved
> columns of air—The edge
> cuts without cutting
> meets—nothing—renews
> itself in metal or porcelain—
>
> whither? It ends—
>
> But if it ends
> the start is begun
> so that to engage roses
> becomes a geometry—
>
> Sharper, neater, more cutting
> figured in majolica—
> the broken plate
> glazed with a rose
>
> Somewhere the sense
> makes copper roses
> steel roses—
>
> The rose carried weight of love
> but love is at an end—of roses
>
> It is at the edge of the
> petal that love waits
>
> Crisp, worked to defeat
> laboredness—fragile
> plucked, moist, half-raised
> cold, precise, touching.[2]

The poem concerns the difference between roses as objects or (since this rose is a design on a plate) geometries, and roses as symbols, now "obsolete," with perhaps a glance as Yeats's Rose poems. More important is the quality of perception—and ultimately of desire—that Williams seeks. It is "crisp," "sharper, neater, more cutting." It is not "regional" or blurred—it awaits us not as a place but as an edge: "It is at the *edge* of the / petal that love waits." And the poem is full of edges, not just in its imagery, but in its sharp enjambments—"The edge / cuts" is how Williams thinks of it—and in its elliptical syntax, always starting, reaching, cutting itself off. That the poem's sharpnesses, edges, geometries, cutting have now, sixty years later, become the ordinary stuff of both poetry and desire is not Williams's fault. He is seeking a perception somewhat Yeatsian in a manner utterly un-Yeatsian. "Cold, precise, touching" sounds like "cold / Companionable streams" or "cold and passionate as the dawn." The "cold familiar wind" of "Spring and All" (from the same sequence) is even closer. Yeats surely would have admired the "stark dignity of entrance" from that poem—in Williams, it is understood as the strangeness of the newly seen object, which comes to be our own strangeness: "Nature is the hint to composition not because it is familiar to us . . . but because it possesses the quality of independent existence, of reality which we feel in ourselves."[3] Yeats, mainly interested in poets whose intensity took them beyond nature, would have found the conclusion of this sentence more interesting than its inspiration. He might have embraced the concept of independence or strangeness Williams develops, for *Spring and All*'s loud echo of Pound's "Make it new" is subtler than it sometimes appears. His concern is pastlessness. Though he can dismiss all history, and though he is less exact a critic even than the mythologizing Yeats, his ambivalence is mainly reserved for the same stretch of the cultural past that Yeats also found deviant. Further, his "poetry of the present," like Lawrence's, is not merely "the poetry of our day," but poetry free of *passing,* poetry that has blocked the Victorian fluidity and restrained its dimming. The newness and freshness he seeks can only surround imaginatively liberated objects, objects made to stand forth separate, hard, cold, wholly present. Yeats could have understood this pastlessness only as the pastlessness of the self, but Williams is there, too. He also tries to "cast out remorse." To accept "remorse," he says, "is to attempt to fit the emotions of a certain state to a preceding state to which they are in no way related." "Imagination," he continues—as Yeats might well continued—"though it cannot wipe out the sting of remorse can instruct the mind in its proper uses."[4] For all their differences, both poets understand their invocation of otherness as a restraint of fluidity.

In the Yeatsian context, it is useful to see Williams's suppression of meter, his shardlike syntax, and his short, sharply enjambed lines not as liberalizations but as new forms of control. In "The Rose" Williams is nearly dictatorial with regard to momentum. The short lines prevent any Tennysonian glide or blur. They seldom "carry" a reader. The play of lineation against syntax, as Charles O. Hartman thoroughly demonstrates,[5] amounts to as much guidance in reading the poem as the expectations of conventional prosody would—more, probably. Attention is almost painfully focused on the edges, falls, quick turns, hesitations. The words, suddenly conscious of the white space between them, seem incapable of flowing together, of becoming the continuous substrate of a Yeatsian "region" or Williamsesque "beautiful illusion."

Williams is looking at a Juan Gris collage and trying to translate its visual disconnections and relations into verbal phenomena. Yeats, too, had looked at modern art, and though he was less enthusiastic than Williams, he also understood the new geometry as a restraint of fluidity: "The radical critics encourage our painters to decorate the walls with those cubes, triangles, ovoids, that are all stiff under the touch, or with gods and goddesses, distorted by Rubensesque exaggeration, dulled by hard doll-like faces that they may chill desire" (*E&I* x). There is more than a little nostalgia here for the dimmed gaze and the beautiful body—this is a man who might well have hung a Rossetti over a Picasso. But though Yeats might have painted Rossettis, he did not want to write them, and the chilling of desire here in the service of criticism is the same and not the same as his "cold passion." The "stiffness" of the paintings is not very far from the stylistic tensions of his poems. The difference,

Yeats might have said, is between the restraint of strength, on one hand, and simple weakness on the other. In any case, he is seeing modern art as having taken just a bit too far a tendency he himself understood and acknowledged. With "cubes, triangles, ovoids," a reader, with some license from Yeats, may think of the pages of obsessively diagrammed historical periodizations of *A Vision:* "I regard them as stylistic arrangements of experience comparable to the cubes in the drawing of Wyndham Lewis and to the ovoids in the sculpture of Brancusi. They have helped me to hold in a single thought reality and justice" (*Vision* 25). With "reality and justice" Yeats's prophetic concerns slip into parallel with his more personal themes—he defines *Will* and *Mask* in *A Vision* as "the Is and the Ought (or that which should be)" (73). Geometry turns out to be another one of those restraints that deepen and define passion: "All, all those gyres and cubes and midnight things / Are but a new expression of her body" (*CP* 444). Whatever the painters themselves would have said, this was not an unusual point of view for a poet. T. E. Hulme characterizes as "space-shy" and "geometrical" the modern art that was replacing an older art of "empathy (*Einfühlung*)." And, like Yeats, he comes to see "how essential and necessary a geometrical character is in endeavouring to express a certain intensity."[6]

Yeats found ways less radical than Williams to purge Victorian momentums, losses, and desires from his poetry. He could have said to him what he actually did say to Pound: "What you are trying to make speech is punctuation without words between them . . . that is my conception of a mathematical world" (*I&R* 1:151). In thus criticizing "pieces composed by ellipsis" (*I&R* 2:235), Yeats thinks of *The Cantos* as in some way analogous to the work of modern painters, a space of abstract relations, and his disgusts cascade—no meaningful relation to speech, no possibility of restraint, no conceivable personality. A poet might as well be a still life.

Yeats would call all this a problem of "syntax." That is a large enough word in any case, but for Yeats it is vast, and important. Often it seems synonymous with all of style: "It was a long time before I had made a language to my liking; I began to make it when I

discovered some twenty years ago that I must seek, not as Wordsworth thought, words in common use, but a powerful and passionate syntax, and a complete coincidence between period and stanza.
Because I need a passionate syntax for passionate subject-matter I
compel myself to accept those traditional metres that have developed with the language" (*E&I* 521–22). "Complete coincidence
between period and stanza" sounds specific, intelligible—and syntactical—but the opening of this quotation seems to ally syntax
with language generally, and the last sentence half-fuses it with
rhythm. In his essays and letters, *syntax* is a word Yeats conjures
with. With a nearby audience of one, however, he realizes he is not
sure what it means. Lady Dorothy Wellesley tells the story:

> *Once, when we were going over a poem of mine, W. B. Y. said to*
> *me: "I don't understand this line". I replied: "I believe that syntax*
> *is one of my weaknesses". To this he answered: "There is nothing*
> *wrong with your syntax; it is perfectly all right." I then said: "I*
> *must confess that I have never understood the true meaning of*
> *syntax. I have always believed it to be the relation of one word*
> *with another." "Neither have I understood it", he replied. At the*
> *end of five minutes' discussion upon this subject he said: "Go and*
> *fetch a dictionary! I think perhaps we ought to know what syntax*
> *is."*

(LDW 192–
93)

Syntax is a friend everyone mentions but no one has looked up
recently—that much of this scene is obvious, and one might fill in
some of its silences. Confronted with an unclear line, Lady Dorothy assumes a syntactical problem. She means, probably, something like a skewed parallelism or a befogged antecedent, all matters
of syntax as she defines it: "the relation of one word to another."
Though other readings of this scene are certainly possible, it seems
that Yeats hesitates because he is surprised to hear the word *syntax* in
this context. The word as Yeats commonly uses it is only sec-
ondarily a matter of relationship or grammar—it could not have
much to do with the *clarity* of a line. It is instead the flow of a
sentence—but, more than that, its sequence and sinew. For him,
syntax is an arch, the path along which the edifice of a sentence
bears weight, transmits its force to the ground. Like a real structural

member, syntax as Yeats feels it is something that can be tensed, bent, compressed, stretched, broken: "Tennyson's syntax is seldom contorted . . . it is perhaps never good speech. It lacks the impulse of passionate life. 'In Memoriam' is detestable because of its syntax."[7]

Syntax, again, is broad, and probably used in a broad protest against features of flow found not only in Tennyson but a range of poets, including early Yeats. Elsewhere, for example, Yeats attributes "the over childish or over pretty or feminine element in some good Wordsworth and much poetry up to our date" to "lack of natural momentum in syntax. This momentum . . . is far more important than simplicity of vocabulary. If Wordsworth had found it he could have carried any amount of elaborate English" (*LY* 710). *Feminine* is a frequent category in Yeats's critical writing. Unmanhandled syntax, he means to say, is part of an effortless, self-releasing poetic flow. This kind of flow both implies and creates a passive relation to experience—it merges poems and readers. In contrast, *contorted* equals "passionate," because Yeats finds in syntactical strain another form of control, another restraint of flow, another hardening of the dimness. This is precisely why he must stop short of the Poundian collage—Donald Davie says it finely: "Because Yeats holds and keeps faith in the discursive language, for instance by the sinewiness of his syntax, as his contemporaries Eliot and Pound do not, a moment . . . when perceptions pass beyond the discursive reason is poignant in his poetry as it cannot be in theirs."[8]

For Yeats, meter and syntax were vital sources of tension, and to dispense with them would have been to purchase the liberty of poetry at the cost of all that there was to liberate in the first place. If he never favored either free verse or "pieces composed by ellipsis" it was because he could not distinguish personality from its restraint.

What Yeats wants from syntax may be a bit vague in theory, but it is fairly clear in practice. Contortions not at all conspicuous will accomplish the hardenings and impedances he seeks. According to Curtis Bradford, for example, the second stanza of "The Wild Swans at Coole" once, in a relatively finished manuscript version, read:

> I am now at the nineteenth autumn
> Since I first made my count
> I make no sound for if they heard me
> All suddenly they would mount
> Scatter and wheel in those great broken rings
> With slow clamor of their wings.[9]

This is only half way to being Yeats. While nothing like the *and . . . and . . . and* of his earlier poems, it hews pretty closely to a narrative or pictorial sequence. The "I" is prominent. "I am this; I do that." Yet the speaker somehow does not seem to exert control over his language. The stanza gives unnecessary explanations ("for if . . .") and seems on the whole slack and clunky, though it contains all the elements of the final version:

> The nineteenth autumn has come upon me
> Since I first made my count.
> I saw, before I had well finished,
> All suddenly mount
> And scatter wheeling in great broken rings
> Upon their clamorous wings.

The startling improvement is curious. The "I," though it still occurs three times, is much less conspicuous. The speaker seems *less* in control of events—the autumn comes upon him and the swans seem to mount more unexpectedly. But the "I" seems *more* in control of the poem's *emotions,* partly because it has interrupted the linearity of the syntax. For example, the draft's "mount / Scatter and wheel in those great broken rings" describes a series of actions. Yeats has tried to harness the imagined rising of the swans to a sequence of verbs. In the final version, "wheeling in great broken rings" freezes action momentarily—it is a second thought, almost parenthetical, actively *inserted.* The most important change, however, is the tucking of the phrase "before I had well finished" between the verb and the direct object. Had Yeats not done this, had he written

> Before I had well finished
> I saw all suddenly mount

> And scatter wheeling in great broken rings
> Upon their clamorous wings

or, worse,

> I saw all suddenly mount
> And scatter wheeling in great broken rings
> Upon their clamorous wings
> Before I had well finished

the phrase in question would have become merely another item in something like a list—to be tolerated and absorbed passively. But the tucking in of the phrase makes syntactical tension bear its weight. The strain of the missing direct object holds it up in the air. "All suddenly mount" is isolated—both more sudden and more energetic because it is *not* as closely tied to a sequence of verbs. More important, the whole sentence, what precedes and follows the phrase, seems tensed and strengthened by the acceptance of this particle of alloy.

Something similar happens in the history of stanza 3 (Bradford uses the *X* to denote a line canceled in manuscript):

> They're but an image on a lake
> Why should my heart be wrung
> X When I first saw them I was young
> The white unwearied creatures
> Delighted me when young
> When I first gazed upon them[10]

This is an early draft and Yeats is still groping through an image which is, in the way of images still too much in the mind and too little in language, simultaneous and omnidirectional. Three over-lapping *when*'s (one canceled) indicate the problem with sequence. The stanza, at this point, is completely invertebrate, but a little later, Yeats has found his syntactical tuck. The *language* of the next version is almost *more* awkward but something important has happened and the edifice steadies, though the unsightly scaffolding of *when*'s is still in place.

> The lovely white unwearied creatures
> Always yet when young

When they flew or clamored overhead
Gave me a lighter tread."[11]

The final version raises a great arch of sky with doubly suspended syntax and sets it all down with unearthly lightness:

I have looked upon those brilliant creatures.
And now my heart is sore.
All's changed since I, hearing at twilight,
The first time on this shore,
The bell-beat of their wings above my head,
Trod with a lighter tread.

There are a several ways Yeats could have straightened the syntax of the middle of this stanza, and all of them would have weakened it. Like a sheet of paper, the sentence will not stand up on its own until it is folded.

"Trod with a lighter tread" is one of the poem's best discoveries, rising in mood with the rising of its sound—from the heavy "trod" to the lighter and higher "lighter tread." We forget for a moment that the exhilaration is in the deep past. "Stepped with a softer step" would not have been close. But not only sound has been managed here—the line would not have worked half as well in any position but the last, nor would it have been half as effective had Yeats's syntactical contortions not postponed it so intricately.

Yeats, indeed, seems to cultivate small tics in his narrative sequence, commonly enfolding causes in a clause after an effect has been partially announced:

(CP 137)   I bade, *because* the wick and oil are spent
And frozen are the channels of the blood,
My discontented heart to draw content.

(CP 133)   I had thought, *seeing* how bitter is that wind
That shakes the shutter, to have brought to mind

These sentences start, drop slightly backwards (not only in time but in the mouth—parenthetical remarks are usually half-swallowed) then surge forward. Events are not a flow but almost an architecture. When Yeats says that Wordsworth, with stronger syntax,

could have "carried" more elaborate English, he is explicitly aware
that a syntax in tension supports masses of language (and perhaps
lengths of attention) that a more elegiac syntax cannot.

A similar achievement of tension through the "folding" of
structure can be seen in Yeats's tinkerings with the overall shape of
"The Wild Swans at Coole." In the first published version, what is
now the final stanza was placed third. The poem consequently
ended with "Passion or conquest, wander where they will / Attend
upon them still." Yeats later found that this made its development
too linear, the conclusion too obviously conclusive. The poem was
narrowed to a lament for lost sexual power. He chose instead to
finish with one of those questions, strangely both reticent and (by a
kind of indirection) assertive that were to become habitual in his
later poetry. The poem ends, as it were, suspended in the air, but
without evasion:

> Among what rushes will they build,
> By what lake's edge or pool
> Delight men's eyes when I awake some day
> To find they have flown away?

The lesson to be learned from Yeats's drafts and outlines—
some surprisingly prosaic and explicit—is a lesson about syntax in
the broad Yeatsian sense. The early drafts quoted above—and
indeed many of his much later drafts—are nearly worthless as
poems, despite the fact they contain all of the images and ideas, and
almost all of the language, of the final versions. For Yeats, a draft is
merely a fence around a cloud—it helps him refind the area of the
brain in which the poem is condensing. More important, finally,
than the individual images and ideas is the way he connects them,
the sequence and tension. Before he finds the one best path through
his mood, the one best structure to transmit its weight, there may
be the poetic, but there is no poem. For Yeats, a poem is more than
something that means, or is, or expresses, or embodies—it must be
something that *works*.

The distancing and strengthening power of syntax is perhaps clarified by Yeats's worries about the fourth section of "Vacillation":

My fiftieth year had come and gone,
I sat, a solitary man,
In a crowded London shop,
An open book and empty cup
On the marble table-top.

(CP 246)

While on the shop and street I gazed
My body of a sudden blazed;
And twenty minutes more or less
It seemed, so great my happiness,
That I was blessèd and could bless.

Yeats had reservations about this paean to caffeine rush and the good moment. He said to James Stephens, who had admired it, "I love that table top poem myself, but I don't think it has the strangeness, the syntax, that makes a great poem" (*I&R* 2:299). Interesting, first of all, is the equation of *syntax* and *strangeness*. Yeats means by "syntax" *his* syntax, and by that, of course, *contorted* syntax. The twisting of syntax, to Yeats, solidifies, alienates, makes strange.

One can guess the point of Yeats's diagnosis without giving up on this attractive poem. Like the earlier version of "The Wild Swans at Coole," it may stick a little too closely to a narrative-descriptive sequence with a prominent "I." Details insufficiently supported by syntax become a trailing list: "An open book and empty cup / On the marble table-top" suddenly opens a window on the merely seen. The second stanza, despite attempts to restrain it with insertions ("more or less," "so great my happiness"), happens (emotionally) rather quickly. Yeats probably feared that the ending, stunning in itself, was unearned. If it is, that is probably attributable more to the poem's shortness than to any inadequacy in its syntax. But Yeats might have replied that syntax is what gives a poem the delay and the weight to make it feel—however long it is—long enough. This dissatisfaction may account for his decision to make the poem part of a sequence where it can tilt toward its successor:

(CP 246)

Things said or done long years ago,
Or things I did not do or say
But thought that I might say or do,

Weigh me down, and not a day
But something is recalled,
My conscience or my vanity appalled.

This clearly belongs near the table-top episode, yet Yeats knows they could never form one piece. How could any poem proceed after "That I was blessed and could bless"? On the other hand, using the table-top poem to reverse the embarrassment here would inevitably seem strained and artificial, and would aggravate any doubts about its "earnedness." The conclusion of "A Dialogue of Self and Soul," however, *does* speak these two poems simultaneously. It convinces partly because it is a longer poem (but one could imagine a very fine poet failing to pull off such a dramatic conclusion despite the length), perhaps because it is wiser (but wisdom is seldom enough), and perhaps because of its estranging syntax:

My Self. A living man is blind and drinks his drop.
What matter if the ditches are impure?
What matter if I live it all once more?
Endure that toil of growing up;
The ignominy of boyhood; the distress
Of boyhood changing into man;
The unfinished man and his pain
Brought face to face with his own clumsiness;

(CP 231–32)

The finished man among his enemies?—
How in the name of Heaven can he escape
That defiling and disfigured shape
The mirror of malicious eyes
Casts upon his eyes until at last
He thinks that shape must be his shape?
And what's the good of an escape
If honour find him in the wintry blast?

This is Yeats at his most wide-ranging and fiercely rhetorical, yet it manages to avoid the false momentum or glossiness he felt in the climax of "Vacillation." "Coincidence of period and stanza" is Yeats's standard. John Holloway explicates: "The thought seems to have no organisation and contour until the very instant of its completion."[12] In such miracles as "In Memory of Major Robert Gregory," the Yeatsian stanza *can* be one sweeping period, but usually, as in the stanzas above, Yeats's drive toward completion is harnessed to bulkier and more miscellaneous materials. One has the sense, at stanza's end, not of inevitable but of *achieved* conclusion.

First of all, the effects of syntax cannot be dissociated from sound. Here, the Yeatsian rhythmic reticence and a more than Rossettian weight of polysyllabic abstraction are virtually hauled along by metrical and syntactic expectations, and we read the tautness of the cables as passionate concentration. Secondly, any potential periodic "sweep" has to work through the expansions and contractions of the stanza form, which constricts in lines 2–3 to a couplet, and in 6–7 not only to a couplet but to four beats.

Yeats begins, as often, by making it hard for himself. Questions are frequent in his later poems, where they function as reticence in comparison to more insupportable direct statements— "boyhood is ignominious," "ditches are impure," "I shall live it all"—they shove to the side. The question mark transforms these phrases into assumptions rather than assertions, and Yeats in effect excuses himself from responsibility. With "What matter" he seems to deny them importance even as he dwells on them, making a typically strong statement without requiring strong agreement. Syntactically, though, the isolated questions are severe qualifications of periodicity—they must be lifted into the larger flow as the poem continues through an enumeration of toils and distresses that seems to struggle more than ordinarily to get over its line breaks.

And then the syntax breaks, as it often does in Yeats, with great effect but inconspicuously. Reading the sequence of "toil of growing up," "ignominy of boyhood," "distress / Of boyhood changing into man," we are taught certain expectations, and the next item in the list "The unfinished man and his pain" does not meet them ("the pain of the unfinished man" would). This phrase, as a result, drops out of syntax and stands forth naked—"unfinished," perhaps, but it is not necessary to go that far. The stanza *is* unfinished, and goes further, overflowing or rather muscling into its successor to finish with "The finished man among his enemies?" The thrust through the stanza boundary is unusual in Yets but the consequent sense of conclusion achieved rather than encountered, earned rather than ordained, is not.

The bravura of the poem's conclusion also depends on silent rhythmical and syntactical restraints, and their silent breaking:

> I am content to live it all again
> And yet again, if it be life to pitch
> Into the frog-spawn of a blind man's ditch,
> A blind man battering blind men;
> Or into that most fecund ditch of all,
> The folly that man does
> Or must suffer, if he woos
> A proud woman not kindred of his soul.

(CP 232)

> I am content to follow to its source
> Every event in action or in thought;
> Measure the lot; forgive myself the lot!
> When such as I cast out remorse
> So great a sweetness flows into the breast
> We must laugh and we must sing,
> We are blest by everything,
> Everything we look upon is blest.

In movement, the concluding four stanzas of the poem are weighty, even ponderous, but the second and third to last lines disconnect expectations and shatter into song. Nearly battering pentameter springs into headless, dipodic tetrameter. It is a different language—a child's or a prophet's lightness—certainly a different speaker. It can hardly be Yeats that is claiming all this: "We must laugh and we must sing, / We are blest by everything."

Then, too, many of the Yeats's strongest emotions are placed in a kind of conditional context that ultimately frees them. Here, even the final ecstasy is multiply insulated. First, it is conditional, occurring only "when" (Yeats knew it was seldom enough) he banished remorse. Second, it is limited to "such as I" (presumably in opposition to the "worst" in whom remorselessness and "passionate intensity" are normal). Finally, the switch to "we" in the last lines is strategic. It may be that self and soul are finally speaking together, but that division is not immediately on the reader's mind this late in the poem. "We," though it might in other contexts be regarded as a presumption, is certainly less baldly egotistical than the alternative:

> *I* must laugh and *I* must sing,
> *I* am blest by everything,
> Everything *I* look upon is blest.

This is so obviously the end the poem is working toward that the present conclusion must be read as specifically avoiding it. What one sees here is Yeats refusing to claim more than his reader is likely to grant him. The power of the conclusion is so obvious that the obliqueness on which it partly depends can easily be overlooked.

There is another typically restrained disconnection in Yeats's final sidestep into ecstasy:

> When such as I cast our remorse
> So great a sweetness flows into the breast
> We must laugh and we must sing,
> We are blest by everything,
> Everything we look upon is blest.

By omitting *that* from "So great a sweetness flows into the breast / That we must laugh and we must sing," Yeats makes "We must laugh and we must sing" stand clear of the sentence's flow, nearly causeless. It becomes almost an outcry, an outcry that gains depth and conviction from straining against, but not quite breaking, syntax. The technique can be clarified by reference to a similar moment in "Sailing to Byzantium":

(CP 191)
> An aged man is but a paltry thing,
> A tattered coat upon a stick, unless
> Soul clap its hands and sing, and louder sing
> For every tatter in its mortal dress.

The literal sense is clear. An aged man is but a paltry thing unless *his* soul claps its hands and sings. But Yeats shifts the line one degree toward impersonality. "An aged man is but a paltry thing unless *the* soul claps its hands," we half-read. But the *the* is only understood, and the isolation of the subjunctive verb from "unless" by the steep break makes the third line seem almost to be spoken by an intruding voice that *commands* the soul to sing. That is, what Yeats has written is halfway to the very different line "Soul, clap your hands and sing and louder sing!" but without any of its naive enthusiasm. The effect, however subliminal, remains. Yeats has invoked us without head-on confrontation. As in "A Dialogue of Self and Soul," the conditional logic does not force us to agree in ecstasy, but as we read, the Yeatsian "I," by a typical indirection, becomes ours.

Another important feature of these stanzas is that they are, like most of Yeats, massively but inconspicuously repetitious. This may seems surprising at first, since one associates heavy repetition with poets who, like Swinburne, aspire to the condition of music. In the final four stanzas of "A Dialogue of Self and Soul," the number of words and phrases involved in full or partial repetition is nearly daunting:

1. living man, blind, what matter, ditches, what matter, live it all, boyhood, boyhood, man, unfinished man, face, face

2. finished man, escape, shape, eyes, casts, eyes, shape, shape, escape

3. I am content, live it all, again, again, life, blind man's, ditch, blind man, blind men, ditch, man

4. I am content, every, lot, lot, cast, we must, we must, blest, everything, everything, blest

Every page of the *Collected Poems* is littered with repetitions that a more finicky writer might consider artless. Auden once said that nineteenth-century poets were rhythmically expert but inexact in diction, whereas their twentieth-century counterparts were rhythmically clumsy but scrupulous in diction.[13] Auden needs little instruction in rhythm, but he sometimes knew too much about diction. A poet of his, or a later, generation, might have reduced the Yeatsian repetition in the service of greater precision and particularity. Yeats would have considered such twiddling neurasthenic. He knew the value of the broad stroke and an apparent "nonchalance of hand" (*CP* 158). These Yeatsian repetitions result not in the early poetry's hypnotic chant, but in rhetorical force. In the rhythmically more reticent and syntactically more shapely environment of the later poems, a repeated word does not blend and blur with its precursor. Rather it seems to reach back across the intervening words to push off from it. Tennysonian and early Yeatsian repetitions are dimming. The repetition of later Yeats has a weighty, accumulating force that helps "earn" each small advance in feeling. Yeats finds in the living tensions of syntax a more effective intensity and drama than the mere shattering of syntax can provide. Here, as in so many ways, his passion is in his restraint.

XI

—◆◇◆—

Dancer and Dance:
One Conclusion

Labour is blossoming or dancing where
The body is not bruised to pleasure soul.
                                        Among School Children

YEATS OFTEN recognized qualities he needed to assimilate in friends and predecessors before he could quite rouse them in himself. At least in autobiographical retrospect, he lived his life as though it were a work of art, and his acquaintances take on the shapes he most needed to confront. They become ways of living, possible poetries, evolutionary hurdles. He often saw them as Tennysonian figures of flow—as dancers, or indeed as their dance.

For the young Yeats, for Tennyson at his most Tennysonian, the greatest beauty was the characterless dimness into which the whole soul could pour effortlessly and without resistance: "And when we love, if it be in the excitement of youth, do we not also, that the flood may find no stone to convulse, no wall to narrow it, exclude character or the signs of it by choosing that beauty which seems unearthly because the individual woman is lost amid the labyrinth of its lines" (*E&I* 243–44). Limitlessness is itself a limitation: vague beauty requires, even creates, vague beholders. Tennyson's attempts to transcend this dimness of "immortal anonymity" led him to imagine figures similar to what Yeats eventually made of Maud Gonne. His Princess Ida, for example, begins in coldness and independence, but he cannot help feeling her resistance as inhuman, and she dissolves in his longing gaze, as does the heroine of *Maud,* whose "cold and clear-cut face" eventually blurs in tenderness. Less uncomfortable with the inhuman, or simply more comprehensive in his definition of the human, Yeats also constructs a goddess and attempts to believe in her, though she is more like Swinburne's ladies of pain—Dolores, Atalanta, and the rest—than anything Tennyson could allow to exist. When he reexplains Maud Gonne with decades of hindsight, Yeats tries to make us see the protracted agony of his courtship as perversely congruent with his artistic and personal needs, as the quest for his antiself. Love is no longer a dimness but an energizing opposite: "When a man loves a girl it should be because her face and character offer what he lacks; the more profound his nature the more should he realise his lack and the greater be the difference" (*Expl.* 430).

In fact, something like this had been on his mind nearly from the beginning of his career. Even pre-Maud, Yeats's desire for an impenetrable other not visible amid his own tremulousness had crystallized as the longing for a heroine he could not see in the literature of his century. The notion is not any more—or less— definite than his concurrent notions of poets and kings, but its tendency is clear: "No one will deny excellence to the Idylls of the King; no one will say that Lord Tennyson's Girton girls do not look well in those old costumes of dead chivalry. . . . Yet here is that which the Idylls do not at any time contain, beauty at once feminine and heroic" (*UP* 1:95). Nor, he says in a letter to the poet Katharine Tynan, are the poets of the next generation any more successful: "Do you not think there is considerable resemblance between the heroines of all the neo-romantic London poets; namely, Swin- burne, Morris, Rossetti and their satellites? For one thing, they are essentially men's heroines, with no separate life of their own; in this different from Browning's. Tennyson's are, I believe, less heroic than the others and less passionate and splendid" (*LKT* 35).

But life, in 1888, seemed to supply the goddess—and the "dance"—that Victorian poetry could not: "I was twenty-three years old when the troubling of my life began. . . . I had never thought to see in a living woman so great beauty. It belonged to famous pictures, to poetry, to some legendary past. A complexion like the blossom of apples . . . and a stature so great that she seemed of a divine race. Her movements were worthy of her form, and I understood at last why the poet of antiquity, where we would but speak of face and form, sings, loving some lady, that she paces like a goddess" (*WBY Mem.* 40). Even goddesses have been known to love men. Part of Yeats, however, needs to see Maud Gonne as so unlike him that she could not possibly return his passion—"Her beauty as I saw it in those days seemed incompatible with private, intimate life" (*WBY Mem.* 41). She served as the utterly public, impersonal, and self-possessed existence toward which Yeats could at this point only vaguely strive, but which, for her, he feigned: "It was natural to commend myself by claiming a very public talent" (*WBY Mem.* 41). Yeats's reformation of poetry would also be a reformation of desire, and Maud Gonne, despite his disavowals of Swinburne, is his Atalanta, "Free, without pity, withheld from woe, / Ignorant."

In contrast, the first draft of the *Autobiography* sees "Diana Vernon" (a pseudonym for Olivia Shakspear), his lover for a year in the nineties and a lifelong friend, as a tamer and less powerful beauty. She has "the nobility of defeated things." Because she is more humanly accessible to him, he cannot imagine her as completely exterior, and she comes in for some of the burden of his self-disgust. Softer and quieter than Maud Gonne, "dark and still," she is more like him, almost sisterly: "I noticed that she was like the mild heroines of my plays. She seemed a part of myself" (*WBY Mem.* 85, 86). Her otherness was insufficient to support his passion, which is a self-denying drive toward his opposite: "It will always be a grief to me that I could not give the love that was her beauty's right, but she was too near my soul, too salutary and wholesome to my inmost being" (*WBY Mem.* 88). Like Swinburne, he needs a love that is penance; the Lady of Pain is another of his furious judges.

Yeats wants us to see his passion for the titanic image of Maud as a rehearsal for the quest he was later to call antithetical emotion. If it was painful and wasteful, he was ready to view the pain and waste in the highest terms, as in "Ego Dominus Tuus." Here, "Hic" has equated Dante's greatness with successful self-expression. He "so utterly found himself" that the image of his "hollow face" has burned itself into the mind's eye. But "Ille" (Pound, amused at the setup, called him "Willie") suggests that what has come down to us of Dante is instead his *antiself*:

                    is that spectral image
         The man that Lapo and that Guido knew?
         I think he fashioned from his opposite
         An image that might have been a stony face
         Staring upon a Bedouin's horse-hair roof
         From doored and windowed cliff, or half-upturned
(*CP* 158)   Among the coarse grass and the camel dung.
         He set his chisel to the hardest stone.
         Being mocked by Guido for his lecherous life,
         Derided and deriding, driven out
         To climb that stair and eat that bitter bread,
         He found the unpersuadable justice, he found
         The most exalted lady loved by a man.

This is Yeats's autobiography of Dante. Preceded in that paradoxical genre by Dante Gabriel Rossetti's "Dante at Verona," whose "steep stairs and bitter bread" (*PR* 2) it echoes, Yeats continues it in *A Vision,* placing Dante with himself and Shelley in Phase 17, the "antithetical man." Interestingly, Yeats could not decide whether *Rossetti* was Keats and Tennyson (Phase 14, nearing "pure beauty," pure Paterian music) or a shadow Yeats (Phase 17—restraining the music, but not so vehemently or abstractly as Blake or Maud Gonne, two inhabitants of Phase 16).[1] To Shelley, he denied the "vision of evil," but his Dante is Browning's "Dante, who loved well because he hated," a personality nearing comprehensiveness or "unity of being."

The passage from "Ego Dominus Tuus" translates fairly easily into the terms of this discussion. Ille insists on what this poem and the whole of "Per Amica Silentia Lunae" say repeatedly—that "the work is the man's flight from his entire horoscope" (*Myth.* 328). Dante is not an elegist, like Tennyson, but an antithetical lover, like Yeats: "I am no Dante scholar and I but read him in Shadwell or in Dante Rossetti, but I am always persuaded that he celebrated the most pure lady poet ever sung and the Divine Justice, not merely because death took that lady and Florence banished her singer, but because he had to struggle in his own heart with his unjust anger and lust" (*Myth.* 329–30). For *Dante,* read "Yeats"; for *Beatrice,*

"Maud Gonne"; for *unpersuadable justice,* read "a love so fixed on its opposite that its very existence is a kind of self-accusation." Though "unjust anger and lust" seem overdramatic for Yeats's somewhat less vivid life, he was not above exploiting his self-divisions—"You think it horrible that lust and rage / Should dance attention on my old age." Our emotions always seem large enough to us, and it is convention, or false modesty, or even a kind of hopelessness that makes us describe them as small. Yeats, at any rate, seems to be thinking again about the uncertainty of borders caused by his inability to balance dim, erotic sympathy and dignified anger. Through Dante, he imagines his life as a continuous self-betrayal that his chameleon self can redeem only by seeking its opposite: Beatrice / Maud, utter integrity, certainty, heroic dignity.

As Yeats moved into middle age he found that both life and poetry required new heroines, for he had begun to see that though Maud Gonne might have been chosen for him by the deep past or intended for him in eternity, she was not to be his in the only life he could live:

> And I that have not your faith, how shall I know
> That in the blinding light beyond the grave
> We'll find so good a thing as that we have lost?
> The hourly kindness, the day's common speech,
> The habitual content of each with each
> When neither soul nor body has been crossed.

(CP 90)

As he himself crystallized and his view of Maud Gonne sharpened and narrowed, he began, justly or not, to think of the self-destructiveness of his passion as a self-destructiveness inherent in *her* character. How could he explain the hopelessness of his longing but by imagining in her an even more hopeless longing?

> Her soul had such desire
> For what proud death may bring
> That it could not endure
> The common good of life.

(CP 123)

It is only apparently ironic that the need for the "*common* good of life" should have been met by an image of the aristocracy, for "common" implies not so much a class of subject matter or society as a way of moving through time and living within life. In the nineties, Yeats had met Lady Augusta Gregory. He found in her not only a patron and co-worker but a friend who, even if he in some ways feared her, was more humanly useful to him than Maud Gonne. In 1897, exhausted, despondent over the course of his affair with Maud, he accepted an invitation to stay at Coole, Lady Gregory's estate: "I found at last what I had been seeking always, a life of order and of labour, where all outward things were the image of an inward life. . . . I think that I was made not for a master but for a servant, and that it has been my unhappiness to see the analytic faculty dissolve all those things that invite our service, and so it is that all images of service are dear to me" (*WBY Mem.* 101–2).

As Yeats gradually takes root in himself order and labour become touchstones, and he discovers in himself "an intense desire for a life of routine" (*WBY Mem.* 171). The aristocracy was many things for Yeats—an Other, a crucial elite, an image to serve, and a model of behavior—"the old nonchalance of hand" in contrast to dim (Victorian, bourgeois) sensitivity. But it is also a matter of houses, family, continuity, comfort. It supplies him with an image of an enlarged domesticity. By 1909, perhaps unwilling to attribute a desire for basic psychic comfort to encroaching middle age, he is avowing deep connections between artists and aristocrats: "Is not all charm inherited?—whether of the intellect, of the manners, or of character, or of literature? A great lady is as simple as a good poet. Both possess nothing that is not ancient and their own" (*WBY Mem.* 140).

The intricacies of Yeats's vision of the aristocratic life have been finely and exhaustively treated by Daniel Harris[2]—here a brief alignment of Yeats's perception of aristocracy with the strengths he had come to covet for his poetry will suffice. Besides the not inconsiderable comforts of routine, Yeats saw in the tradition-founded life of the aristocrat an antidote for uncertainty, awkwardness, embarrassment. Daily life was transformed into an art. "Aristocracies have made beautiful manners, because their place in the world puts them above the fear of life" (*E&I* 251). The high artifice of aristocratic life becomes for Yeats the highest naturalness, a formal behavior the best vehicle for instinct. "In life courtesy and self-possession, and in the arts style, are the sensible impressions of the free mind, for both arise out of a deliberate shaping of all things, and from never being swept away, whatever the emotion, into confusion or dullness" (*E&I* 253). The firm sense of borders, the successful manner, the resultant "nonchalance of hand," are equivalent to artistic poise, to style. Courtesy and self-possession, the shaping forces of behavior, are analogous to his necessary poetic reticence. And as difficultly balanced. It is well to keep that difficulty in mind, as Yeats surely did, when reading the ecstatic resolutions of such poems as "A Dialogue of Self and Soul," "Among School Children," and "A Prayer for My Daughter." Though uttered with prophetic certainty, they urge courses Yeats knew ran counter to some of his deepest impulses. His poetry, any poetry, is as much compensation and remedy as self-depiction, and even his recommendations of self-acceptance are full of self-denials, for he seems to believe that happiness is not, for him at any rate, natural. It must be made possible—by making the self for which it is possible.

Not surprisingly, then, the deepest division in the later Yeats is between the desire, on one hand, to live within life and make a whole of its exploding fragments, and, on the other, his fiercer transcendences and more fiery objectifications. In practice, the poles are not quite so clear, and in the arrangement of his volumes, Yeats likes to pair near-opposites. "The Second Coming" is answered by "Prayer for My Daughter", and "Sailing to Byzantium" is reconsidered by "The Tower." In each of these pairs the second and more affirmative poem seems richer. Life demands neither acceptance nor rejection, but Yeats seems less likely to posture (and more likely to vacillate) when he at least considers the possibility of living within it. "A Prayer for My Daughter" confronts the noble heroine with the aristocrat in what amounts to an exorcism of Maud Gonne:

(CP 186)

> In courtesy I'd have her chiefly learned;
> Hearts are not had as a gift but hearts are earned
> By those that are not entirely beautiful;
> Yet many, that have played the fool

For beauty's very self, has charm made wise,
And many a poor man that has roved,
Loved and thought himself beloved,
From a glad kindness cannot take his eyes.

The immense relief of self-acceptance makes this surely one of Yeats's most poignant stanzas, but "courtesy" perhaps needs amplification. It is, first of all, contrasted with "murderous innocence," which, though directly attached to the sea refers indirectly to the weather, the European war, and implicitly (and almost explicitly, through her likeness to "that great Queen that rose out of the spray") to Maud Gonne. Maud has the "ignorance" of Swinburne's ladies of pain. Far from Yeats, almost (so it once seemed to him) "incompatible with private, intimate life," she is mythologized as innocent partly because she is, to him, so impenetrable as to seem nearly uncaused, and partly because she is, unlike the aristocrat, unshaped by ceremony and courtesy, unaccommodated to the needs of others or to this life.

On the other hand, as Yeats once said, "The highest life unites, as in one fire, the greatest passion and the greatest courtesy" (*Expl.* 162). Daniel Harris comments, "Courtesy was the shaping restraint of energy which wrought passion to its uttermost intensity."[3] The daughter's courtesy is, therefore, the father's labor or reticence— the restraint that makes all expression possible. In this poem, at least, Yeats can believe it is the principle of both happiness and art. "Self-delighting" is his word for it. It is also Pater's word, and that it occurs in the essay on Coleridge is perhaps not coincidental, given this poem's clear debts to "Frost at Midnight": "The work of art is likened to a living organism. That expresses truly the sense of a self-delighting, independent life which the finished work of art gives us: it hardly figures the process by which such work was produced."[4] Both Pater's agreement and his reservation are relevant to Yeats's poem, which strives for an end that denies its own origin in struggle, for a grace that would have no need of further words. If his daughter becomes more art than artist, that is in a large sense what Yeats often wanted for himself. The poem's "radical innocence" is, as Yeats says elsewhere, "an innocence that is no longer a mere accident of nature, but the human intellect's crowning achievement" (*A* 251–52). Yeats would be the last to underestimate the role of anger and hatred in forming the individual soul, and he, with his uncertain borders, would probably be the last to achieve to his own satisfaction the sureness of balance here described so yearningly and so well. His prayer for his daughter is a prayer for himself, but it must be read against its impossibility.

In "Some dance like shadows on the mountains" (*CP* 361), from *The Wandering of Oisin,* the dancers are what a flickering candle throws against a wall, another of Yeats's shifting dimnesses. Their fluidity is an image for the movement the early poems wish to be drawn into. Such a dance may be beautiful—more likely fascinating and forgetful—but it cannot have grace, which supposes gravity and mass, difficulties to be not quite effortlessly overcome and "shaping restraints of energy." The play of shadows is a dance wholly inside the mind—a dance, perhaps, without a dancer. On the other hand, there are plenty of scarecrows and stiltmen in Yeats—they are will and fate, mind and body, mismatched. For Yeats, embarrassing clumsiness, naked abstraction, killing difficulty, and hopeless love are dancers with no dance.

The dancer of "Among School Children" represents a life and a flow that is between these two extremes. She is labor with grace, and also, like the daughter of "Prayer for My Daughter" and the Self of "A Dialogue of Self and Soul," an image for the part of the Yeats that strives to claim his past and live within life. The poem is in many ways a Yeatsian "Tintern Abbey"—like it, arising in the poet's alienation from life's flow—but it responds differently and moves through an utterly different element, for by the time of "Among School Children" Yeats's incorporation of labor and weight into the momentum of the line is complete. Grace replaces the effortlessness of the early poems. The Wordsworth that Yeats invokes in his criticism is a paragraphic, blank verse poet. Yeats himself was seldom comfortable in this form outside of the plays— or too comfortable. George Moore reports him as saying he "could write blank verse almost as easily as prose, and therefore feared it; some obstacle, some dam was necessary."[5] One might say, there-

fore, that the first and largest restraint of "Among School Children"
is that it is not in blank verse.

Yeats's new movement is also evident on the slightly larger
scale of the poem's odelike progression. The streaming, pooling,
and trailing of Wordsworth's blank verse paragraph is the murmur
of memory, a fluidity that dissolves boundaries and heals breaches.
Yeats dams this fluidity by organizing his poems in more abrupt
strophes and antistrophes, substituting for Wordsworth's prolonged moments and entranced gaze ("we are laid asleep / In body")
a series of disconnections, breathtaking turns. This fondness for
isolating thoughts, even setting them against each other, is perhaps
the source of Yeats's interest in dialogue poems and his increasing
tendency to number his stanzas or write sequences. It is certainly a
different sense of what is interesting in human consciousness, what
the edges of thoughts are like. More than that, Yeats's stanzas are
not merely rhymed paragraphs ended after a preordained number
of lines. They are not streamlike—they do not trail off or peter out.
They seem to *make* their endings—they achieve a difficult, constel-
lated balance. The opening stanza of "Among School Children" is,
however much punctuation strives to say otherwise, several sentences and several tones pressing against each other:

> I walk through the long schoolroom questioning;
> A kind old nun in a white hood replies;
> The children learn to cipher and to sing,
> To study reading-books and history,
> To cut and sew, be neat in everything
> In the best modern way—the children's eyes
> In momentary wonder stare upon
> A sixty-year-old smiling public man.

(CP 212–3)

Yeats begins, as often, with the raveled edges, making it hard
for himself. The first two lines scuff along casually—is this going to
be a poem, or notes? The next two mime the sing-song of the nun's
reply and continue with primitive advertising lingo: "In the best
modern way." The second half of that line—"the children's eyes"—
uses a word the nun has used. It could be hers, but it turns out to be

Yeats's. "Momentary," a soft, polysyllabic explosion, suddenly brings us into the poem. The glance of the children may be brief, but Yeats's own wonder is not. He is left with himself, dawdling through the resigned falling rhythm of "a sixty-year-old smiling public man." "Me only cruel immortality / Consumes," he might have said.

It is easy, given the myriad concerns and difficulties of "Among School Children," to forget that it is, most simply, a poem about the past—or, like most poems about the past, a poem about the threat of pastlessness. Here "Tintern Abbey" and "Tithonus" are again more than casually relevant. All three poets confront a past suddenly crystallized, suddenly separate and unreachable. All feel their lives broken in half and set against the stream of time, and all image their alienation as a problem of flow—that is, a physical and existential *awkwardness.* Wordsworth contrasts his uncomfortable exposure with the graceful unconsciousness of boyhood "when like a roe" he "bounded o'er the mountains" or the intensity of his adolescence when passion carried him like a wind, and Tennyson's "Me only" and his "cold my wrinkled feet / Upon thy glimmering thresholds" are eloquent. Yeats is less likely than Wordsworth or Tennyson to image self-alienation as distance from a landscape. Largely indifferent to visual imagery, and seeing the landscape as another form of the "regional," or worse, pictorial, temptations of his youth, Yeats regarded love of nature as a peculiarly English sentimentality— "Why can't you English poets keep flowers out of your poetry," he once groused at Lady Dorothy Wellesley (*LDW* 190).

Instead Yeats settles on the image of the "old scarecrow," the "tattered coat upon a stick" of "Sailing to Byzantium," to express the painful and clumsy mismatch of interior and exterior—in this case the soul's struggle with a body and a life that no longer fit it like a glove. "Decrepit age that has been tied to me / As to a dog's tail." The awkwardness of the scarecrow images the isolation of the momentary self from the flow of its own life and the inability to forge a continuous self from the fragments of past and present. The dancer sits out the dance: "Better to smile on all that smile, and show / There is a comfortable kind of old scarecrow."

But that is to skip some stanzas. Hung between these two sharp present moments like a subordinate clause, and framed by them, is what would have been the Tennysonian dissolve:

2

I dream of a Ledaean body, bent
Above a sinking fire, a tale that she
Told of a harsh reproof or trivial event
That changed some childish day to tragedy—
Told, and it seemed that our two natures blent
Into a sphere from youthful sympathy,
Or else, to alter Plato's parable,
Into the yolk and white of the one shell.

(CP 213)

3

And thinking of that fit of grief or rage
I look upon one child or t'other there
And wonder if she stood so at that age—
For even daughters of the swan can share
Something of every paddler's heritage—
And had that colour upon cheek or hair,
And thereupon my heart is driven wild:
She stands before me as a living child.

Here is, almost, the Tennysonian twilight, the sinking fire of "When You Are Old," the mask of age no longer a mask. But "I dream" in this decade of Yeat's career is not quite a swoon but almost one of those Yeatsian summonses John Holloway identifies:

(CP 230)   I summon to the ancient winding stair

(CP 159)   I call to the mysterious one

            I . . . send imagination forth
(CP 193)[6]   Under the day's declining beam, and call
            Images and memories

The feelings, at any rate, do not fade much. All that Yeatsian rhythmic restraint is here to keep dimness an idea rather than an environment. The lines, even when they run over, do not trail or

fade, but instead stop and surge: "I dream of a Ledaean body, bent /
Above a sinking fire." And there are restraints in the language.
"Trivial event" puts the familiar Yeatsian distance on an old emotion, as does, more subtly, "some childish day." The Wordsworthian *some* is always slightly mysterious in its reference:

> With *some* uncertain notice, as might seem
> Of vagrant dwellers in the houseless woods,
> Or of *some* Hermit's cave, where by his fire
> The Hermit sits alone.

But Yeats's is laconic—"some childish day." So is his ubiquitous
that—"And had that colour upon cheek or hair" (this line, dropped
unexpectedly in mid-stanza, is a fine example of *achieved* rather than
inevitable syntactical closure). "That" provides the gesture of specificity and the authority of summoning, without the burden of
detail. Another control is imposed by "Ledaean." Heard even by
initiated Yeatsians as technical, this is one of those "wrong words"
that Yeats uses for astringent strangeness, for it is estrangement as
much as symbolism, nonmeaning as much as meaning, that Yeats
seeks from his philosophical systems. To be effective, this kind of
private language has to remain at least partly unfamiliar even to its
creator.

   Nor is the syntax elegiac. The Yeats poem of this period is
structured not with the fading *and* but with his more relational
that—three of them here. The first two, at least, are a kind of
controlled recession. The second clause opens a window within the
window of the first:

> a tale *that* she
> Told of a harsh reproof or trivial event
> *That* changed some childish day to tragedy—
> Told, and it seemed *that* our two natures blent

And passes, lets go. *That* holds, but veers. Finally, the image of
merger is not quite a merger.

> Into a sphere from youthful sympathy,
> Or else, to alter Plato's parable,
> Into the yolk and white of the one shell.

Sympathy, the limit and limitlessness of the early poems, is qualified as "youthful"—as in the revisions of those poems it is almost a criticized feature of the style. That the image is vaguely metaphysical and Metaphysical also serves to fix our distance from the poem. First of all, a Yeatsian "idea"—though only a very Wildean critic would want to subordinate the content of the poems utterly to their style—is at least partly a means to a tone (Yeats was himself not un-Wildean). Here, the very *sense* of thinking qualifies with irony or astringency the instinctive response of the vestigially Victorian limbic system to any image of blending. And "the yolk and white of the one shell" is hardly so direct a fade-out as Tennyson's "Be lost in me." Like Donne's comparison of lovers to stiff twin compasses, it seems to arrive with relatively few previous associations—we do not refer it to similar images. It means only what the poet makes it mean as we watch, and no poet will ever be able to use it again without seeming to quote. In this sense it is a nonparticipatory, a nonregional image, relying, no matter how many times it is read, not on the reader's prior knowledge but on the author's control.

Wordsworth's poem moves on from its self-alienation by remembering remembering. So does Yeats's. Maud's recollection of childhood tragedy inspires him with all the ambiguously possessive tenderness we feel seeing photographs of lovers taken before we knew them. It is now not only his own past but hers that he wishes to repossess: "And thereupon my heart is driven wild: / She stands before me as a living child."

By odd exchanges, the past has almost literally become desire. At least to give up one, in this poem, is to give up the other. To deny the body of life—personal history—is to deny the physical body, to pull dancer from dance. Many of the poem's exemplary figures have made this unacceptable choice. Maud is "hollow of cheek" because she is drained by what Yeats saw as her abstract fury ("withered old and skeleton-gaunt, / An image of such politics" [*CP* 229]). In the stanzas on nuns and mothers, he examines the heart's abstractions, finding them, regretfully, heartbreaking idealizations, "self-born mockers of man's enterprise." Both systems and philosophers are "Old clothes upon old sticks to scare a bird," first because of the inadequacy of their skeletal schemata to the whole of life, and secondly because they have made the old man's choice Yeats refuses to make. "Little more than intellectual abstractions themselves," Pater calls them, though specifically excepting Plato,[7] they exalt only what they know will persist through old age—the mind over the body, the form over the body of life. They deny what they fear is already lost, but Yeats in this poem is not having anything to do with their, or his own, compensations. He is bent, instead on heroic antielegy, an impossible denial of loss.

The last stanza, with its extraordinary balances, is one of those Yeatsian conclusions whose vast reservations are often overlooked amid its ecstasy. It attempts to solve almost by decree the problems of flow that have been the subject of this essay:

> Labour is blossoming or dancing where
> The body is not bruised to pleasure soul,
> Nor beauty born out of its own despair,
> Nor blear-eyed wisdom out of midnight oil.
> O chestnut-tree, great-rooted blossomer,
> Are you the leaf, the blossom or the bole?
> O body swayed to music, O brightening glance,
> How can we know the dancer from the dance?

(*CP* 214)

"How can we know the dancer from the dance?" is less a question than a wish, or even an imperative. "Among School Children" is, after all, full of killing mismatches of dancer and dance—minds rattling in bodies, selves broken off from their lives. There are scarecrow poets and philosophers, Maud Gonne's beauty hollowed by the abstract wind, nuns and mothers drained with wishing beyond life. If these are not enough, the opening lines of this stanza give three more examples of dancer and dance out of kilter—each with specific relevance to Yeats himself as lover, poet, and philosopher. It is all too *easy* to say who the dancer is, and which the dance. If Yeats speaks loudly here, he is exhorting himself to that faith which is of all faiths the most difficult for him.

From a slightly different perspective—that of "Tintern Abbey"—the dance embodies the Wordsworthian, Tennysonian, and now Yeatsian, concern with the continuity of the self through time. In this context, the final question means something like "How can we distinguish the self at any one moment from its progress through the years?" Or rather, "Would that we could not," for all three poets begin with time shattered into isolated, awkward present and irretrievable past. But the very wish to become all of himself, "content to live it all again," just as the chestnut tree is all of its parts and all the seasons they symbolize, is poignant and important. The dancer, as a perfect balance of labor and grace, passion and restraint, is a Yeatsian ideal of flow. Neither dimming trance nor killing impediment, she touches time. She is embodiment embodied.

That is one conclusion—that there is no conclusion. "Man can embody truth but he cannot know it," Yeats wrote a few weeks before his death. "The abstract is not life and everywhere draws out its contradictions. You can refute Hegel but not the Saint or the Song of Sixpence" (*LY* 922). It is difficult to know whether this remark arises from deep faith or deep skepticism, and therefore whether it was a deeper faith or a deeper skepticism that made him half disbelieve it. A poet who more than anything else knew the difficulty of being with the whole heart could never wholeheartedly make the choice between dancer and philosopher, with all it implied to him. He would see on one hand that ideas were gestures of the dance, and on the other that the very unconsciousness of the dance was itself an idea. Yeats found truth in the remark that "the intellect of man is forced to choose / Perfection of the life, or of the work" (*CP* 242), and at times he thought he knew which choice he had made. All lives, it may be, fail, and all poems, but Yeats could not substitute one for the other, because there was, finally, no way of telling them apart. He had to believe what all poets must believe, that a way of moving a poem is a way of living a life.

Abbreviations

Notes

Index

Abbreviations

A	*The Autobiography of William Butler Yeats.* New York: Macmillan, Collier Books, 1965.
AT Mem.	Hallam Lord Tennyson. *Alfred Lord Tennyson: A Memoir by His Son.* 2 vols. New York: Macmillan, 1897.
CP	*The Collected Poems of W. B. Yeats.* Definitive Edition. New York: Macmillan, 1956.
E&I	W. B. Yeats. *Essays and Introductions.* New York: Macmillan, Collier Books, 1968.
Expl.	William Butler Yeats. *Explorations.* New York: Macmillan, Collier Books, 1973.
I&R	*W. B. Yeats: Interviews and Recollections.* Ed. E. H. Mikhail. 2 vols. New York: Macmillan, 1977.
Lang	*The Pre-Raphaelites and Their Circle.* Ed. Cecil Y. Lang, 2d ed., 1968. Reprint Chicago: Univ. of Chicago Press, Phoenix Books, 1975.
LDW	*Letters on Poetry from W. B. Yeats to Dorothy Wellesley.* Ed. Dorothy Wellesley. London: Oxford Univ. Press, 1940.
LKT	*W. B. Yeats: Letters to Katharine Tynan.* Ed. Roger McHugh. Dublin: Clonmore and Reynolds, 1953.
LR	*Letters of Dante Gabriel Rossetti.* Ed. Oswald Doughty and J. R. Wahl. 4 vols. London: Oxford Univ. Press, 1965–67.
LY	*The Letters of W. B. Yeats.* Ed. Allan Wade. London: Rupert Hart-Davis, 1954.
Myth.	William Butler Yeats. *Mythologies.* New York: Macmillan, Collier Books, 1969.
PR	*The Poetical Works of Dante Gabriel Rossetti.* Ed. William M. Rossetti. London: Ellis and Elvey, 1903. For poems not in Lang.
PS	*The Poems of Algernon Charles Swinburne.* 6 vols. New York: Harper and Brothers, 1904.
Ricks	*The Poems of Tennyson.* Ed. Christopher Ricks. Annotated English Poets. New York: Norton, 1972.
UP	*Uncollected Prose by W. B. Yeats.* Vol. 1, coll. and ed. by John P. Frayne. New York: Columbia Univ. Press, 1970. Vol. 2, coll. and ed. by John P. Frayne and Colton Johnson. New York: Columbia Univ. Press, 1976.
V. Ed.	*The Variorum Edition of the Poems of W. B. Yeats.* Ed. Peter Allt and Russell K. Alspach. New York: Macmillan, 1957.

Vision	W. B. Yeats. *A Vision*. New York: Macmillan, Collier Books, 1966.
WBY Mem.	*W. B. Yeats: Memoirs (Autobiography—First Draft, Journal)*. Transcr. and ed. by Denis Donoghue. New York: Macmillan, 1973.

Notes

Introduction

1. *Selected Writings of Walter Pater,* ed. Harold Bloom (New York: Columbia Univ. Press, Morningside Books, 1982), "Conclusion" to *The Renaissance,* 60.

2. *Further Letters of Gerard Manley Hopkins,* ed. Claude Colleer Abbott (London: Oxford Univ. Press, 1938), 72.

3. Alan Sinfield, *The Language of Tennyson's In Memoriam* (New York: Barnes and Noble, 1971), 84.

4. George Saintsbury, *History of English Prosody,* 3 vols. (London: Macmillan, 1906), 3:205.

5. Christopher Ricks, *Tennyson* (New York: Macmillan, Collier Books, 1972), 228; G. K. Chesterton, "The Bones of a Poem," in *A Handful of Authors: Essays on Books and Writers,* ed. Dorothy Collins (New York: Sheed and Ward, 1953), 105.

6. Charles Kingsley, unsigned review, in *Tennyson: The Critical Heritage,* ed. John D. Jump (London: Routledge & Kegan Paul, 1967), 183.

7. Ezra Pound, "A Retrospect," *Literary Essays of Ezra Pound,* ed. T. S. Eliot (New York: New Directions, 1968), 11; idem, Epigraph to "Revolt," *Collected Early Poems of Ezra Pound,* ed. Michael John King (New York: New Directions, 1982), 96; *A Concordance to the Poems of W. B. Yeats,* ed. Stephen Maxfield Parrish (Ithaca: Cornell Univ. Press, 1963), 206–7; T. S. Eliot, "Yeats," *On Poetry and Poets* (New York: Farrar, Straus and Giroux, Noonday Press, 1961), 300.

I: Vanishing Lives, Vanishing Landscapes

1. Browning to the Storys, Nov. 10, 1861, *Browning to His American Friends: Letters between the Brownings, the Storys and James Russell Lowell, 1841–1890,* ed. Gertrude Reese Hudson (London: Bowes and Bowes, 1965), 83–84.

2. See, for example, letters 16 and 18 in *The Brownings to the Tennysons: Letters from Robert Browning and Elizabeth Barrett Browning to Alfred, Emily and Hallam Tennyson, 1852–1889,* ed. Thomas J. Collins, *Baylor Browning Interests,* no. 22, May 1971 (Waco, Tex.: Armstrong Browning Library), 35, 36–37.

3. William Allingham, *William Allingham's Diary,* introduction by Geoffrey Grigson (Fontwell, Sussex: Centaur Press, 1967), 290.

4. Ibid., 326.

5. *The Letters of Robert Browning and Elizabeth Barrett Browning, 1845–1846,* ed. Elvan Kintner, 2 vols. (Cambridge: Harvard Univ. Press, 1969), 2:701; *Dearest Isa: Robert Browning's Letters to Isabella Blagden,* ed. Edward C. McAleer (Austin: Univ. of Texas Press, 1951), 328.

6. *Robert Browning and Julia Wedgwood: A Broken Friendship as Revealed by Their Letters,* ed. Richard Curle (New York: Frederick A. Stokes, 1937), 48, 56.

7. James Knowles, "A Personal Reminiscence," *Tennyson: Interviews and Recollections,* ed. Norman Page (London: Macmillan, 1983), 92.

8. Ibid., 92.

9. Graham Hough, "Tears, Idle Tears," in *Critical Essays on the Poetry of Tennyson,* ed. John Killham (London: Routledge & Kegan Paul, 1960), 187–88; Saintsbury, *History of English Prosody,* 3:212.

10. To Benjamin Bailey, 8 Oct. 1817, *The Letters of John Keats,* ed. Hyder Edward Rollins, 2 vols. (Cambridge: Harvard Univ. Press, 1958), 1:170.

11. W. David Shaw, *Tennyson's Style* (Ithaca: Cornell Univ. Press, 1976), 76.

12. Ricks, *Tennyson,* 45.

13. A. Dwight Culler, *The Poetry of Tennyson* (New Haven: Yale Univ. Press, 1977), 56.

II: The Language of Absence

1. Allingham, *Diary,* preface and 84.

2. Ricks, *Tennyson,* 201.

3. Ibid., 202, 252.

III: The Limit of the Self

1. Arthur Henry Hallam on *Poems, Chiefly Lyrical* (1830), reprinted in Jump, *Tennyson: The Critical Heritage,* 42.

2. A. Dwight Culler expands and corrects the legend in "Tennyson we cannot live in art," in *Nineteenth Century Literary Perspectives: Essays in Honor of Lionel Stevenson,* ed. Clyde de L. Ryals (Durham, N.C.: Duke Univ. Press, 1974).

3. Carol T. Christ, *The Finer Optic: The Aesthetic of Particularity in Victorian Poetry* (New Haven: Yale Univ. Press, 1975), 19. In "Tennyson's Optics: The Eagle's Gaze," *PMLA* 92 (1977):420–28, Gerhard Joseph says, "Where, however, Christ emphasizes a categorical Tennysonian penchant for stark individuation, I see a dialectical movement between particularity and indefiniteness" (427n). This statement, though it oversimplifies Christ's valuable book, is closer to the view taken by the present essay and first outlined by Arthur Hallam.

4. Sinfield, *The Language of In Memoriam,* 178.

5. W. K. Wimsatt, Jr., and Monroe C. Beardsley, "The Concept of Meter: An Exercise in Abstraction," *PMLA* 74 (1959):597.

6. Charles O. Hartman, *Free Verse: An Essay on Prosody* (Princeton: Princeton Univ. Press, 1980), 15.

IV: The Tennysonian Flow

1. Pater, "Wordsworth," *Selected Writings,* 136; Northrop Frye, "The Drunken Boat: The Revolutionary Element in Romanticism," *Romanticism Reconsidered: Selected Papers from the English Institute* (New York: Columbia Univ. Press, 1963), 16; Virginia Woolf to Vita Sackville-West, 16 Mar. 1926, *The Letters of Virginia Woolf,* vol. 3, *1923–28,* ed. Nigel Nicolson (New York: Harcourt, Brace, 1977), 247.

2. Donald Davie, *Articulate Energy: An Inquiry into the Syntax of English Poetry* (London: Routledge & Kegan Paul, 1955), 30.

3. "George Chapman," in *Swinburne as Critic,* ed. Clyde K. Hyder (London: Routledge & Kegan Paul, 1972), 156–57.

4. Jean Brooks, *Thomas Hardy: The Poetic Structure* (Ithaca: Cornell Univ. Press, 1971), 45.

5. Saintsbury, *History of English Prosody,* 3:39.

6. Knowles, "A Personal Reminiscence," 93.

7. Coventry Patmore, "Essay on English Metrical Law," in *Poems,* 2 vols. (London: George Bell and Son, 1886), 2:232.

8. Morris Halle and Samuel J. Keyser, *English Stress: Its Form, Its Growth, and Its Role in Verse* (New York: Harper and Row, 1971). See especially chap. 3, sect. 3, "Iambic Pentameter."

9. Pope to Walsh, 22 Oct. 1706, *The Correspondence of Alexander Pope,* ed. George Sherburn, 5 vols. (Oxford: Oxford University Press, 1956), 1:23. It has been pointed out that Pope's dating of this letter is probably specious.

10. Hartman, *Free Verse,* 55–56.

11. In Jump, *Tennyson: The Critical Heritage,* 160.

12. Ricks, *Tennyson,* 122.

V: Repetition and Resolution

1. R. W. Rader, *Tennyson's Maud: The Biographical Genesis* (Berkeley: Univ. of California Press, 1963).

2. Sir Charles Tennyson, *Alfred Tennyson* (New York: Macmillan, 1949), 245.

3. Gerhard Joseph, *Tennysonian Love: Strange Diagonal* (Minneapolis: Univ. of Minnesota Press, 1969). See, for example, "the clarification of Tennyson's melancholia into a sharply focused mourning" (72).

4. James D. Kissane, *Alfred Tennyson* (New York: Twayne, 1970), 100.

5. Florence Emily Hardy, *The Life of Thomas Hardy* (1962; rpt. Hamden, Conn.: Archon Books, 1970), 209–10.

VI: Dante Gabriel Rossetti: The House of Lives

1. Pater, "Dante Gabriel Rossetti," *Selected Writings,* 203; ibid., 204; "The Critic as Artist," *Complete Works of Oscar Wilde* (London: Hamlyn, 1963), 878.

2. William E. Fredeman, "Rossetti's *In Memoriam:* An Elegiac Reading of *The House of Life,*" *Bulletin of John Rylands Library* 47 (1965):323, 334; Pater, "Aesthetic Poetry," "Rossetti," *Selected Writings,* 198, 204

3. George H. Ford, *Keats and the Victorians* (1944; rpt. Hamden, Conn.: Archon Books, 1962), 137; Culler, *The Poetry of Tennyson,* 7.

4. Jerome J. McGann, "Rossetti's Significant Details," *Victorian Poetry* 7 (1969):44.

5. Christ, *Finer Optic,* 48–49.

6. Richard Poirier, *Robert Frost: The Work of Knowing* (Oxford: Oxford Univ. Press, 1979), 34–37.

7. Dante Gabriel Rossetti, *The House of Life,* ed. Paull Franklin Baum (Cambridge: Harvard Univ. Press, 1928), 8; Wendell V. Harris, "A Reading of Rossetti's Lyrics," *Victorian Poetry* 7 (1969):300–301.

8. Joseph F. Vogel, *Dante Gabriel Rossetti's Versecraft* (Gainesville: Univ. of Florida Press, 1971), 21–25.

9. Baum, 34; *Dearest Isa,* 336; Helen Rossetti Angeli, *Dante Gabriel Rossetti* (London: Hamilton, 1949), 168.

10. Oswald Doughty, *Dante Gabriel Rossetti, a Victorian Romantic* (New Haven: Yale Univ. Press, 1960), 125.

11. Susan P. Casteras, "The Double Vision in Portraiture," in *Dante Gabriel Rossetti and the Double Work of Art,* ed. Maryan Wynn Ainsworth (New Haven: Yale Art Gallery, 1976), 11, 14.

12. McGann, "Rossetti's Significant Details," 45.

VII: Swinburne: Purity and Pain

1. E. K. Brown, "Swinburne: A Centenary Estimate," in *Victorian Literature: Modern Essays in Criticism,* ed. Austin Wright (New York: Oxford Univ. Press, 1961), 300; Lionel Stevenson, *The Pre-Raphaelite Poets* (New York: Norton, 1974), 223; George Saintsbury, "Mr. Swinburne," in *Swinburne: The Critical Heritage,* ed. Clyde K. Hyder (New York: Barnes and Noble, 1970), 201.

2. Derek Attridge, *The Rhythms of English Poetry* (London: Longman, 1982), 100–101. This scrupulous, accessible, marvelously practical book surely deserves to become the standard work on English poetic rhythm.

3. John D. Rosenberg, introduction to the Modern Library *Swinburne: Selected Poetry and Prose* (New York: Random House, 1968), viii.

4. Ibid., xiv.

5. Ibid., vii; Jerome J. McGann, *Swinburne: An Experiment in Criticism* (Chicago: Univ. of Chicago Press, 1972), 166; T. S. Eliot, "Swinburne as Poet," *The Sacred Wood* (1920; rpt. London: Methuen, 1950), 49–50.

6. *Dearest Isa,* 333.

7. Rosenberg, introduction, x; McGann, *Swinburne,* 156.

8. Rosenberg, introduction, xxxi.

9. Pater, "Aesthetic Poetry," *Selected Writings,* 193.

10. Harold Bloom, introduction to Pater, *Selected Writings,* xxviii.

11. Eliot, "Swinburne as Poet," 150.

12. *Swinburne Letters,* ed. Cecil Y. Lang, 6 vols. (New Haven: Yale Univ. Press, 1959), 1:57.

13. David Riede, *Swinburne: A Study in Romantic Mythmaking* (Charlottesville: Univ. Press of Virginia, 1978), 163.

VIII: Into the Twilight

1. *Letters to the New Island by William Butler Yeats,* ed. Horace Reynolds (1934; rpt. Cambridge: Harvard Univ. Press, 1970), 98–99.

2. David G. Riede, *Dante Gabriel Rossetti and the Limits of Victorian Vision* (Ithaca: Cornell Univ. Press, 1983), 231.

3. W. D. Paden, *Tennyson in Egypt: A Study of the Imagery in His Earlier Work* (1942; rpt. New York: Octagon Books, 1971), 53.

4. *Life of Thomas Hardy,* 210.

5. Katharine Tynan, *The Middle Years* (Boston: Houghton Mifflin, 1917), 45.

6. T. S. Eliot, "Yeats," *On Poetry and Poets,* 300.

7. Graham Hough, *The Last Romantics* (1949; rpt. New York: Barnes and Noble, 1961), 216.

8. See the readings of "Pictor Ignotus" and "Andrea del Sarto" in Constance W. Hassett, *The Elusive Self in the Poetry of Robert Browning* (Athens: Ohio Univ. Press, 1982).

IX: Discoveries of Restraint

1. Richard Ellmann, *Yeats: The Man and the Masks* (1948; rpt. New York: Norton, 1978), 5.

2. *The Poetical Works of Robert Browning,* ed. G. Robert Stange, Cambridge Ed. (1895; rpt. Boston: Houghton Mifflin, 1974), 1009.

3. Robert Langbaum, *The Mysteries of Identity: A Theme in Modern Literature* (1977; rpt. Chicago: Univ. of Chicago Press, Phoenix Books, 1982), 147–74.

4. Journal of Jan. 1929, quoted in Richard Ellmann, *The Identity of Yeats,* 2d ed. (New York: Oxford Univ. Press, 1964), 239–40.

5. *Dearest Isa,* 336.

6. Hugh Kenner, *A Colder Eye: The Modern Irish Writers* (New York: Knopf, 1983), 58.

7. *A Critical Edition of Yeats's* A Vision *(1925),* ed. George Mills Harper and Walter Kelly Hood (London: Macmillan, 1978), Notes, 3.

8. *Letters of Keats,* to Richard Woodhouse, 27 Oct. 1818, 1:387.

9. Ibid.

10. Christopher Ricks, *Keats and Embarrassment* (London: Oxford Univ. Press, 1974).

11. *Letters of Keats,* to J. H. Reynolds, 27 Apr. 1818, 1:273.

12. W. H. Auden, *The Dyer's Hand* (New York: Random House, 1962), 97–98.

X: Yeatsian Shapes

1. Kenner, *A Colder Eye,* 59.

2. *The Collected Poems of William Carlos Williams,* vol. 1, *1909–1939,* ed. A. Walton Litz and Christopher MacGowan (New York: New Directions, 1986), 195.

3. Ibid., 207–8.

4. Williams, *Kora in Hell: Improvisations,* in *Imaginations,* ed. Webster Schott (New York: New Directions, 1971), 38–39.

5. Throughout his *Free Verse,* cited above.

6. T. E. Hulme, "Modern Art and Its Philosophy, *Speculations,* ed. Herbert Read, 2d edition (1936; rpt. London: Routledge and Kegan Paul, 1949). "Geometrical character . . . intensity" (81); "empathy" (85); "space-shyness" (86).

7. Quoted in Thomas Parkinson, *W. B. Yeats: Self-Critic* and *The Later Poetry,* in one volume (1951, 1964; rpt. Berkeley: Univ. of California Press, 1971), 185.

8. Donald Davie, "Michael Robartes and the Dancer," *An Honoured Guest: New Essays on W. B. Yeats,* ed. Denis Donoghue and J. R. Mulryne (London: Edwin Arnold, 1965), 86.

9. Curtis Bradford, *Yeats at Work,* abridged ed. (New York: Ecco Press, 1978), 59.

10. Ibid., 50.

11. Ibid., 50–51.

12. John Holloway, "Style and World in *The Tower,*" *An Honoured Guest,* 99.

13. *Nineteenth Century British Minor Poets,* ed. W. H. Auden (New York: Dell, Laurel Editions, 1966), 23.

XI: Dancer and Dance: One Conclusion

1. *Critical Edition of A Vision,* Notes, 19–20.

2. Daniel Harris, *Yeats: Coole Park and Ballylee* (Cambridge: Harvard Univ. Press, 1974).

3. Ibid., 36.

4. Pater, "Coleridge," *Selected Writings,* 152.

5. *Lady Gregory: Interviews and Recollections,* ed. E. H. Mikhail (Totowa, N.J.: Rowman & Littlefield, 1977), 1.

6. Holloway, "Style and World in *The Tower,*" 95–98.

7. Pater, "Plato and Platonism," *Selected Writings,* 225.

Index

Vogel, Joseph F., 107

Wedgwood, Julia, 16
Wellesley, Lady Dorothy, 166–67,
    198–99, 221
Wilde, Oscar, 99, 161
Wilding, Alexa, 100
Williams, William Carlos, 193–97
Wimsatt, W. K., Jr., 50–51, 52
Woolf, Virginia, 64–65, 75
Wordsworth, Dorothy, 62
Wordsworth, William, 6, 19, 21,
    24, 26, 35, 48, 57, 60–65, 68–
    75, 80, 85–86, 89–90, 176,
    198–99, 202–3, 219–21, 223

Yeats, William Butler, 10, 24, 57,
    77, 103, 129, 130, 133, 136
  "Adam's Curse," 177–80
  "After Long Silence," 169
  "Among School Children," 165,
    176–79, 217, 219–26
  "The Blessed," 153
  "The Dawn," 144
  "Dialogue of Self and Soul," 179,
    189, 205–10, 217, 222
  "A Dream of Death," 170–71
  "Ego Dominus Tuus," 161, 167,
    222
  "Ephemera," 153
  "The Fascination of What's Diffi-
    cult," 182
  "Fergus and the Druid," 156
  "The Fisherman," 190
  "The Gift of Harun Al-Rashid,"
    140
  "He Tells of a Valley Full of
    Lovers," 153

"He Thinks of Those Who Have
    Spoken Evil of His Be-
    loved," 151
"He Wishes His Beloved Were
    Dead," 152–55
"In a Drawing Room," 149
"In Memory of Eva Gore-Booth
    and Con Markiewicz," 226
"In Memory of Major Robert
    Gregory," 179, 202, 206
"The Indian to His Love," 153
"Into the Twilight," 151
The Island of Statues, 144–47
"King and No King," 215
"The Living Beauty," 202
"A Prayer for My Daughter,"
    179, 217–19
"Sailing to Byzantium," 208–9,
    221
"The Scholars," 169
"The Second Coming," 169
The Shadowy Waters, 149–50
"The Sorrow of Love," 163–68,
    197
"That the Night Come," 215
"To a Friend Whose Work Has
    Come to Nothing," 181–83
"The Tower," 179, 222
"The Two Trees," 168
"Vacillation," 186, 203–5
A Vision, 161, 188–89, 197
The Wanderings of Oisin, 145–48,
    149, 219
"When You Are Old," 155
"Who Goes with Fergus?" 150,
    153
"The Wild Swans at Coole," 166,
    190–93, 199–203

 is a series of monographs on literature
covering the years from 1830 to 1914.
Contributions may be critical (historical or theoretical),
biographical, bibliographic, comparative, or interdisciplinary.